DANCING WITH STRANGERS

INGA CLENDINNEN

Dancing with Strangers

TEXT PUBLISHING MELBOURNE AUSTRALIA

The Text Publishing Company
171 La Trobe Street
Melbourne Victoria 3000
Australia

First published in 2003 by The Text Publishing Company

Designed by Chong
Map by Tony Fankhauser
Typeset in Granjon 12.2/17 by J&M Typesetting
Printed by Griffin Press

National Library of Australia
Cataloguing-in-Publication entry:

Clendinnen, Inga.
Dancing with strangers.

Bibliography.
Includes index.
ISBN 1 877008 58 3.

1. Aborigines, Australian - New South Wales - Sydney Region - Effect of colonization on. 2. First Fleet, 1787-1788. 3. Australia - Colonization.

994.410049915

This project has been assisted by the Commonwealth Government through the Australia Council, its arts funding and advisory body.

*For
Anastasia
and for
Gilchrist*

Acknowledgments

I thank the staff at the Borchardt Library, La Trobe University, and at Townsville Regional Library, whose kindness went well beyond duty.

I thank Michael Heyward at Text for luring me into this adventure in the first place. He promised I would enjoy myself, and I have. He has proved yet again an incomparable editor.

I thank my old colleagues at La Trobe University History Department for their continuing affection and interest over the years, especially Alan Frost, John Hirst and Richard Broome for generous aid and comfort.

I thank the host of writers who will find no acknowledgment in the text, but who have filled my days and shaped my thinking over the years.

And I thank Miss Cantwell, third-grade teacher at Newtown and Chilwell State School sixty years ago, who finally managed to teach me to read.

History…is made up of episodes,
and if we cannot get inside [episodes] we
cannot get inside history at all.
E. P. Thompson

Man proceeds in a fog. But when he looks
back to judge people of the past, he sees no fog
on their path. From his present, which was their
far-away future, their path looks perfectly clear
to him, good visibility all the way. Looking back
he sees the path, he sees the people proceeding,
he sees their mistakes, but not the fog.
Milan Kundera

CONTENTS

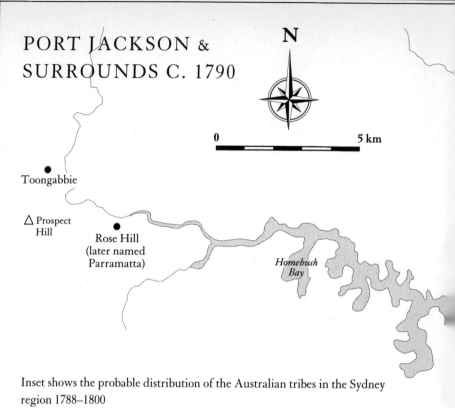

PORT JACKSON &
SURROUNDS C. 1790

N

0   5 km

● Toongabbie

△ Prospect
Hill   ● Rose Hill
(later named
Parramatta)   Homebush
Bay

Inset shows the probable distribution of the Australian tribes in the Sydney region 1788–1800

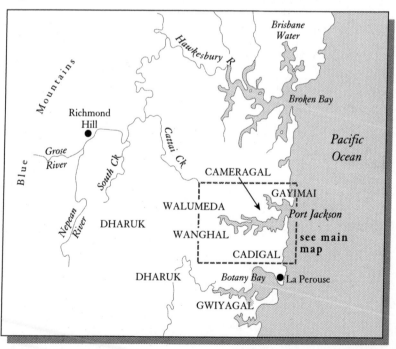

Brisbane
Water

Hawkesbury R

Mountains

Broken Bay

Richmond
Hill ●

Pacific
Ocean

Grose
River

Blue

South Ck

Cattai Ck

CAMERAGAL

GAYIMAI

Port Jackson

Nepean River

DHARUK

WALUMEDA

WANGHAL

see main
map

CADIGAL

DHARUK   Botany Bay ● La Perouse

GWIYAGAL

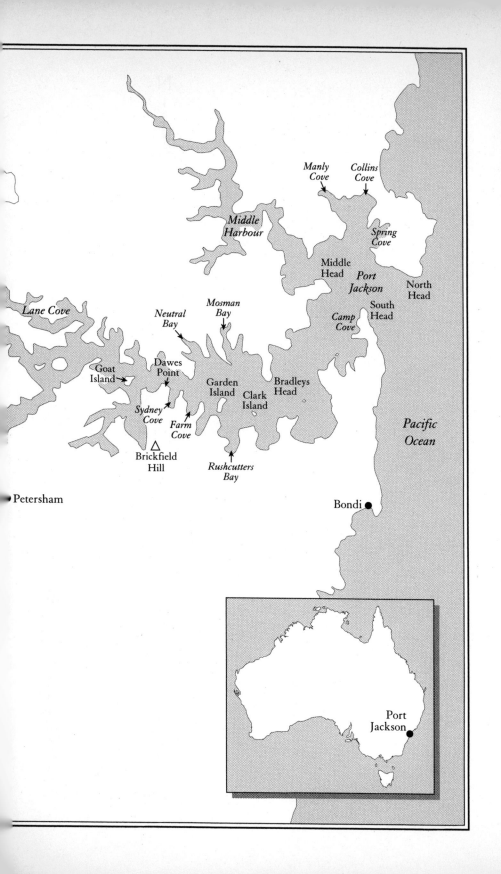

INTRODUCTION

This is a telling of the story of what happened when a thousand British men and women, some of them convicts and some of them free, made a settlement on the east coast of Australia in the later years of the eighteenth century, and how they fared with the people they found there.

My telling of it has its origins in a place, and in a person. For the place: a few years ago I took a boat trip with my husband across the top of Australia. We stopped briefly at a place called Port Essington, or 'Victoria', on the Cobourg Peninsula. Nowadays it is a ranger's headquarters, but it was built and garrisoned in the first half of the nineteenth century as a fort against the French. The French didn't come, and after about eleven years the soldiers were withdrawn.

It is desolate country, hot, sweaty and, despite its flatness, somehow claustrophobic. The sea up there glitters like new silver, but it's full of crocodiles. Even the tough young ranger didn't swim, despite the heat, despite the boredom. He said the crocodiles were too crafty. If you went in at the same place twice the odds were one of them would be waiting for you, and they would pick up the sound of the splashing anyway and slide along to check out the prospects. He also warned us about the snakes, and listed some of the diseases the local mosquitoes were eager to trade for a sip of human blood. There wasn't a lot to do. We looked through the tiny museum, peered into a couple of the dark little stone houses where the married soldiers used to lived, and walked a long hot way up to the cemetery. It was a big cemetery for so small a place, spreading over a bluff. From the headstones it looked as if childbirth and infant fevers had been the big killers. No medical assistance in the 1840s, or not at Port Essington. A lot of women and children had been left behind when the soldiers pulled out.

It was a melancholy place, and I was glad to leave it. Then I forgot about it, or thought I had. It came back when I was given a book written by a fellow with the odd name of Watkin Tench, a marine officer who came out to Australia with the First Fleet. I fell in love with Tench, as most of his readers do. He is a Boswell on the page: curious, ardent, gleefully self-mocking. He didn't fit my image of a stiff-lipped British imperialist at all. The visit to Port Essington had made me realise that the past—those early settlements in Australia—had once been as real as the present, which is always an electrifying realisation. Before I quite knew what was happening I had started work on the remarkably accessible documentation for the early years of the British presence at Sydney Cove. Through those British sources I also met the beach nomads of Australia. My aim in what follows is to understand what happened between these un-like peoples when they met on the edge of a continent 20,000 kilometres from England.

The imperial adventure in Australia was played out by a very small cast. A handful of British observers are our main informants as to what happened between the races during Arthur Phillip's governorship, which began in January 1788 and effectively ended with his return to England in December 1792. In 1796 his friend and secretary David Collins also went home. Nine years is a brief time span, but in my view much of what mattered most in shaping the tone and temper of white–black relations in this country happened during those first few years of contact.

Doing history teaches us to tolerate complexity, and to be alert to the shifting contexts of actions and experience; anthropology reminds those historians who still need to be reminded that high male politics isn't everything, and that other cultures manage to get along using accounts of the world we find bizarre, even perverse. Historians' main occupational hazard is being culture-insensitive, anthropologists' is insensitivity to temporal change. Both can be insensitive to the reciprocating dynamic between action and context. Together, however, they are formidable, and in my view offer the best chance of explaining what we humans do in any particular circumstance, and why we do it. In what follows I have tried to bring the two methods together in the analysis of a number of sequential episodes, interspersed with short explanatory essays when I think the reader might need to pause for breath.

Coming to the field of Australian history late in life and fortuitously, I did not know the archival material for the early British–Australian encounters. But the published documentation is rich and can be found in most good libraries, where it takes up not much more than one solid shelf. My hope is that readers will be stimulated to read some of that material themselves, possibly as they read this book. I promise they will be rewarded.

The reports, journals and letters I have used are notably well ordered, with the episodes I discuss being described over a handful of pages. I have therefore consolidated the relevant references, with their appropriate page spans, at the end of each chapter. The exception is David Collins, whose combination of dogged record-keeping and occasional anecdote sometimes demanded an inelegant string of page numbers. My aim is simple: that readers be able to find the precise passage they want to check in less than a minute's search. I would prefer, of course, the old style, with a protective bristle of footnotes hanging off every page, but now those days are gone.

There were, of course, difficulties in deciding how to proceed. The first might seem trivial, but is not: what to call the people the British found living around what was to become Sydney Harbour. 'Aborigine' is anachronistic: a colonial construct crusted with later stereotypes. It also smoothes away that people's variousness, and their sheer unexpectedness. The British called them 'natives' or 'indians' or sometimes, not always pejoratively, 'savages', which at least captures their strangeness and the intruders' unease. I call them 'Australians', which is what they undoubtedly were, just as the British were certainly other—'them' as against 'we people here'. The word 'British' also gave me pause, given the mix of nations among soldiers, sailors and convicts of the first fleets, but I could find no better alternative.

Readers will be frustrated to discover that some of the most intriguing questions about the Australians cannot be answered from the 'outsider' sources we have. Our informants had been schooled by their professions to be scrupulous observers, but whole areas of local life, especially of thought and sensibility, remained invisible to them. Working on the Mexico of five hundred years ago I was able to retrieve something of the Indians' thinking as to what was happening in their sacred unseen worlds from the elaborate descriptions of ritual life collected from native lords, and detailed Spanish reports of the transformations in Indian ceremonial life over the first fifty years of colonisation. That kind of reconstruction is impossible for my own country, where contact began a mere two hundred years ago, not least because after the first few years the Australians ceased to be of much interest to the British, while in Mexico the friars remained committed to the pursuit of souls. In my view the sacred world of the Australians in 1788—the world of mind and spirit, none of it written but stored in landscape, artefact, dance and story—is closed to us outsiders. My interest therefore focuses on the Australians' secular life: on what we can learn from British observers during those first few years of contact, before cynicism set in, about a remarkable people.

I have another hope, at once deeper and more tentative: that by retracing the difficulties in the way of understanding people of a different culture we might grasp how taxing and tense a condition 'tolerance' is; and how we might achieve social justice between Australia's original immigrants, and those of us who came later.

The Australians and the British began their relationship by dancing together.

DANCING WITH STRANGERS

On a December evening in 1832 the *Beagle* entered a bay in Tierra del Fuego and gave young Charles Darwin his first view of the famously savage Fuegians. Through the gloom he could distinguish some remarkably tall men, naked except for long skin cloaks slung from their shoulders, perched on the edge of a wild promontory, shouting and waving their cloaks. He watched as they followed the ship along the coast to its overnight anchorage.

Darwin was an eager member of the party which went ashore the next morning to meet the wild men. There were four of them, and Darwin was fascinated: 'I could not have believed how wide was the difference between savage and civilised man; it is greater than between a wild and domesticated animal…their very attitudes were abject, and the expression of their countenances distrustful, surprised, and startled.' That vast gulf shrank slightly over the next minutes. The wild men accepted the Englishmen's gifts of scarlet cloth, which they tied around their necks, and in return they gave their own welcome. An old man paired himself with Darwin, clucked like a chicken, patted the Englishman on the breast, gave him three hearty, simultaneous slaps on the back and chest, and then bared his bosom for Darwin to return the compliment.

What to do next? Clearly words were useless: Darwin thought the men's language was no language at all, being as savage as they were, a 'barely articulate' matter of raspings and hawkings with a few gutturals mixed in. So parallel gabbling gave way to a more elastic mode of expression: competitive face-pulling. The British began it ('Some of our party began to squint and look awry'); the savages eagerly reciprocated, winning the contest when one young Fuegian with black-painted face and a white band across the eyes 'succeeded in making far more hideous grimaces'. Then they mouthed words at each other, and again the Fuegians won: 'They could repeat with perfect correctness each word in any sentence we addressed them, and they remembered such words for some time'; and Darwin paused to wonder why savages should have a natural bent for mimicry.

Then the British reclaimed the initiative. They began to sing and to dance, and this time they struck gold: 'When a song was struck up by our party I thought the Fuegians would have fallen down with astonishment. With equal surprise they viewed our dancing.' But they recovered quickly, and 'one of the young men, when asked, had no objections to a little waltzing'. Later in the day there was more dancing, and by the evening, Darwin tells us, 'we parted very good friends; which I think was fortunate, for the dancing and "sky-larking" had occasionally bordered on a trial of strength'. The wild men had truly descended from their 'wild promontory' to mingle and dance on the beach. We leave Darwin and his company peacefully waltzing with savages in the Land of Fire.

*

We don't readily think of dancing as a phase of the imperial process, but rather more than forty years before, when a fleet of British ships berthed on the east coast of Australia, first at the place they named Botany Bay and then at 'Sydney Cove', a surprising amount of interracial dancing went on. On 29 January 1788, three days after landfall, Lieutenant William Bradley, second in command of HMS *Sirius*, was dutifully charting the harbour when he had his first meeting with the Australians. It was a remarkably friendly encounter, the British party being welcomed ashore by unarmed men who pointed out a good landing place 'in the most cheerful manner, shouting and dancing'. (At this point we have to suppose 'dancing' meant no more than 'caperings': 'the giving of direct physical expression to sensations of pleasure and excitement', as my dictionary dourly puts it.) From the strips of cloth tied around their bodies Bradley knew that at least some of these friendly fellows must have met with Governor Arthur Phillip the previous day, with the bright rags the spoils of their meeting.

Then, Bradley tells us, 'these people mixed with ours and all hands danced together'. The next day at Spring Cove there was another impromptu dance party when about a dozen of the local men came paddling in soon after the British landed, left their spears in their canoes as a sign of friendship, and all proceeded to more 'dancing and otherwise amusing themselves'. Then they embarked on an even more intimate interaction: the combing of never-before-combed hair. I would have thought this exercise painful for the people who suffered it and distasteful to the Europeans who performed it—the hair, Bradley tells us, was 'clotted with dirt and vermin'—but excitement and curiosity overcame fastidiousness, and it seems all parties enjoyed themselves.

We can imagine the hair clipping, but what can this mysterious 'dancing together' have looked like? Rollicking British hornpipes followed by elegant Australian knee-lifts? Wild hoppings and leapings from some cultural no-man's land? Bradley, having thickened the mystery with words, clarifies it with paint in a charming watercolour, signed 'WB' and titled *View in Broken Bay, New South Wales, March 1788*: that is, two months after landfall. (The picture is reproduced on the cover of this book and in the plate section.) The dancing is presented as a decorative foreground to the 'view', so Bradley probably constructed this particular representation from several incidents, but as he was a serious young naval lieutenant who set great store by accuracy, I think we can rely on him. What he shows us is the British and the Australians dancing hand in hand like children at a picnic: that is, dancing in the British style. (Darwin's 'waltzing'—bodies facing and lightly embraced—had not yet become respectable in Britain. That had to wait on the loosening effect of Napoleon and Waterloo.) Furthermore, the pairs are scattered over the whole foreground, with none of the local preference for formation dancing, which reinforces my suspicion that it was the British who took the initiative.

The First Fleeters also invoked the power of song. When Surgeon-General John White fell in with a large body of Australians at Botany Bay soon after landing, he was anxious to make them realise the fatal power of the short metal sticks the British redcoats carried, both to preserve the peace and to save local lives. He therefore concocted a vivid visual demonstration: he borrowed a warrior's shield, propped it as a target, and fired his pistol at it. Alarm erupted, both at the noise and because the ball passed clean through the shield. White does not bother to tell us what happened next (his journal is a rather shorthand affair) but Watkin Tench of the marines, with his eye for the speaking detail, does. White began to whistle 'Marlbrooke has gone to the wars', the tune we know as 'We won't get home until morning'; the locals took up the fetching little air; the panic subsided; and 'Marlbrooke' became a favourite item in the Australians' expanding repertoire of borrowed songs. Six months later, with relations souring and some British blood spilt, White still trusted in the pacifying power of song when some canoes ventured to fish behind the point on which the hospital was built. After some friendly exchanges with one couple, White persuaded one of the British gentlemen with him to sing. The women in the canoes responded: they 'either sung one of their own songs, or imitated him, in which they succeeded beyond conception'. The impromptu songfest had gone on for some time when an Englishman happened to appear with a gun and the panicked Australians paddled away. White ordered the gun set aside, his people kept right on singing, and the canoes came back to their fishing and their friendly conversation-through-song.

Some encounters were raunchier. Lieutenant Philip Gidley King of the *Sirius* gives an amiably binocular account of what the locals might have been seeing during his own first contact with a band of Australians. As the first man was being coaxed to approach by the offer of the usual trinkets King noted that he 'seemed quite astonished at ye figure we cut in being cloathed'. And then, reflectively and not altogether in bad faith, 'I think it very easy to conceive ye ridiculous figure we must appear to these poor creatures, who were perfectly naked.' It was King who later took the direct way to resolve another mystery. Because the British were both beardless and came swaddled in 'cloathing' there had been baffled speculation among their hosts as to their sex: speculation which had already generated gusts of nervous laughter. Australians followed different protocols for the genders even more earnestly than did the British, so any ambiguity in this area was deeply embarrassing. Accordingly, King had one of his men unbutton and publish his privates, at which sight the locals made 'a great shout of admiration'—or so King interpreted it. A happy survivor of the sexual excesses of Tahiti, he was constantly pressing for closer contact with Australian women, and on this unbuttoned occasion he had a rare triumph: he contrived to lure one girl sufficiently close to 'apply [a] handkerchief where Eve did ye fig leaf', and again her countrymen set up another 'very great shout'. It seems that, whatever their cultural backgrounds, lads will be laddish.

An element of contest was mixed in with the good will. Much later, in 1790, during what can only be described as a peacemaking party (the sharing of food, a great deal of shaving and beard-clipping), the two groups, Tench tells us, 'began to play and romp' with each other, with one hefty Englishman contriving to lift two lean Australians at once, while they could not budge him. So not dancing this time, but a chest-to-chest, thigh-to-thigh schoolyard test of strength. John Bayley has written of 'those moments in the past between explorers and savages, when some sort of clowning pantomime on the part of the former seems…to have evoked instant comprehension and amusement'. 'Clowning pantomimes' catches the mood of these early encounters exactly. Nor do I doubt the amusement. But how real was the comprehension?

MEETING THE INFORMANTS

It is a commonplace rediscovered every decade or so that individuals see what they see from their own particular perspective, and that perspectives change through time. These disenchanted days we know there are no I-am-a-camera observers, and we also know that even cameras lie. This recognition has not stopped would-be historians from piecing together snippets derived from a range of narratives, perspectives and sensibilities in chronological order, and calling the resulting ribbon patchwork 'objective history'.

Making coherent stories out of the fragments we find lying about is a natural human inclination, and socially a necessary one, but when doing history it must be resisted. My own preferred metaphor comes from snorkelling, where at first we are uneasy interlopers, with both the flitting shapes and the social geography vague. Then, after sufficient hours of immersion, we begin to reconstruct in our minds the salient formations—the context—and to be able to follow the opalescent inhabitants as they go about their engrossing affairs—the action. This submerged world is never as clear as the airy world above, but it is the more absorbing for that.

The historians' situation is complicated because we have to look through other people's masks if we are to see anything of the world we want to fathom: that is, we have to read their words instead of using our own eyes. Fortunately for us, some of Governor Phillip's senior officers entered into agreements with publishers even before they left England: John Hunter, commander of the *Sirius*; John White, surgeon-general to the entire expedition; and Governor Phillip himself. Judge-Advocate David Collins began his journal partly through a sense of duty and partly for private distraction, but after only a few months he had decided to keep it in a form suitable for later publication. A venturesome publisher also contracted the relatively lowly Watkin Tench, captain-lieutenant of marines, to prepare an account of his experiences in the new colony. Cook's journals had set the style and established the taste for dramatic doings in exotic places which could be elevated to science by the inclusion of a flow of observations of curiosities encountered along the way: of birds, plants, animals and savages, usually in that order.

An unvoiced 'we' dominates the journals, which admit us to an unfamiliar culture: the close-knit world of serving British naval and marine officers overseas. Habituated to maintaining solidarity against lesser men, subordinates or foreign, they saw their colony-planting endeavour as unitary—'for England'—and their individual narratives as expressions of a collective enterprise. Patriotism and caste loyalty routinely trumped competitiveness, with borrowings being generously offered and acknowledged; indeed the whole of David Collins' second volume, published in 1802 six years after he quit the colony, was compiled from the reports of other men.

Supplementing the formal published accounts are more private narratives. There is a particular charm about journals of private record, both in the freshness of their observations and our illicit pleasure in reading what we shouldn't. Philip Gidley King, who knew the hazards of a seafarer's life, wrote the following words at the front of his private journal:

> As I write this journal for my own satisfaction, I do beg & request, that, into whatever hands it may fall, (in case of any accidents happening to me) To give or forward it to the hands of His Excellency Governor Phillip or, in the case of his demise, to Lieut. William Dawes of the Marines, who I instruct to destroy it; if any of the materials can be of service he is perfectly welcome to them.

These sentiments neatly encapsulate the themes mentioned above. The right to privacy belonging only to the living, King's instructions were posthumously ignored. Here is an entry from his private diary for 17 August 1788, six months after he was sent to plant a tiny settlement on Norfolk Island:

> Moderate Breezes and very pleasant Weather. Sowed 1 & ½ Rood of Ground with Wheat received by the Supply—opened a cask of Beef & one of Flour, the latter of which had a large Rats nest in it & several dead young ones. This Cask came by the Supply [from Sydney] & wanted 50 lbs of the weight.

By the end of these few lines we know both King and his situation better.

Two days later he took himself off on an adventure, away from rats and housekeeping:

> I went up the Cascade which is beautifull but at the same time tremenduous [sic] we had to ascend some perpendicular rocks by

going from the branches of one tree to another, when arrived at the Summit, we found a very pleasant levell piece of Ground watered by the Rivulet, which supplies the Cascade & which is large and deep.

Part exploration, part jaunt, and altogether a glorious day. This time we glimpse not only his situation, but his sensibility.

Lieutenant William Bradley of the *Sirius* was twenty-nine years old and married, but like his brother officers was compelled to leave his wife behind in England. Establishing settlements was a masculine affair, at least for officers. Bradley wrote a professional journal enlivened by the occasional personal aside. Even more usefully, he painted a sequence of careful watercolours which provide many of the illustrations for this book.

Letters are another beguilingly informal source. Writing home must have filled many empty evenings, but it would rise to fever pitch when a ship was due to leave for England or the Cape. Then whole days could pass in writing letters, often in several copies (these men knew the perils attending long sea voyages). Despite shared experiences, the letters which survive are marvellously various in tone. Assistant-Surgeon Worgan from the *Sirius* had somehow contrived to bring his piano with him (he beguiled his fellow-officers with concerts in ports along the way), so he must have spent time on his music. Given the tough conditions in the new land, he must also have been much occupied by his work. Nonetheless, we see him writing vast letters to his beloved brother Dick, as if, as he wistfully says, he were sitting opposite him by the fire. His love for his distant sibling is as palpable as his loneliness. The eagerness of publishers brought the antipodean colony very close to those left at home—as its editor points out, the compilation known as *An Historical Journal of the Transactions at Port Jackson and Norfolk Island*, which appeared in

London under John Hunter's name at the beginning of 1793, described events to the close of 1791, a mere twelve months before. To the exiled colonists, home was very far away. Worgan reported on local affairs, he made a few scientific observations, but his main endeavour was to entertain that ghostly fraternal presence on the other side of the fire with running jokes and racy tales, especially about 'the savages'.

Marine-Lieutenant Ralph Clark wrote to his wife Alicia about his dreams (he tenderly recalls her interpreting his dreams as they lay in bed of a morning), his longing for her, and his frequent atrocious toothaches. He did not tell her about the baby girl borne him by a convict woman in 1791 during his year at Norfolk Island, although he named the child, presumably with some emotional confusion, 'Alicia'. There are others, like Major Ross, commander of the marines, who these days exist mainly as writers of furious letters of complaint, and others again, for all we know more important to the evolving life of the colony, who do not exist for us at all because they wrote nothing, or nothing that survived. Getting into the historical record is a chancy business.

These were impressive men. While an individual might acknowledge ignorance of a particular area (Captain Hunter allowed he didn't know much about agriculture), the collective assumed its competence over a wide range of scientific and artistic endeavours. Some painted, most sketched, some botanised; some sang, some studied the stars; some constructed lexicons of Australian words and struggled to fathom Australian grammar; Worgan played his piano. And nearly all of them wrote: fine, flowing sentences infused with their own individual flavour, with nuances of judgment, mood and emotion effortlessly expressed. As we will see, this is true even of Marine Private Jonathan Easty, whose wildly ambitious spelling marks him as an untaught man, but one in love with words and their protean possibilities.

The display of solidarity sustained through the hardest times is also impressive. It is true that the solidarity was to a degree self-interested. Senior officers could not afford a reputation of being unable to handle their men; junior officers needed the recommendation of their seniors for promotion. As the slow months passed there would be tensions enough in the cramped little society at Port Jackson, with every face familiar and caste divisions deep, but they are largely excluded from the public record. It is private letters which tell us most about such abrasions. When Lieutenant Daniel Southwell of the *Sirius* writes to his mother we hear his chagrin at being exiled and, as he thought, forgotten at the lookout at South Head for the best part of two years, from February 1790 until he went home at the end of 1791. He had to watch from the sidelines as young Lieutenant Waterhouse, more than a year his junior but always at the governor's side, found daily opportunity to shine. (Southwell cheered up briefly when Phillip, noticing his sulks, distinguished him with marked cordiality.)

The stress of maintaining a decent affability was also tested by cantankerous personalities like Major Ross, a social monster in any circumstances but close to intolerable in the claustrophobic confines of the settlement. We would expect him to be worse when Phillip seized the chance to send him to command Norfolk Island, but there he seems to have performed rather better. The fusses Ross provoked could not be kept out of official correspondence, but they were loyally excluded from the journals, and the loathing he inspired was revealed only in private letters. The normally discreet Collins confided to his father that he could have wished Ross drowned when a ship carrying him was wrecked on the reef at Norfolk Island, and that he would choose death rather than share a ship for the long voyage to England with the execrable major.

For the few respectable females of the settlement social constrictions must have been even more painful. Pious Mrs Johnson was the only lady in Sydney until the arrival of lively young Elizabeth Macarthur in July 1790, and Elizabeth found her sadly dull. Later Elizabeth would lament every reduction in her tiny circle of friends when, with their terms of duty ended, her favourite officers went home: gaining Mr Worgan's piano was no compensation for losing Mr Worgan, while the loss of Captain Tench was scarcely to be borne.

While the letter-writers might have more immediate verve than the formal journal-keepers, it is the Big Five of Tench, White, Hunter, Collins and Phillip himself who provide us with most of our information regarding life in the young colony. This is our most reliable information too, because by publication they opened themselves and their accounts to contemporary challenge and correction.

Initially I saw these men, members as they were of a self-conscious officer caste, as cut from much the same stern cloth, but with increasing familiarity their individual personalities insisted on asserting themselves. People always look most alike when we know them least. So let me introduce them to you.

GOVERNOR ARTHUR PHILLIP

Commander Arthur Phillip was a naturally cautious man, and having risen to the top of the naval hierarchy from its lowliest position (he had begun as ship's boy), he was well-practised in presenting a controlled image in public and on the page. His personal journal has been lost, but I suspect it would not have been very personal. His style for all seasons and purposes was clear, concise and conscientiously free from flourishes or affect which, given the mass of necessary communications and the scant time he had to write them, was a sensible decision. Nearly all his writings from Sydney come to us at second hand as selections from his official dispatches made by John Hunter, who drew on Phillip's official correspondence for the 'narrative' he incorporated into his *An Historical Journal of Events at Sydney and at Sea 1787–1792*, which appeared in 1793, or by the publisher's scribes back in London who put together the rather more crisply titled *The Voyage of Governor Phillip to Botany Bay* to catch the market in 1789. It is clear from a comparison of their versions with Phillip's extant dispatches that his scribes had sufficient respect both for the man and for official documents to follow the contours of the original texts closely. It is therefore possible to map the attention given particular topics and so to discover Phillip's hierarchy of concerns.

We see more of Phillip the man of action in the account of a lay outsider. Arthur Bowes Smyth, surgeon to the *Lady Penrhyn*, hired only for the voyage out, and as a landsman a nervous observer, thought Phillip was a hasty sailor. He noted on 10 December 1787, after Hunter had taken over the *Sirius* and the command of the rest of the fleet while Phillip hurried on ahead with the four fastest vessels, that the remaining seven ships kept together well, 'as Capt. Hunter does not carry such a press of sail as the Commodore used to do'. Bowes Smyth was also distinctly disaffected when Phillip insisted on moving the whole fleet out of Botany Bay to Port Jackson on a day when the wind was up. (Phillip probably decided to overlook weather conditions and make a dash for the more favoured harbour after the astonishing arrival at Botany Bay of two ships, the *Bousoule* and the *Astrolabe,* comprising an official French expedition under the command of Comte Jean de La Pérouse.) The British ships only got out of the bay with the 'utmost difficulty & danger wt many hairsbreadth escapes' and quite a lot of bumping into each other, 'with everyone blaming the rashness of the Governor in insisting upon the fleets working out in such weather, & all agreed it was next to a Miracle that some of the Ships were not lost'.

Bowes Smyth was also a touch sardonic regarding Phillip's on-shore performance. He gave a full account of the governor's formal reading of his commission, embellished with bands and marching and the processing of colours, and then the gentlemen gathered at the centre, with the convicts around them sitting on the ground and the soldiery forming an outer circle. Listening to the commission, Bowes Smyth judged it to be 'a more unlimited one than was ever before granted to any Governor under the British Crown', Phillip being accorded 'full power and authority' to do whatever he needed to, with no requirement to take any counsel of anyone.

Bowes Smyth reports that the governor proceeded to outline his regimen. Phillip was admirably direct. He warned the convicts that he had reason to think most of them incorrigible, and that his discipline would be accordingly stern: that anyone attempting to get into the women's tents at night would be fired on; that if they did not work they would be let starve; that given their situation any stealing of 'the most trifling Article of Stock or Provisions' would be punished by death. Then came a gentler conclusion: they would not be cruelly worked, and 'every individual shd. contribute his Share to render himself and Community at large happy and comfortable as soon as the nature of the settlement would permit it'. It was, given the circumstances, as encouraging a harangue as could be expected. But Bowes Smyth swiftly realised the governor's court would be exclusively an officers' club, noting crossly that only officers were invited to the governor's tent for supper while he and the other free men come from England were left to fend for themselves.

Nor was he impressed by Phillip's on-shore discipline. Within a month of disembarkation he thought the convicts out of control and already carving out their own territory, the men being 'ready to seize on any Sailors on shore who are walking near the Women's Camp, beat them most unmercifully, & desire them to go on board'. (Sailors had used their opportunity to establish alliances with some of the convict women on the long voyage out.) He also thought the 'justice' dealt out in the governor's courts was no justice at all. A marine who got in among the convict women and bashed a girl who had been his lover ('a most infamous hussy', splutters Bowes Smyth) was given a hundred lashes with a hundred more to come, while a convict who had struck a sentry received a mere one hundred and fifty. His comment: 'The severity shewn to the Marines and Lenity to the Convicts has already excited great murmurings & discontent among the Corps & where it will end, unless some other plan is adopted, time will discover.' He was even more outraged when Phillip ordered a naval steward who had bought 'an animal of the squirrel kind' from a convict and paid him in rum to suffer one hundred lashes, reduced to fifty when 'several gentlemen' urged greater leniency. (The steward had bought the 'squirrel', presumably a possum, on an officer's behalf; trade with convicts was forbidden.) He had no complaint about the death sentence imposed on three convicts found guilty of stealing bread, pork and other provisions, or the three hundred lashes awarded a fourth man who had been their accomplice. In the event only one of the three died, being hanged before the assembled convicts on 26 February. The two others were twice granted a stay of execution for twenty-four hours, and finally reprieved once more, which might seem to us a purely sadistic display of power, but which was intended to impress its victims with the mercy lurking within the terrible justice of the Crown. The two men were condemned to be 'transported' yet again when somewhere could be found to send them, and another convict who had stolen food and wine in the interim was granted his life only if he would take on the hideous role of public executioner.

All this and more, within a month of landing. Bowes Smyth's agitated cluckings give us some sense of the challenges Phillip faced in bringing each level of this unruly new society to hear and to heed his words. Phillip's own correspondence is notably smoother, largely having to do with the anxious business of housekeeping and the balancing of eroding provisions against reducing rations.

Phillip was also the patriarch of an expanding community:

managing his officers, sustaining the morale of the soldiery in a hardship post, struggling to restore the health of diseased and ailing convicts and then to get useful work out of them, and then, when he was able, finding new land, establishing new settlements. Given the urgency and the consequence of all these concerns, the energy Phillip expended on his relationship with the Australians is to my mind remarkable. I have come to think him close to visionary in his obstinate dream of integrating these newly discovered people into the British polity.

Phillip had arrived burdened with an armful of instructions on how to handle natives. As early as 1769, when Cook's *Endeavour* was about to embark on its voyage, the Earl of Morton, President of the Royal Society, presented Cook with a list of 'hints' for dealings with native peoples met along the way. The hints have the whiff of the candle about them; of pleasurable hours spent in desk-bound explorations. Beautifully clear principles were enunciated. The shedding of native blood was prohibited as 'a crime of the highest nature', these people being equal in the eyes of their Maker to 'the most Polished European'. Nor could they be deprived of their land without consent. Moreover, they could justly resist invaders whom 'they may apprehend are come to disturb them in the quiet possession of their country, whether the apprehension be well or ill founded'.

Morton realised that this last principle might be difficult to maintain, given that the British would have to get water and fresh food where they could. How to communicate the innocence of their intentions? So he set himself to devising a basic-needs alphabet in sign language. We watch his imagination take fire as he wrestles with this delightful problem:

Amicable signs may be made which they could not possibly mistake—Such as holding up a jug, turning it bottom upwards, to shew them it was empty, then applying it to the lips in the attitude of drinking, [or] opening the mouth wide, putting the fingers towards it, and then making the motion of chewing, would sufficiently demonstrate a want of food.

A question arises. Will the chewing always be understood to mean, 'We want to eat?' Might it not, under certain circumstances and in certain company, mean, 'We want to eat you'? But Morton does not falter, and proceeds smoothly to the next phase. Music, but only music of a soothing kind, should be employed. The natives should not be alarmed 'with the report of Guns, Drums, or even a trumpet', but rather 'be entertained near the Shore with a soft Air'. Thus, with savage breasts calmed, a landing could be effected and a few trinkets ('particularly looking Glasses') laid upon the shore. The newcomers would then tactfully withdraw to a small distance to observe the locals' response before a second landing was attempted. Furthermore, 'Should they in a hostile manner oppose a landing, and kill some men in the attempt, even this would hardly justify firing among them.'

Then, at last, comes the crucial qualifier: 'till every other gentle method had been tried'. In the last resort, the landing must be effected whether the natives resisted or not. Why? Because the expeditions' aims were scientific, and therefore virtuous. The British could land, even in the face of resistance. They could trade. All they could not do was to occupy the land without consent.

There is something disarming about these solemn lessons in mannerly imperialism, but as we would expect the 'hints' proved somewhat wanting as guides to action. Cook's first landing in New Zealand ended with his men withdrawing to their ship leaving their gifts of nails and beads on the corpse of a chief pierced through the heart by a musket shot. Cook already knew something the noble deskman did not: a lot of 'savages' enjoyed fighting. His New

Zealand experiences were only some among many initially peaceable encounters which had swirled into violence: as he coolly observed of the chief-killing episode, 'Had I thought that they would have made the least resistance I would not have come near them, but as they did not I was not to stand still and suffer either my self or those who were with me to be knocked on the head.' For once, Joseph Banks agreed with him. He thought the Maori were shockingly eager to fight, almost making a game of it: 'They always attacked, though seldom seeming to mean more than to provoke us to show them what we were able to do in this case. By many trials we found that good usage and fair words would not avail the least with them, nor would they be convinced by the noise of our firearms alone that they were superior to theirs.' The only thing to do was to fire to wound, because 'as soon as they had felt the smart of even a load of small shot and had time allowed them to recollect themselves from the effects of their artificial courage...they were sensible of our generosity in not taking the advantage of our superiority'. For Banks gunfire, not music, was the way to the savage heart.

Official instructions, however utopian, have a longer life than the stories drawn from hard experience. Governor Phillip brought a determination verging on obstinacy to the business of persuading the local population to friendship; a determination rare, possibly unique, in the gruff annals of imperialism. He pursued Morton's strategies from refusing to use guns, even at the cost of taking casualties, down to the detail of the ribbons and looking-glasses. (It is true that he also resorted to kidnap to convey his benevolent intentions, but that rough way to useful intercourse predates Columbus.) In a letter probably written in the July of that first hectic year of 1788 he gave the following detailed observations on the local inhabitants. (The capitals might imply pomposity to us, but not to a contemporary):

The Natives are far more numerous than expected, I reckon from fourteen to sixteen hundred in this Harbour, Broken Bay, and Botany Bay, and once [we fell in with] Two hundred and twelve Men in one part...The Women are constantly employed in the Canoes where I have seen them big with Child, and with very young Infants at their Breasts, they seem less fond of ornaments than the men. And I have [never?] seen them with their hair Ornamented with the Teeth of Dogs […] etc. as the Hair of the Men is frequently Ornamented.

I have reason to think that the Men do not want personal Courage [,] they readily place a confidence and appear to be a friendly and inoffensive people unless made Angry and which the most trifling circumstance does at times. Three convicts have been killed by them in the Woods and I have no doubt but that the Convicts were the [aggressors?].

They...are fond of any very Soft Musick, and will attend to singing any of the Words which they very readily repeat. But I know very little at present of the people. They never come into the Camp, and I have had few hours to seek them out. There are several roots which they Eat, and I have seen the Bones of the Kangurroo and flying Squirrel at the entrance to their huts, but Fish is their principal support which on these Shores is very scarce and I believe many of them are Starving.

Contrast this with Darwin's dismissive diagnoses regarding the Tierra del Fuegian 'savages' a mere fifty years later. Phillip grants no gulf in nature. We are still in the dawn of the world, with friendship between unlike peoples a blossoming hope—given the universality of reason and local good will.

Phillip was further disarmed by his first meetings with Australians, when his calm, weaponless advance and the offering of gifts led to the consummation of hand meeting hand in The

Handshake, to him a universal pledge of peace and friendship. (That same experiment could turn out differently. The historian Greg Dening tells a story of a British officer who was powerfully offended when another native on another beach grasped his extended hand, turned it over to see if it had anything in it—and then let it drop. The Britisher crossly concluded that these were an unpleasantly avaricious people.)

Phillip's serene account of the Australians' response to the British presence is obliquely confirmed by the gleeful descriptions George Worgan provided his brother in a letter written a month later. Worgan told of a string of meetings with locals whom he described as behaving like excited children at a Christmas party, holding out their hands for their presents, laughing heartily, jumping 'extravagantly', and whooping with pleasure as they examined the clothes, hats and hair of the newcomers. They also allowed themselves to be tricked out in 'different coloured Papers, and Fools'-Caps which pleased them mightily'. Even allowing for Worgan's determined jocularity these still look like astonishingly amiable meetings, incorporating startling hands-on intimacies. Worgan describes 'a Fellow' picking up a quill and 'trying to poke it through my Nose and two or three other Gentlemen's', as he checked to see whether their nasal septums were pierced or not, and then giving up and 'shewing Us that he could not wear it in his own, and shaking his head'.

Phillip, reading these scenes not with Worgan's irony but for the trusting good will he thought he saw demonstrated, was confirmed in his chosen policy. That policy and his personal example would keep the British and the local men on sufficiently peaceful terms for as long as they were under his eye. But he could not control attitudes. Here is a paragraph from Worgan, again to his brother, on what he really thought about the new people, beginning with his estimation of the charms of their women.

'It must be merely from the Curiosity, to see how they would behave...that one would be induced to touch one of Them, for they are Ugly to Disgust, in their countenances and stink of Fish-Oil and Smoke, *most sweetly*.' They are shapely enough; he allows that if some of them were cleaned up they might excite lust 'even in the frigid breast of a philosopher', but in their natural state the fish-oil and soot would keep more than philosophers away. He concludes: 'To sum up the Qualities Personal and mental...they appear to be an *Active, Volatile, Unoffending, Happy, Merry, Funny, Laughing, Good-natured, Nasty Dirty,* race of human Creatures as ever lived in a state of Savageness.' (Worgan's italics throughout.) He knew these people to be 'savages', and therefore creatures utterly unlike himself.

Pragmatic David Collins recognised the fish oil to be a sensible protection against both the ferocious local mosquitoes and the cold. Nonetheless he acknowledged that 'the oil, together with the perspiration from their bodies, produces, in hot weather, a most horrible stench' (the British had made landfall in late January, on the brink of the hottest month). He recorded he had seen some natives 'with the entrails of fish frying in the burning sun upon their heads, until the oil ran down over their foreheads'. Later we will see that the first thing the British did with their kidnap victims was to dump them in a tub, crop their hair and give them a thorough scrubbing before stuffing them into shirts, trousers and jackets. We can't know what the victims thought about any of this, only that they were terrified. It is also likely that the Australians found the stink of unwashed British flesh sweating in unwashed woollen clothing in Sydney heat at least as repellent, but in such encounters it is the literate who do all the complaining.

Less contemptuous and more curious observers than Worgan, and less complacent ones than Phillip, could be baffled as to Australian intentions. Surgeon John White had this to say about an unexpected and potentially dangerous encounter with 'about three hundred natives' at Botany Bay on 1 June:

> This was the greatest number of the natives we had ever seen together since our coming among them. What could be the cause of their assembling in such great numbers gave rise to a variety of conjectures. Some thought they were going to war among themselves. Others conjectured that some of them had been concerned in the murder of our men, notwithstanding we did not meet with the smallest trace to countenance such an opinion, and that, fearing we should revenge it, they had formed this convention in order to defend themselves against us. Others imagined that the assemblage might be occasioned by a burial, a marriage, or some religious meeting.

'A burial, a marriage, or some religious meeting'—or perhaps a preparation for war. It was certainly a deeply uncanny situation. It is against this background of casual contempt and intelligent anxiety that we have to locate Phillip's determined optimism. From the beginning, and remarkably, he recognised the Australians' wants and expressions to be as powerfully felt as his own, and as we will see he acknowledged some conflicts. But he also remained persuaded of something not at all evident: that in time the Australians would inevitably come to recognise the benefits of the British presence among them, not only in material matters, but in the unique, incomparable gift of British law.

First, for things material. Phillip:

> It is undeniably certain that to teach the shivering savage how to clothe his body, and to shelter himself completely from the cold

and wet, and to put into the hands of men, ready to perish one half of the year with hunger, the means of procuring constant and abundant provision, must confer upon them benefits of the highest value and importance.

Phillip did not regard this conviction as prior and ideological, but as the fruits of observation. He had watched these people suffer hunger when fish supplies dropped off in colder weather. He noted the meagreness of their vegetable resources, and how long and painfully the women laboured to collect and prepare them. He watched them in bad weather, and knew they suffered: 'While they have not made any attempt towards clothing themselves, they are by no means insensible to the cold, and appear very much to dislike the rain. During a shower they have been observed to cover their heads with pieces of bark, and to shiver exceedingly.' His response was typically direct. He decided that the moment he established good contact with these poor cold savages he would introduce them to the benefits of clothing. He therefore requested the immediate dispatch from England of 'a supply of frocks and jackets to distribute among them', urging that the garments be made long and loose 'so they would be useful to both men and women'.

Phillip, unlike some of his compatriots, acknowledged that sensibilities might differ between the races. He noted, for example, one Australian's disgust at the smell of salt pork lingering on his fingers after he had touched a piece. He thought such differences to be trivial and ephemeral, and that civilising savages would be easy because, as rational beings, they would readily recognise the superiority of British material and moral arrangements. Like most of us, Phillip believed his home culture to be universally advantageous and desirable. Furthermore, he believed it to be universally applicable and therefore transportable; that it could flourish in any clime. The irony of this vision, given the total British dependence on imported supplies and their near-starvation in a milieu where Australians had survived for millennia, quite escaped him. I doubt it escaped the Australians.

Every Britisher thought their superiority manifest in their possessions, especially their manufactured goods—clothing, guns, tools—but also what Tench calls 'toys': the baubles brought to charm and disarm the natives. All of the officers and some of the men had brought stocks of such objects to barter for native artefacts, which were enjoying a vogue at home since the voyages of the great, good, and martyred Captain Cook.

The model for pacification through trade had been established in Tahiti, that terrestrial Paradise. There Cook had seen an earth so spontaneously productive that 'in the article of food those people may almost be said to be exempt from the curse of our forefathers; scarcely can it be said that they earn their bread with the sweat of their brow, benevolent nature hath not only supply'd them with necessarys but with abundance of superfluities'. The human population also seemed blessed with superfluities of physical grace and natural intelligence. Immediately recognising the desirability of European goods, they leapt into enthusiastic trade, happily exchanging warm female flesh and a wondrous variety of fresh foods for European products, especially iron nails. (The British ships, surreptitiously denailed, were soon in danger of falling apart.)

The responsiveness of these delightful savages had given their new trading partners a reassuring illusion of the 'naturalness' of trans-cultural understanding. The sturdiness of Tahitians' appetite for British goods—'red and yellow cloth, some tomahawks, axes, knives, scissors, shirts, jackets, etc.'—together with the convenience of a 'king' ready to accept the personal reward of 'a mantle and some other articles of dress decorated with red feathers, together with six muskets and some ammunition', meant that as early as 1801 such items could be shipped to Tahiti from infant Sydney in full confidence that they would be exchanged for the pork the British hungered for.

After such encounters with village-dwelling agriculturalists long familiar with the benefit of trade, naked nomads—lacking pigs, fruits and kings, and cautiously frugal with their women—had to come as something of a disappointment, even to men uncorrupted by the mellow exchanges of Tahiti. These people did not covet the trinkets the British waggled at them. They seemed to lack a proper passion for novelties. Gifts of ribbons and neck-cloths were accepted, worn for a day, then hung on a bush and forgotten. They seemed also to regard most British foods as inedible. Nor did these natives have an 'abundance of superfluities' of their own available for exchange: it quickly became clear that every one of their hand-crafted multi-purpose possessions was essential for the daily business of surviving, and was duly cherished. They coveted only those British products which replicated the functions of their own tools, like metal hatchets or fishhooks. Tench himself, engaging in his first day of serious trading, found that a man whose spear he wanted would part with it only in exchange for a hatchet, and Tench had to have himself rowed all the way back to Sydney from the northern shore of the harbour to get him one.

The British should have paid more attention to the experiences of their predecessors. A hundred years before Cook, William Dampier visited the north-western coast of Australia and met some of the inhabitants. He did not stay long—not more than two months—but that was time enough to identify some disturbing characteristics of these particular natives. He could define them only by the negatives of all the things they did not have: no clothes, no houses, no beds, no gods; no sheep, no poultry, no cultivated foods.

And no decorum, either: they lived, he said, in heaps, twenty or thirty men, women and children piled together, sharing what they ate and eating what they could find. They were, in his opinion, 'the miserablest People in the World'.

However, despite all the negatives they seemed amiable enough, and with his experience of the docile workers of the islands behind him, Dampier thought they might as well be put to useful work. This is what happened next:

> We had found some Wells of Water here and intended to carry 2 or 3 barrels of it aboard. But as it was somewhat troublesome to carry it to the Canoes, we thought to have got these Men to carry it for us. And therefore we gave them some old Clothes: to one, a pair of old Breeches; to another, a ragged Shirt; to the third, a Jacket that was scarce worth owning, which would have been very acceptable in some of the places where we had been…We put them on them, thinking that this finery would have brought them to work heartily for us. And having filled our Water in small long Barrels, about six Gallons in each…we brought our new Servants to the Wells, and put a barrel on each of their Shoulders for them to carry to the Canoe.

So there they were, appropriately laden. Then came an unexpected difficulty:

> …all the signs we could make were to no purpose, for they stood like Statues without motion, and grinned like so many Monkeys, staring one upon another. For these poor Creatures do not seem accustomed to carrying Burdens, and I believe that one of our Ship-boys of ten years old would carry as much as one of them. So we were forced to carry our Water ourselves. They very fairly put the Clothes off again, and laid them down as if Clothes were only for working in. I did not perceive they had any great liking for them at first.

No talent for work, no taste for European clothing, and no admiration for 'anything we had'. We seem to hear the echo of ghostly black laughter rising from the page. This brief encounter set the tone for later ones: Australian incomprehension in the face of European exhortations, an obstinate disinclination to covet European goods, and an absolute refusal to embrace their predestined roles as hewers of wood or, in this case, haulers of water. Nomads have their own ways of managing the world.

One thing is clear to us. These radically modest local wants, which led to such confusion over what constituted grounds for legitimate exchange, ensured that in Australia trade could never become the Grand Pacifier it had proved elsewhere.

Phillip had read Dampier. What he seems to have remembered best was Dampier's comment that many of the men were lacking the upper right incisor. He happened to have lost that same tooth himself in some long-ago accident. He did not know how much that would matter, and he did not take the Dampier lesson regarding Australian recalcitrance at all. How could he, given the strength of his convictions regarding 'savage teachability'?

Consider his account of an early trans-racial meeting at Port Jackson. His strategy of mimed trust and the offer of gifts seemed to be working as well there as it had in Botany Bay, so confirming, as he thought, the excellence of his diplomatic technique. (Oddly, it rarely occurred to the British that the Australians might be in communication with each other, with information about the white men running before them. Like imperialists earlier and later, they tended to take each meeting as *de novo* and 'the natives' as perennially innocent.) At the Port Jackson meeting Phillip was particularly delighted to find a man fascinated by his first sight of an iron pot full of boiling water. Phillip reports:

He...went on with me to examine what was boiling in the pot, and exprest his admiration in a manner that made me believe he intended to profit from what he saw, and which I made him understand he might very easily do by the help of some oyster shells...by these hints, added to his own observation, he would be able to introduce the art of boiling among his countrymen.

The art of boiling introduced to Australia by Phillip's solemn dumb-show. I suppose teachers everywhere tend to overestimate the effectiveness of their teaching, if only to avoid despair.

But it was the moral challenge which most enthralled him. Given that these Australians were intelligent beings, capable of reciprocating trust and assessing consequences, they were also capable of being 'civilised' in the fullest (British) sense. Being fully confident that British superiority must have been obvious to all parties, he was able to interpret what were probably displays of Australian insouciance or tolerant courtesies extended to uncouth strangers as admiring recognitions of superiority. Experience kept confirming his reading, as experience will. One example: at the cove he had named Manly to mark his high estimation of the impressive men he met there, a noisy group of Australians who had been 'very troublesome when we were preparing our dinner' quietly subsided when he drew a circle in the sand and gestured that they should stay outside it, so that he and his officers could eat in peace. They sat in silence outside the circle; the British ate. Phillip took this as 'another proof of how tractable these people are, when no injury or insult is offered, and when proper means are used to influence the simplicity of their minds'. That they might have been shocked into silence by the ignorance of these extraordinary guests, who sat down without invitation, and who then gobbled their food with no hint of sharing even between each other, much less with their hosts, did not occur to him. How could it? Phillip knew nothing of nomad protocols of food-sharing.

More damningly, and, as time was to show, most damagingly, he believed these people to be bereft of formal rules to live by, and so confidently assumed that his greatest gift to them would not be British manners or cooking techniques, desirable as they were, but the gift of British justice mediated by British law. In time he would learn, slowly, painfully, that Australians were rather less teachable than he had thought. It would be on deep disagreements regarding the moral foundation of law that his dreams of enduring reconciliation would founder.

CAPTAIN JOHN HUNTER, COMMANDER OF HMS *SIRIUS*

Jane Austen exclaimed that her naval-officer brothers 'write so even, so clear, both in style and penmanship, so much to the point, and give so much intelligence, that it is enough to kill one'. In her novels she allowed herself to become positively girlish in her effusions of admiration for naval men like Fanny's brother William or Anne Elliot's Captain Wentworth, and quite lost her characteristic irony when she considered the nobility of their profession.

I confess that as I read John Hunter's journal I felt something of the same flutter. I liked what he said, and I liked his silences, too. He was silent as he watched his big, beautiful *Sirius* pounded to pieces on a reef at Norfolk Island in February 1790, knowing he would have to face a court-martial for its loss; knowing its loss to be unavoidable; knowing that he and his men would be marooned on the island for unknown months to come (eleven, as it turned out), being treated as so many extra mouths to feed and ignominiously subordinate to a mere marine. He was silent regarding his loathing of that marine, Major Ross, new governor of the island: officers do not denigrate their fellow-officers. But he was unhesitatingly brisk in his criticism of unseamanlike behaviour, as when a ship's captain en route to China decided not to waste valuable time calling in on the forlorn little sub-colony of Norfolk, leaving the islanders bereft of provisions, news, and the hope that they had not been forgotten. Here was the very model of an eighteenth-century British sea captain.

I especially liked watching how his few mannerisms fell away when he wrote on matters nautical. Reading the accounts of those naval officers today, we recognise a shared view of what mattered and how what mattered should be ordered. New territories like Port Jackson were described in accordance with a formula: geographic form, terrain, bays, rivers and creeks; human inhabitants considered under the headings of economic organisation, social organisation, political organisation (if discernible), religious thought (if decipherable); local fauna, local flora. Their laconic recording of events in stern chronological order derived from their habituation to the grid-form of ships' logs, with their topics typically following the model of the journals of the great Cook. They also acquired a daunting array of skills. They were responsible for their own charts, maps and 'views' (exaggerated profiles of coastlines for easy visual identification), and their written sailing directions would be crucial guides for all later mariners entering those waters. That training in naval draughtsmanship meant that once landed they could supply land maps, sketches, landscapes, and even carefully precise drawings of previously 'non descript' creatures and plants. There were three especially skilled draughtsmen on board the *Sirius*: Captain Hunter himself, his first mate Lieutenant Bradley, and young George Raper, appointed midshipman on the voyage out, possibly the most gifted of the three, who would never see England again. He would die of fever off Batavia when he was twenty-four.

These men were sons of the English scientific enlightenment, and proud of it. But they were seamen first of all. On all professional matters—the location of reefs, shoals and currents, the seasons and habits of treacherous winds—Hunter's easy exactitude reminds us of something we landlubbers forget. For men like Hunter, as for Phillip, the 'trackless oceans' were well-signed thoroughfares linking familiar ports and provisioning centres, and thick with memories, familiar to them in ways the land spaces of the colonies could never be.

Hunter's unusual insouciance regarding land-based catastrophes presumably derived from his conviction that worse things happen at sea. On land he used his fine measuring eye to assess, for example, the accuracy and the killing power of native spears, crucial information to the intruders and also, as we will see, to us, as we struggle to retrieve Australian intentions from British accounts of their aggression. (Preliminary example: did spears which fell short miss deliberately, or through lack of skill or power?) Hunter could recognise the strategic deployment of Australian warriors in situations which to less experienced eyes would look like savage chaos.

He was also, by his own confession, rather too quick to resolve ambiguous situations by force. During an apparently friendly encounter with some of the local people, but after several British stragglers had been speared by unknown assailants, a warrior suddenly flung a spear. It whistled a good six feet over the startled Britishers' boat, so the gesture was probably theatrical, but Hunter snatched up his gun, intending to discharge it into the midst of the clustered Australians. The gun misfired, the men fled, and no permanent damage was done, but Hunter knew he had been hasty: 'It was perhaps fortunate that my gun did not go off; as I was so displeased by their treachery, that it is highly probable I might have shot one of them,' which would have been directly contrary to Phillip's requirement of restraint. Hunter was normally obedient to his superiors, but he was not of a temperament to give second chances.

As an artist Hunter drew with stern devotion to accuracy. Although we might feel that his representations of, for example, the platypus or the wombat fall far short of capturing the creatures' distinctive forms of life, we have to remember he was often drawing from a corpse or even from an emptied skin—although we have to remember too that the great George Stubbs, also working from a skin, could re-create a marvellously vivid kangaroo back in England. But Hunter's birds are unfailingly marvellous and his written account is alive with images no one else thought to mention. Painted dancers at a little distance 'appeared accoutred with cross belts'; others, with 'narrow white streaks around the body, with a broad line down the middle of the back and belly, and a single stripe down each arm, thigh and leg', gave the wearers 'a most shocking appearance; for upon the black skin the white marks were so very conspicuous, that they were exactly like so many moving skeletons'.

Despite his artist's eye we might judge Hunter to be unpleasantly haughty in his accounts of the Australians, rather like a squire observing the doings of a beagle pack. He was eager to control situations, and rather too fond of taking calculated liberties. One example: when on one occasion he suspected that the local women were being deliberately kept at a distance, he exerted himself to lure them closer, and was triumphant when he succeeded—or was permitted to succeed. He took little interest in Phillip's civilising mission; he thought the Australians physically repellent because they were 'abominably filthy', and he describes their filthiness with his usual visual exactitude:

they never clean their skin, but it is generally smeared with the fat of such animals as they kill, and afterwards covered by every sort of dirt; sand from the sea beach, and the ashes from their fires, all adhere their greasy skin, which is never washed, except when accident, or the want of food, obliges them to go into the water.

And he gives no hint that he thought the Australians even potentially educable: when 'passion' overcame them, he said, 'they act as all savages do, as madmen'.

Were this all we knew of him, we would not like him. But there was good humour in him, and male competitiveness, too. To return to dancing: Hunter was one of the white guests invited to the corroboree staged by Baneelon and Colbee early in 1791, just after the 'coming in'. He was particularly impressed by a remarkable feat performed by the male dancers, achieved by 'placing their feet very wide apart, and, by an extraordinary exertion of the muscles and thighs, moving the knees in a trembling and very surprising manner'. Then he adds, casually, 'which none of us could imitate', and suddenly we know that at some stage of the evening Hunter and other Englishmen were on their feet and in the ring, furiously wobbling their knees. I have a subliminal vision of tourists visiting indigenous territories nowadays being pulled to their feet and made to stumble through a parody of an Australian dance, to the covert giggles and overt shouts of encouragement of the locals.

Hunter also chose to report an apparently trivial episode in detail. In June 1789 'the Governor, Captain Collins (the judge-advocate), Captain Johnston of the Marines, Mr White, principal surgeon of the settlement, Mr Worgan, Mr Fowell and myself, from the *Sirius*' plus 'two men, all armed with muskets', set off for Broken Bay to explore the Hawkesbury River. Notice that these imperialists had to do without the glamour and ease of horse-borne exploration, the one stallion and three mares belonging to the colony being far too precious to risk in such adventures. They had to walk, and to carry their own supplies, in this case 'several days provisions, Water, Arms and ammunition', and we wonder what Australian warriors, moving so lightly over the land, would have made of these grotesquely burdened travellers.

This time the tents and poles and extra provisions could be ferried to the agreed beach rendezvous by boat, and by afternoon the walkers were setting up their base camp. Then someone stumbled upon a girl, still weak from the smallpox epidemic which had swept the area a month before, crouching in the wet grass close by the camp. The whole party trooped off to look at her, scaring her even further out of her wits. Hunter reports: 'She was very much frightened on our approaching her, and shed many tears, with piteous lamentations.'

The gentlemen went into a flurry of action. A fire was made, grass dried, birds shot, skinned and laid on the fire to broil 'along with some fish', and water, of which she was in great need, given her. Then they stacked up fuel for her fire, put her to bed by covering her with warm dried grass, and retired contentedly to their tents.

The next morning the girl was rather less frightened, and when the British party returned from their day's walking late that afternoon they found she had moved to a little bark hut on the beach. Now she had a little girl with her, whom she was trying to protect from falling rain by covering her with her body. The child was, in Hunter's bachelor opinion, 'as fine a little infant of that age as I ever saw', but desperately afraid of the strangers: however much they coaxed 'it could not be prevailed on to look up; it lay with its face upon the ground, and one hand covering its eyes.' (Note again the visual detail.) Again they plied the mother with meat, fish and fuel, this time heaping dried grass over her hut to keep her warmer, and in the morning, when they visited again, the baby was ready to hold a British hand. I hope it was Hunter's. He has just betrayed an unexpected tenderness towards small children. Then, leaving the mother with good supplies of fuel, food and water, they set off on their expedition upriver. When they returned after a few days' (inconclusive) exploring, their friend and her child had gone.

I cite this episode because it tells us a great deal about Hunter we would not otherwise know. It also reminds us how precarious are the edifices we build from surviving fragments from the past. Hunter might have left out the incident as trivial; or his publisher might have struck it out as behaviour unbecoming to serious-minded Britons. Instead he chose to memorialise it on the title page of the first edition of Hunter's *Historical Journal.* There is the naked woman cowering with her baby in a curved grass shelter; there are the tall Englishmen standing protectively around her like a wall. The image provides no model for the future: not very much later, Australian women, and Australian babies too, would die of British bullets. Nonetheless, we have been permitted to see these men bustling about arranging for the comfort of a frightened woman.

The accident of our knowledge of this particular incident also reminds us how many other Britishers, articulate in their own time, have been retrospectively struck as dumb as Lot's reckless wife because no record of their actions happens to survive. The 'historical record', with its silences, absences and evasions, accidental and deliberate, is a most imperfect mirror of 'what happened'.

SURGEON-GENERAL JOHN WHITE

By his own account Surgeon White enjoyed playing the gallant on the voyage out. Thirty years old and unmarried, he sought the company of women, whether Dutch or Brazilian, in the ports along the way and flirted zestfully with them. In Rio he was charmed to discover that the Portuguese, reputedly a jealous race, were so delighted by compliments paid their womenfolk that they were ready to grant a delightful degree of access to them, as he discovered when a gentleman asked him to help rebind the magnificent floor-length hair he had ordered his wife to loose so the charming English officer could properly admire its abundance. While other officers on shore leave no more than glimpsed feminine shadows behind latticed windows, White spent tender hours at convent grilles in halting conversation with the lovely novices within. He enjoyed every aspect of his stay in Rio except for the lack of coffee-houses, an odd absence to claim for Brazil, especially when we know that the masters of the different vessels 'all adjourn'd to a Coffee house to Breakfast [where] they had Coffee in great plenty, sweatmeats [sic] & a great variety of rich cakes' after they had done their marketing, a treat they enjoyed so much they described it in detail to Arthur Bowes Smyth, cooped up on the *Lady Penrhyn*.

Surprisingly, White enjoyed Capetown nearly as well as exotic Rio. During three years spent in the West Indies he had been sickened by the British style of slavery: 'The bare retrospect of the cruelties I have seen…there excites a kind of horror that chills my blood.' By contrast the Dutch, cruel as they were to delinquent compatriots (they were slowly broken on the wheel) treated their slaves with 'great humanity and kindness'. And if the Dutch ladies were not quite as fetching as the dark-eyed Brazilians, they were of a 'peculiar gay turn', cheerfully allowing liberties unthinkable in England. No tender sighings here: in Capetown he found he had to adopt more robust ways to be 'the favourite with the fair'. The local style, he found, was to '*grapple* the lady' (his italics), 'and paw her in a manner that does not partake in the least of gentleness'. A gallant was also expected to 'ravish kisses even in the presence of her parents', as White gallantly did. Other countries, other customs.

White was also a fine surgeon, and proud of it. In Rio he displayed his professional skills before a sceptical local audience by amputating a man's leg by a new method, and silenced the scoffers when the stump healed in as many days as the weeks it usually took. And for all his playboy style in port, throughout the voyage he maintained an active concern for the health of the people in his charge, convict and free. When he joined the fleet assembling for the voyage to Botany Bay at Portsmouth he was told by 'a medical gentleman from Portsmouth' that a 'malignant disease' was loose among the convicts on the *Alexander* which would demand their immediate re-landing, a daunting undertaking. When White hurried below to test the truth of the story, he found several men suffering from 'slight inflammatory complaints' but badly frightened by gloomy prognostications, others physically and mentally debilitated by long imprisonment, and others again keeping to their beds 'to avoid the inconvenience of the cold, which was at this time very piercing'. With a David Collins these diagnoses would have led to scoldings and angry rousings-out, but White thought the malingerers' strategy perfectly sensible, given that their 'wretched clothing' gave them no protection from the cold. He briskly reassured the invalids that the prognostications were false and that they would surely recover, and on the spot promised the rest of his eager listeners that warm clothes would be found for those who needed them, and that the salt rations they had been living on for the last four months while moored in a British port would be immediately replaced by fresh beef and vegetables. He also arranged with the ship's master for the convicts to be brought up on deck daily, 'one half at a time...in order that they might breathe a purer air'. Then, with matters sorted out below, he hurried back to the quarterdeck to demolish the interfering 'medical gentleman', who was unwise enough to repeat his destructive nonsense.

This energetic common sense made White an excellent surgeon for a convict fleet. He had been able to act so decisively because Phillip, who knew him from earlier voyages (remember how small a world this was), had given him authority to order what was necessary for the health and well-being of 'the people'. We have an account from the lower deck of White's precautions from the marine private Jonathan Easty, who records the time he spent scrubbing and whitewashing in the first days of the voyage. White continued alert to threats to his charges' health, and was inventive in removing them: when the women convicts showed so pertinacious a desire to get into the men's quarters that the hatches had to be kept closed, White prevailed on Phillip to have gratings made, which kept the sexes apart but at least let them breathe.

When White unloaded his convict cargo at Sydney Cove in late January 1788, there had been a mortality rate of only one in seventeen for the whole voyage, despite its miserable beginnings. This was a remarkable feat, especially when contrasted with the human catastrophe wrought among the convicts of the Second and Third fleets by greed and neglect. (The death rate for the Second Fleet is said to have been one in four, and for the Third Fleet one in eleven.) An officer of the New South Wales Corps travelling with the Second Fleet judged that 'the slave trade is merciful to what I have seen in this fleet'. Twenty-one months after first landing, with the health of the settlement in White's charge, Phillip could report that there had been only seventy-two deaths, including some by execution and misadventure, and with twenty-six due to long-standing causes. Even after the mayhem of the 1790 convict fleets, and despite increasingly desperate shortages of food, blankets and supplies, White somehow kept most of the people in his charge alive and sufficiently healthy.

Some time during 1790, with life in the colony harsh and getting harsher, White found solace with a young convict woman, Rachel Turner, first his housekeeper, later his mistress. Rachel bore him a son in September 1793. He was proud of his boy, and when he returned to England on the *Daedalus* in December 1794 he took his fifteen-month-old child with him, and found him a loving carer in the sister of his old friend Lieutenant Henry Waterhouse, which indicates how close-knit the friendships wrought in the course of colonial tours of duty were. Meanwhile White's convict mistress, presumably aided by his good offices, had landed on her feet: in 1797 she was granted a special dispensation from the governor succeeding Phillip to marry a free settler, and together they went on to become one of the most prosperous couples in the colony. White himself did not marry until 1799, and then he brought his natural son into his growing household. Andrew Douglas White continued a source of pride to his father, joining the Royal Engineers and fighting at Waterloo. Then early in 1823, a year after his father's death, the young man travelled back to Sydney to be reunited with his mother, now a respectable colonial matron. Clearly the meeting was a success: Andrew Douglas later willed his mother his cherished Waterloo medal.

White's enthusiasm for the fauna of the new continent was evident from first contact, but how did this brusque, warm-tempered man respond to its human inhabitants? He was, as we might expect, charmed by the women. Out on an expedition with the governor late in August 1788, the British fell in with a large party of Australians at Manly Cove, and the women, who seemed to stand 'in very great dread' of their menfolk, were coaxed into accepting gifts: 'Every gentleman,' White tells us, 'singled out a female and presented her with some trinkets…' Commenting appreciatively that 'many of the women were strait, well-formed, and lively', White decked his chosen girl with strips of cloth torn from his pocket and neck handkerchiefs. Then, 'having nothing left except the buttons of my coat, on her admiring them, I cut them away, and with a piece of string tied them round her waist'. Chivalrous indeed, with the weather chill and not the least prospect of any more buttons. 'Thus ornamented,' White continues happily, 'and thus delighted with her new acquirements, she turned from me with a look of inexpressible archness.' He was more than content with the exchange.

For all his stay, White would display a good eye for details of Australian behaviour and an easy tolerance in matters of race. In the autumn of 1789, when the Australians were ravaged by a smallpox epidemic, White did his best to save some of the afflicted, and took a survivor, a six-year-old boy called Nanbaree, into his household. He was content to keep Nanbaree on a very light rein, leaving him free to visit his kin at will, to sustain his duties to them and to fulfil his ritual obligations as required. Throughout his life, Nanbaree was to move between the two worlds with more confidence and at less personal cost than any of his Australian contemporaries.

From his first days in the colony White deeply enjoyed tramping through the bush taking pot-shots at novel animals and birds. He made what he insisted was an 'excellent soup' out of a white cockatoo and a couple of crows, and he was delighted to discover that the 'New Holland Cassowary', the bird we call the emu, tasted 'not unlike tender young beef'. He had begun collecting specimens on behalf of a friend, but the favour flowered into a passion, and he quickly became a dedicated naturalist himself. His journal covered only the first ten months of his time at Sydney, with the first edition being published in 1791, only a year after Tench's engaging narrative and the weightier compilation from Phillip's dispatches titled *The Voyage of Governor Phillip to Botany Bay*. The White volume was angled towards a particular market: the growing band of amateur natural scientists. Its title declared its ambition: *Journal of a Voyage to New South Wales with Sixty-five Plates of Non Descript Animals, Birds, Lizards, Serpents, curious Cones of trees and other natural Productions by John White Esq., Surgeon General to the Settlement*. Those sixty-five plates must have taken some organisation. Despite his powers of exact observation (for evidence see any one of his bird descriptions), White lacked the co-ordination of hand and eye of a draughtsman, and had to corral any available talent to secure his illustrations.

However—there is a strange absence from White's accounts of

the local birds, and from the accounts of his fellow diarists too. None of them describe the extraordinary noises made by so many Australian birds: no reference to the souls-in-torment shrieking of the sulphur-crested cockatoo or the kookaburra's Mrs Rochester laugh; no reference to the vocal pyrotechnics of the rufous whistler— although Tench does allow that 'in the woods are various little songsters, whose notes are equally sweet and plaintive'. Most insulting of all, while Collins gives a careful description of the feathers of the lyrebird, which he thought a type of bird-of-paradise, he fails to mention its golden voice. Did no one bother to listen? (It is evening and roosting time now, and the racket outside is tremendous.) Did sounds not interest classifying scientists? Or is it that we only 'hear' the birdsongs of our youth?

JUDGE-ADVOCATE DAVID COLLINS

David Collins, also thirty years old in 1788, accepted the post of judge-advocate in the new colony when his useful but undistinguished career in the Marine Corps was interrupted by the ending of the American war. Within months he also became Phillip's secretary and, in time, his friend, although never, I think, his confidant. Phillip was by nature and policy a secretive man.

Collins had minimal legal experience, but he was a man of steady intelligence and conventional mind, and discharged his judicial duties to the satisfaction of his more reasonable colleagues. Such duties in a convict colony must have been onerous enough, but Collins was a prodigious worker, choosing to take his position as secretary to mean he should keep a quasi-official chronicle of events suitable for later publication. As early as July 1788 George Worgan knew Collins was preparing such a narrative, and in a letter to his brother declared he stood ready to recommend it 'in preference to any other, because from his Genius I am certain it will be the most Entertaining, Animating, Correct and satisfactory of any that may appear'.

Worgan was of a sardonic turn of mind, especially when writing to his brother, so there may be a joke here. From what Collins has left on the page it is difficult to imagine him 'entertaining' or 'animating'. His aim, it seems, was to be Master of Plod. But he was as 'correct' as human frailty allows, and profoundly 'satisfactory' in a range of ways: for example, without him we would never know the favourite petty derelictions of convicts, and so could not know which deprivations chafed them most. Professionally close-mouthed regarding trouble between officers, his occasional rumbles against the obnoxious Major Ross are the more revealing. And we could not know the enigmatic Phillip half so well if we did not have this big, solid fellow always at his heels, providing his own commentary on Phillip's sometimes ambiguous actions.

During the colony's infant years, Collins found the climate, land and problems of supply so intractable that he had little faith in its survival. Nonetheless he enumerated every new building, whether prison, provisions shed, windmill or granary, and soberly redrew the map of material progress at the end of each month. His favourite metaphors for growth came from agriculture. It was a vegetable growth he looked for, with steady expansion and increasingly rich fruits the sure reward of postponed gratification and systematic labour. I think this was one reason why he found convicts so repellent. Content merely to scratch the soil so that precious seeds withered, seeming to lack any sense of communal responsibility, they were also incurably improvident, gobbling their weekly rations and then living from day to day by thieving from their fellows.

Paradoxically, he was at least as offended by evidence of convict solidarity: 'There was such a tenderness in these people to each other's guilt, such an acquaintance with vice and the different degrees of it, that unless they were detected in the fact, it was generally next to impossible to bring an offence home to them.' Six months of close contact was enough to persuade him that, a very few individuals excepted, convicts were a race apart and crime the convict soul made visible: irremediably feckless, with no inner discipline and no recognition of consequences.

His diagnosis was not, as ours might be, of class solidarity forged out of shared experience. For Collins character was not the product of circumstance. He thought what bound convicts together was their natural amorality. They were the scourings of society, and only a few had the least chance of rehabilitation.

His most scathing condemnations were reserved for Irish convicts, and for all convict women. But despite his animus, and despite his warmly conjugal communications with his wife Maria, Collins himself soon took a young convict girl as his mistress. At seventeen Ann Yates was sentenced to hang for stealing a bolt of printed cotton. Reprieved to transportation, she bore a child to a seaman called Theakston during the voyage out on the *Lady Penrhyn*. The boy was later baptised by the Reverend Johnson and given his father's name, but Theakston sailed for China and out of Ann's life early in May 1788. In November 1791, she bore Collins his first child, a daughter, and in June 1793 his only son, and she remained his lover for the rest of his years in the colony. They never cohabited. Yates, who in time received her freedom, continued to live in the convicts' quarters with her children, while Collins preferred to live in the governor's house, close by his friend and his work. Such liaisons were common—most officers had some enduring connection with convict women—but I still wonder what Collins found to say as he glided out of the governor's house of an evening.

Collins neglected neither Ann nor his children by her. He bequeathed her a holding of 100 acres of land on the Hawkesbury when he left the colony late in 1796 to return to the embraces of his loyal wife Maria, who had assuaged her loneliness during his long absence by writing romantic novels. Ann and the two children happened to travel back to England on the same ship, probably disembarking at Liverpool on their way to Ann's native Yorkshire. The little family of three returned to Australia in July 1799, and the children were later reunited with their father during his governorship of Tasmania.

Collins already was, or was to become, a susceptible man. Travelling to Australia in 1803, again without Maria, to establish a colony first and abortively at Port Phillip, then successfully at Hobart, he met the pretty young wife of a convict on the voyage out and became enamoured of her. The relationship scandalised Hobart Town throughout Collins' governorship, especially given the cuckolded husband's affable compliance, the privileges Collins granted the pair, and the trio's relaxed conduct in public.

Collins is especially important to us because without his dutiful recording it would be difficult to trace the interactions between Australians and British in the years after the Australians decided to 'come in' to Sydney Town. As his passion for agricultural metaphors suggests, he was a perfect representative of the moral and material economy of European culture. It was these assumptions he brought to his analysis of the convict condition, and which he initially brought to the encounter with the very different culture and economy of the nomad people of Australia.

He began by seeing them as nuisances, as, for example, in the matter of fishing. At first, he said, they had been happy to help draw the great nets of the British, and to wait quietly for a share of the catch. (They must have been both impressed and appalled by the efficiency of British net-hauling in contrast to their hook-and-line or spearing techniques.) Then, with winter coming on and fish scarcer, a British party had been drawing in a big haul when warriors swept down and 'took by force about half of what had been brought on shore', while spearmen stood with spears poised for throwing. We might think that leaving half the catch to predatory uninvited guests was generous, but while Collins allowed that the natives were hungry, he saw the action as both irrational and wantonly hostile. He was as yet no readier to grant intelligent motivations to savages than he was to convicts.

His initial philosophical response to the nature of Australian existence was nonetheless surprisingly perceptive. From the beginning Collins exempted the Australians from the commitment to progress and accumulation he required of civilised men. He recognised that their way of life was timeless, reiterative rather than progressive, and his expressed hope was that even after the arrival of the British they could be left in their timeless universe 'under a dispensation to keep them happy in their liberties'. However, precisely because their ways of thinking and being were incompatible with those of the British, they would have to continue their timeless existence elsewhere, beyond the expanding British colony (remember that in his understanding the rest of the land was 'empty'). These people were certainly fully human, but they were also *sui generis*, and therefore unassimilable.

Collins was accordingly contemptuous of Phillip's efforts to incorporate the Australians into British society over those first years, dismissing his tireless negotiations as time and energy wasted on 'amusing ourselves with these children of ignorance', as he grumpily put it. Better, he thought, to drive them away, and keep them away, by the judicious use of muskets. He continued to believe that separation would have been the best policy for both peoples. But as the slow years pass we watch David Collins ripen into an absorbed observer of native conduct, and a man capable of recognising, indeed of honouring, a quite different way of being.

WATKIN TENCH,
CAPTAIN-LIEUTENANT OF MARINES

Watkin Tench of the Royal Marines, unmarried but already a veteran of the American wars, was about thirty when he landed at Port Jackson. His reports from the new colony immediately outsold his loftier competitors', and continue to outsell them today. He is one of the handful of writers who are an unshadowed pleasure to meet on the page. Through that familiar miracle of literacy where pothooks transform into personality, it is not so much his information as his presence which delights us. His parents are said to have run a dancing academy, and it tempting to think that their son's grace on the page has something to do with a melodious, light-footed upbringing. He has the kind of charm which reaches easily across centuries. If he lacks Montaigne's intellectual sophistication and unwavering moral clarity, he shares with him the even rarer quality of sunny self-irony.

Almost all we know of the man is here, in the two and a half hundred pages of his two books, and yet we think we know him. George Worgan dismissed him as a lightweight incapable of producing anything beyond 'fireside chit-chat', but it is precisely

Tench's cosy informality, together with his eye for the apparently redundant detail, which charms as it informs.

The best reason for reading Watkin Tench is that he reminds us of two important things surprisingly easy to forget: that the past was real, and that this likeable man whose words are on the page before us was actually there. In his writings Tench lives again, as he makes the people he sees around him live, especially the men and women rendered near-invisible or unintelligible in too many other accounts: the indigenous inhabitants of the Sydney region.

The great anthropologist W. E. H. Stanner, reflecting on the long alienation between European and Aboriginal Australians, believed that the grossly unequal relationship that developed in the earliest days of the colony—he says within the first five years—continued to inflict injustice and injury on generations of Aboriginal Australians to his own day. He believed that those serial injustices found their root in the British failure to comprehend, much less to tolerate, legitimate difference: an intolerance which then sustained itself in the face of a long history of practical intimacy; of long-term work and sexual relationships, even childhoods spent in one another's company. He believed crippling incomprehension continues to rule because 'a different tradition leaves us tongueless and earless towards this other [Aboriginal] world of meaning and significance'.

As we will see, there is much truth in that. But if Watkin Tench was initially rendered 'tongueless and earless' by the strangeness of the people he fell among he was never eyeless, even at the beginning, and with experience and reflection he came to hear a little of what was being said, and to tell us about it. That little is precious.

In new colonies race relations are shaped quickly, usually during the first few years of contact, and not by rational decision but by hugger-mugger accidents, casual misreadings, and unthinking responses to the abrasions inevitable during close encounters of the cultural kind. Tench was in the colony for only four years. By the time he left, in December 1791, and despite the good will of leaders on both sides, rapprochement was a fading dream, but Tench's eager gaze and pleasure in the unfamiliar holds out the hope that, by reading him and his peers, we might be able to identify the small events, and the compounding errors, which were to have such large and finally tragic consequences.

What made Tench incomparable among good observers is that he treated each encounter with the strangers as a detective story: 'This is what they did. What might they have meant by doing that?' This glinting curiosity is uniquely his. (Compare him with John Hunter, who also watches keenly, but at a condescending distance: the squire watching his beagles.) Tench always saw the Australians as fellow humans, and their conduct as therefore potentially intelligible. This focus on action is essential in ethnohistory, which is what we call history when the people we are curious about have left no easily decipherable records of their own, and when their intentions and understandings have to be constructed out of descriptions given by literate outsiders who often do not know what they are looking at (a wedding?...a war party?). At best we can hope for the documentary equivalent of a silent film shot by a fixed camera—a camera which cannot know precisely where the focus of action is. It is that alert, steady gaze that Tench grants us.

Tench was a marine, but his journals do not follow the naval model. It is true that on the voyage out he gives triumphantly precise measurements of latitude and new-fangled longitude, that marvellous fruit of the new science, and like any young man involved in grand affairs he brims with advice: potential settlers may buy their poultry, wines and tobacco in Tenerife, the Madeiras, the Cape of Good Hope, anywhere—but they must buy their sheep and hogs in England, and bring all their clothing, furniture and tools with them. But that was on the voyage. Once arrived in Australia he left such matters to others, nor did he bother with visual illustrations beyond a single map. While he was astonished by the weirder fauna and delighted by some of the flora, his natural tendency was towards philosophising rather than science, and his descriptions of the land's human inhabitants come sequined with reflections and anecdotes. An example: while he, like his competitors, provided the conventional description of the physical attributes of the Australian—long-muscled, skin char-black, hair wavy, beards scant—only Tench thought to tell us that the Australians' 'large black eyes are universally shaded by the long thick sweepy eyelash'. He finished with a dancing-school flourish which does not quite come off—'[the sweepy eyelash is] so much prized in appreciating beauty, that perhaps hardly any face is so homely that this aid can to some degree render interesting; and hardly any so lovely which, without it, bears not some trace of insipidity'—which leaves us slightly dizzy. But we will not forget those eyelashes.

Tench also had a sharp eye for what the anthropologists call 'material culture'. He was especially intrigued by the Australians' canoes, as James Cook had been in his time. In New Zealand Cook had been impressed by the 'great ingenuity and good workmanship in the building and framing of [Maori] Boats or Canoes', which he described as 'long and narrow and shaped very much like a New England Whale boat', that universal model of fine small-boat design. They were also splendidly large, the largest being capable of carrying up to one hundred men along with their arms. By contrast, he was outraged by the sheer effrontery of Australian canoes: 'The worst I think I ever saw, they were about twelve or fourteen feet long made of one piece of the bark of a tree drawn or tied up at each end and the middle kept open by means of pieces of sticks by way of thwarts.'

Bradley of the *Sirius* recorded his contempt for the flimsy craft, so unlike the sleek double-hullers he knew from Tahiti—no more than a narrow strip of bark, he said, inelegant, unstable, and propelled by ludicrous paddles 'in shape like a pudding stirrer' held one in each hand. Nonetheless, Bradley had to allow that in these apologies for canoes the local men went astonishingly fast: sitting back on their heels with knees spread to hold out the sides, with bodies erect and paddling furiously with their pudding-stirrers, they could slice through a heavy surf (and we know how big the surf around Sydney can be) 'without oversetting or taking in more water than in smooth seas'.

In these same horribly unstable craft men would leap to their feet and proceed to spear fish with four-metre-long spears, or alternatively lie athwart the canoe, heads fully submerged to get a clear view, spears at the ready, while a companion did his best to keep the craft balanced for the thrust. Thinking of Sydney Harbour we think of sharks, but the Australians kept themselves out of the water unless there was no help for it—and what use would a heavier canoe be against a white pointer with murder in its heart? (Tench: 'Sharks of an enormous size are found here. One of these was caught by the people on board the *Sirius*, which measured at the shoulders six feet and a half [two metres] in circumference.')

Tench recognised the élan of these men, paddling kilometres into the open sea in mere twists of bark. But (typically) he looked beyond male flamboyance to the women, and they impressed him even more. A woman would go out in her skiff, 'a piece of bark tied at both ends with vines, and the edge of it just above the water', with a nursling child precariously perched on her shoulders and gripping her hair. The baby would be swung down to the breast when its grizzling grew too loud, and then swung up again so the mother could get on with her hook-and-line fishing in woman's style. Hunger being a close companion, both men and women nurtured small fires on clay pads in the bottom of their canoes, cooking and eating the first fish as they were taken, and taking the rest of the catch back to shore to be shared.

Captain Hunter of the *Sirius* also recognised seamanship when he saw it, even in women, and again we see his endearing concern for the well-being of infants. A mother, he said, might take out two or even three tiny children with her, all of them packed into 'a miserable boat, the highest part of which was not six inches above the surface of the water, washing almost in the edge of a surf, which would frighten even an old seaman to come near in a good craft', but with the smallest baby tucked between her breast and her raised knees, 'where it lay secure and safe as in a crib'.

Where Tench excels is in the reporting of encounters, moods, and above all conversations. He conversed with everyone—or, more exactly, with everyone who interested him: fellow-officers, settlers and (long before he had any of the language, and intensely) with the Australians, who, with his American experience behind him, he nonchalantly called 'Indians'.

Consider his first meeting with the local people.

Late in January 1788, after three days at anchor in Botany Bay, Tench was walking for the first time on an Australian beach. He had the company of a few friends, and he was hand-in-hand with a little boy of about seven who had also been cooped up too long. (There were seventeen children belonging to the officers and men on the

First Fleet, and sixteen children of convicts. On the *Charlotte*, Tench's ship, there were only three: two children belonging to convicts, and one 'free' child. Was this Tench's small friend?)

Tench tells us that as the British party strolled along 'we were met by a dozen Indians, naked as at the moment of their birth', also out for a stroll. The two groups, one clothed, one naked, both armed, and presumably neither ready to give the advantage to the other, advanced warily. Tench had seen 'Indians' during his American sojourn; he had read Cook and the others on the blessed inhabitants of Polynesia, but he was not prepared for what he saw that day: naked black men, with wild hair and scrubby beards, hair, faces and bodies shining with fish oil, and every one of them hefting a businesslike spear. This was Encountering the Other with a vengeance.

Tench seems not to have turned a hair. Noting that the sight of the little boy roused particular interest, Tench, with the confident intuition and the quick invention which were to characterise his contacts with the Australians, opened the lad's shirt so the strangers could appreciate the dazzling whiteness of his skin, and continued to walk steadily towards them. One 'hideously ugly' old man was especially charmed by the child: drawing close, 'with great gentleness [he] laid his hand on the child's hat and afterwards felt his clothes, muttering to himself all the while'. When the boy grew restless under the handling, Tench contrived to send him back to the rest of his party 'without giving offence to the old gentleman', who he was confident would understand his protectiveness because 'some youths of their own, though considerably older than the one with us, were kept back by the group'.

This is probably about as good as it gets in encounters between strangers. The recognition that 'natural' impulses—curiosity, tenderness towards the young, a nervous good will—were probably shared by both naked Australians and swaddled Europeans is a denial of the dangers of otherness not often met with. Tench—alert, intelligent, curious, compassionate—demonstrates here his genius both for the 'natural' human response, and for the quick recognition of unfamiliar styles of dignity, treating the old man with a sensitive courtesy which assumed not only a common humanity, but a shared delicacy of feeling. He was in no doubt as to the political relationship between the two peoples—he had just recorded Governor Phillip landing on the north shore of the bay 'to take possession of his new land and bring about an intercourse between its old and new masters'—but for Tench the assumption of political domination did not preclude mutual understanding and respect.

Over the next months his view was to harden. By the completion of his first report, 'A Narrative of the Expedition to Botany Bay' to which a postscript was added in October 1788, with the first cheerful encounters a fading memory and contact shrunk to occasional tussles between fishing parties, his hopes of friendly exchanges had dimmed. He claimed to have come to share the bleak evaluation of Australians made by Cook eighteen years before: these were an ugly, dirty people, miserably under-equipped for life. He declared himself shocked by their lean-tos, their nakedness, the crudeness of their few tools. Nonetheless, he continued sensitive to details of their behaviour, noting, for example, the contrast between the men's domination over their women and their egalitarianism between themselves: 'Excepting a little tributary respect which the younger part appear to pay those more advanced in years, I never could observe any degree of subordination among them.' The absence of visible marks of deference must have been startling for a young captain-lieutenant, whose every action was modulated by the niceties of rank.

Then once again Tench displays his distinctive flair. The early encounters had taken place around the coves of the harbour: that is, on the Australians' home ground, which the British, of course, assumed to be neutral, or more correctly empty, given there were no obvious permanent habitations. Only once did two old men venture into the settlement, and we wonder if staying away from guests' camps was an Australian courtesy. Tench decided their hesitancy might have a different origin: that in the face of 'our repeated endeavours to induce them to come among us…they either fear or despise us too much to dare be anxious for a closer connection'. 'Fear' was the conventional and comfortable British interpretation of native caution. But 'despise'? Could these naked savages dare 'despise' officers of the British Crown? That Tench thought they might marks him as a man of unusual imaginative flexibility.

As for himself, he took every chance he could to 'converse' with these interesting people. During the brief period of good will immediately after the move to Port Jackson when Australians were still frequenting the fringes of the settlement, he began collecting all the words and phrases in the local language he could. He made some surprising discoveries: for example, that it was Cook and the British who had introduced the word 'kangaroo' to the local people, whose word for that surprising creature was *patagorang*. They seemed to have started applying 'kangaroo' as the British word for any and all the large animals the newcomers had brought with them, excepting the familiar dog, or, as they called it, 'dingo'. Tench deduced all this when he came upon a group of men 'busily employed in looking at some sheep in an enclosure, and repeatedly crying out "kangaroo, kangaroo"!' Always ready to augment innocent amusement, he was trying to point out some horses and cows at a little distance when the men's attention was deflected by the appearance of some convict women, upon which they 'stood at a distance of several paces, expressing very significantly the way in which they were attracted', but 'without offering them any insult'. This is a pleasant and, in its way, a remarkable scene. I cannot see a Spanish captain standing by while 'savages' openly assessed the charms of Spanish women.

(Some of these attempts at language learning can only have compounded confusion. Tench tells us that the British had been nearly three years in Port Jackson before they realised that the native word they used as meaning 'good' in fact signified 'no', or at least demurral. The consequences are too daunting even to contemplate.)

Tench had deeply enjoyed these fleeting encounters with Australians before the general alienation. Then on the second-last day of 1788 an Australian man was taken captive on Phillip's orders, and Tench's talent for personal relationships could at last come into play.

JANUARY 1788–SPRING 1790
SETTLING IN

The two French ships which had followed the First Fleet into Botany Bay remained at anchor there for the best part of six weeks, which allowed for a number of polite exchanges with the British now ensconced at Port Jackson. Philip Gidley King, fluent in French, especially enjoyed the French officers' company, their conversation and the delicacy of their manners. Without King's journal we would know very little about this small, beautifully equipped expedition and its courteous officers: the two ships sailed out of Botany Bay into oblivion, lost somewhere in the Pacific. In the event, King had sailed even earlier, being informed by Phillip on 31 January that he was to head a tiny settlement at Norfolk Island, another even more remote site identified by Cook as promising. On the morning of 15 February King and his little band of settlers—seven free men and fifteen convicts, six of them women—embarked on the *Supply*, to be dumped on a beach with their baggage and provisions piled around them with orders to make a new society. Naval obedience came at a high price.

Before he left King made the most of his time with the French. He reports the Comte de La Pérouse as notably less well disposed to the local people than was Phillip. His wariness was natural enough: at a landfall only a handful of weeks before, the expedition had lost two longboats and more than a dozen men, among them the captain of the *Astrolabe* and eight other officers, in a surprise attack by natives. (Up to that time they had not lost a single man.) Their assailants were islanders, probably Samoans, 'a very strong & handsome race of men scarce one among them less than 6 Feet high, & well-sett', who over several days had seemed perfectly friendly, and then, after what seemed to the French a trivial incident, had swung their clubs with killing effect. The French estimated that about thirty islanders fell to their guns.

Retrospectively La Pérouse read the episode as a textbook example of 'savagery': of unpredictable fluctuations in mood, unpredictable eruptions of murderous violence. At Botany Bay he built a stockade around his tents, mounted two small guns, and kept his guns at the ready.

Phillip built no stockades and he set no guards, or not against the Australians. He intended to persuade the local people that the newcomers were their friends. But his first task was to settle his own people, and once the flurry of disembarkation was over, with its inescapable disorder—the orgiastic scenes on the night of the disembarkation of the convict women have become legendary— officers, soldiers and convicts set about making themselves at home.

First, the alien landscape had to be mapped and its strangeness tamed by naming. Spectacular landmarks were given the names of distant patrons—Pittwater, Norfolk Island—but with their duty done to the grandees, the new arrivals could celebrate themselves and their adventures—Tench's Hill, Bradley's Head, Collins Cove,

Dawes Point. The names, used daily and inscribed in letters to kin and friends, must in time have come to seem 'natural'. Both Phillip's sturdy mind and conciliatory ambitions are suggested by his decision in mid-1791 to reject the wistful romanticism of Rose-Hill for the new up-river settlement in favour of the local name, Parramatta, which meant something like Where Eels Meet—that is, a place of feasting and fecundity.

Outposts of empire are lonely places. But calendars count time at the same rate everywhere, so the settlers celebrated their first King's Birthday on 4 June with all the pomp and alcohol they could muster. No news came from the real world: they could not know whether they were at war with France on any particular day, and these ardent patriots were to hear the King was well again before they had known he was ill. Remote though they were from the centres of action, distance brought none of the liberties remoteness can bring. The bounds of settlement were crushingly narrow. Officers could look forward to occasional 'expeditions' on land or on the water, but convicts were penned within settlement boundaries, unless they were given specific duties outside it. They were always being admonished for 'straggling'—wandering in the bush without permission—which they continued to do whatever the consequences in floggings or spear wounds.

Officers settled to a range of genteel diversions. As we have seen, some made music, some collected specimens, some drew or painted. Some kept journals, giving form to otherwise featureless days: 'this happened, then that happened'. A few, like Major Ross, squabbled. Irritability helps pass the time. And, as we know, everyone, or everyone literate, wrote letters home. They wrote in the hope that, barring shipwrecks, the words they were writing would be read months or years later by a known loved someone in some known loved place. George Worgan bursts into what reads like a post-modernist riff on time, sound and distance as he considers that, however long the chain of words he is hurling towards his brother, 'the First Word will not have reached one quarter over the Seas that divides Us, at the time the last is tumbling out of my Mouth', and decides he will let fly each one 'with such an impulsive Velocity…as to make their Way against the Resistance of Rocks, Seas and contrary Winds and arrive at your Street-Door with a D——l of a Suscitation…' A 'suscitation' indeed, with the force of love, gales and several seas behind it. Worgan was missing his brother badly. Two transports were about to sail. He planned to put a letter to Dick on each, and reflected on the melancholy possibility that neither would arrive. Then Dick, in lieu of his living, loving words, would have to make do with the narratives being prepared by Collins or Tench for news of his young brother. The two ships were sailing in the morning. Worgan confided he had thirty-one letters, five of them almost as long as this forty-page monster, 'to Close, Seal, Enclose and direct' and get on board before the ships raised anchor. Then comes a forlorn postscript: 'I have sent you 2 letters beside this.' For all its compulsive chirpiness, Worgan's huge letter breathes loneliness.

There were the immediate pleasures of local conviviality. From their first days in the colony gentlemen were deploring the convict passion for rum and the wickednesses they would commit to get it, but not only the lower orders were addicted to alcohol. Surgeon White gives a genial description of the toasts drunk during that first extravagant King's Birthday. The lower orders had been catered for: the governor had issued every soldier a pint of porter in addition to his usual allowance of rum-and-water grog, and to every convict a half pint of rum 'that they might all drink his Majesty's health'. Then the gentlemen settled to their pleasures. After the midday gun salutes the officers attended the governor in his house, and sat down to dinner to the pleasant accompaniment of the band playing 'God Save the King' followed by 'several marches'. Worgan gives us the menu: they ate 'mutton, pork, ducks, fowls, fish, kanguroo, sallads, pies and preserved fruits': foods handsomely outside the usual salted or dried rations. Then the cloth was removed, and they had the toasts. White lists them: 'His Majesty's health was drank with three cheers. The prince of Wales, the Queen and royal family, the Cumberland family, and his Royal Highness Prince Henry William…his Majesty's ministers were next given.' Then, the obligatory public toasts drunk, they began on the private and the particular, with the governor opening the new round with a toast to their own 'Cumberland County', the first British-style county in the new world, existing as yet only in the mind, but, as Phillip proudly declared, 'the largest in the world'. Its name, he said, would be 'Albion'.

So the toasts continued. Worgan (these surgeons seem to have been devoted drinkers) recorded the officers drank 'PORT, LISBON, MADEIRA, TENERIFFE and good Old English PORTER' (his capitals), which 'went merrily round in bumpers' through a long afternoon. Then, after joining in the democratic jubilation around a great bonfire, the officers went back to the governor's house for supper and a night-cap or three. We have to assume that by bedtime most of them were thoroughly drunk. Nonetheless, they were affronted the next morning to discover that during their loyal celebrations some of their tents had been looted: 'We were astonished at the number of thefts which had been committed during the general festivity, by the villainous part of the convicts, on one another, and on some of the officers, whose servants did not keep a strict lookout after their marquees.' White harrumphed: 'Availing themselves thus of the particular circumstances of the day, is a strong instance of their unabated depravity and want of principle.' A young convict would hang for the crimes he committed in the course of that festive night.

White provides the frankest account we have of officers' drinking, and some of his own conduct implies a ready tolerance of inebriation. At another celebration in August 1788, the governor's dinner to honour the birth of the Prince of Wales, White and William Balmain, one of his assistant surgeons, had a difference of opinion, rose from the table, went outside, and, without seconds (so avoiding the risk of bloodless reconciliation) fought a pistol duel. Ralph Clark claimed that each fired several shots at the other, but that the only injury sustained was a slight wound to Balmain's thigh, which implies either remarkably bad marksmanship or incapacitating drunkenness. As White on a good day was capable of bringing small birds down from trees, we have to diagnose inebriation exacerbated by a warm temperament. By the end of the same year White was ready to settle another dispute with pistols, this time with an adjutant of marines, until friends managed to persuade him he was in the wrong. Phillip would need a cool head to keep such effervescent fellows in amity.

The second King's Birthday celebrated in Sydney was marked by a play, George Farquhar's *The Recruiting Officer*, watched happily by governor and officers, but acted, directed and produced by convicts—which sheds an unexpected light on convict conditions and caste relations in the new colony. Tench:

> I am not ashamed to confess that the proper distribution of three or four yards of stained paper, and a dozen farthing candles stuck around the mud walls of a convict hut, failed not to diffuse general complacency on the countenances of sixty persons of various descriptions who were assembled to applaud the representation.

That is: they enjoyed it. There were more mundane pleasures to be taken in tending exotic menageries of pets like parrots or dingos or possums or lizards. The Australians' alert, handsome dingos especially caught the dog-loving British eye. In flagrant defiance of an 'all dogs ashore' order Phillip had given in Portsmouth, a number of officers had brought their dogs with them on the voyage. The dogs contributed unpleasantly to the horrible crowding of shipboard life, already burdened with a Noah's Ark of 'useful', meaning edible, animals, and there are indications that sailors resented cleaning up after them, more than a few fetching up overboard. On Ralph Clark's *Friendship* five dogs, including his own, had mysteriously vanished before the voyage was much more than half over. Soon after they landed the dog-deprived British were searching the countryside or bartering with dog-rich Australians for dingo puppies.

What happened next could have served as an early warning of deeper incompatibilities. John Hunter, studying the dingos as carefully as he studied all the creatures of the new continent, discovered them to be fatally flawed. Despite their notable good looks, they had an ineradicable propensity to kill all and any small animals. Some packs could even drag down kangaroos. Hunter writes, regretfully:

> Of those [native] dogs we have had many which were taken when young, but never could we cure them of their natural ferocity; although well fed, they would at all times, but particularly in the night, fly at young pigs, chickens, or any small animal which they might be able to conquer and immediately kill and generally eat them. I had one which was a little puppy when caught, but notwithstanding I took much pains to correct and cure it of its savageness, I found it took every opportunity, which it met with, to snap off the head of a fowl, or worry a pig, and would do it in defiance of correction. They are a very good-natured animal when

domesticated, but I believe it to be impossible to cure that savageness, which all I have seem to possess.

Governor Phillip himself supplied an assessment of this interesting animal, based on his study of a living specimen he had sent as a present to Under-Secretary Nepean:

> It is very eager after its prey, and is fond of rabbits or chickens, raw, but will not touch dressed meat. From its fierceness and agility it has greatly the advantage of other animals much superior in size: for a very fine French fox-dog being put to it, in a moment it seized him by the loins, and would have put an end to his existence, had not help been at hand. With the utmost ease it is able to leap over the back of an ass, and was very near worrying one to death, having fastened on it, so that the creature was not able to disengage himself without assistance; it has also been known to run down both deer and sheep.

An impressive animal, but an alarming one. David Collins put the dilemma with his usual pragmatic economy: 'The dogs of this country...have an invincible predilection for poultry, which the severest beatings could never repress. Some of them are very handsome.'

If it's meat and it moves, grab it. These nomad dogs knew nothing of the pastoralists' distinction between 'stock' and 'game'. Meanwhile the offspring of the dogs the British brought with them, especially little terriers and spaniels, were eagerly coveted by the Australians. They were dog lovers too: their dingos were allies in the hunt and companions around the campfire. But dingos, bred to stalk flighty marsupials, did not bark. British dogs did. Through their centuries of living in agricultural settlement they had developed a strong sense of property, so they barked at strangers, especially strangers who came softly in the night. Translated to Australian conditions, those British-bred spaniels and terriers could give warning of night attacks. One of the skills of the Australian warrior was to move stealthily through the night, and kill an enemy who had mortally offended him as he lay by his own campfire.

To each culture its own canine. The 'mindless' slaughter of stock and the consequent murderous reprisals which were to embitter British–Australian relations through later decades were implicit in this energetic early trade between dog lovers.

Isolation, with desolation lurking within it, remained the temporary settlers' worst enemy. William Bradley has left us a watercolour of the settlement at Sydney Cove in early 1788 (see plate section): a scatter of tents, a few huts, a handful of larger structures, a flagpole— and that is all. The land constructions are given substance and focus by the two ships riding at anchor in the clear water. For officers, sailors and marines those ships spelt security even in a storm, and breathed of home. Mind and spirit were refreshed by the clustered signs of European, indeed of British, technological ingenuity. Later, when officers condescended to play host to parties of Australian sightseers, leading them around the assemblage of cunning arrange- ments which constitute a ship, they were offended to find the tourists thoroughly bored, coming alive only when weapons or animal skins stimulated their curiosity. If for some of these men the sea was an open highway to England, by February 1789 the big ships had all sailed away, and even the faithful *Supply* was gone on a mission to Norfolk Island. The settlers were left with only the poor fruits of their own labour: huts, tents, a canvas house for the governor, some scars in the earth, some trees felled. With the harbour empty, Sydney Cove must have seemed to cling to the edge of the world.

For convicts, some uncertain as to whether they would ever return home, others knowing they would not, the isolation must have been worse. We can measure their despair by the fantasy which sent many of them off along the sea-shore or into the scrub in search of 'China', which they thought lay a long walk and across a river somewhere, or to another place where a copper-coloured people would welcome them, and there would be peace and no more labour. We hear their own exhaustion and the echoes of sailors' tales here, and sweet memories of that earthly paradise, Tahiti.

Nature offered scant solace. Splendidly tall, straight trees proved useless when felled: riddled with fissures, they oozed thick blood. The soil was no more than a pretty skin over rocks, and the flowers, so sweet in their brief season, withered under the oven-hot blasts of the summer winds. As relations with the local people worsened, unarmed convicts or even soldiers who ventured too far into the scrub might not return, killed by the Australians, or simply lost, wandering and calling in the featureless wilderness. Of necessity they used the Australians' paths, and some of those, like the path used to visit the French at Botany Bay, came to be marked by evil memories. In the October of that first year a convict sent to gather 'vegetables' and known to be a steady fellow somehow strayed from the group. His body was found on that path, 'his head beaten to a jelly, a spear driven through it, another through his body, and one arm broken'. What had been done to him before he died? A contingent went out immediately to bury the corpse, but three times in the next month it was reported to be above ground again. They thought it had been dug up by the natives' dogs.

Even as the newcomers were beginning to mark their presence on the land with their buildings and garden plots, their names and their stories, the complicated scribble of deeply-indented coves defied mental mapping. The normally phlegmatic David Collins lets us glimpse a moment of existential dread, confessing that:

> In many of the arms [of the harbour], when sitting at my ease with my companions in a boat, I have been struck with horror at the bare idea of being lost in them; as from the great similarity of one cove to another, the recollection would be bewildered in attempting to determine any relative situation. It is certain that if destroyed by no other means, insanity would accelerate the miserable end that must ensue.

By the end of that first year many of the interlopers must have lost heart in their power to tame this strange place and its strange, elusive people, but it was Major Ross, officially second-in-command, who fired off an uninhibited denunciation to Under-Secretary Nepean, designed to scuttle the whole enterprise. (His letter is also a model of applied nastiness):

> From our governor's manner of expressing himself, for he communicates nothing to any person here but to his secretary (Captain Collins), he has, I dare say, described this country as capable of being made into the Empire of the East. But notwithstanding all he may from interested motives say—and as this letter is for your own private perusal—I do not scruple to pronounce that in the whole world there is not a worse country than what we have yet seen of this. All that is contiguous to us is so very barren and forbidding that it may with truth be said that here nature is reversed; and if not so, she is nearly worn out, for almost all the seed we have put into the ground has rotted, and I have no doubt but will, like the wood of this vile country when burned or rotten, turn to sand…if the minister had a true and just description given him of it he will not surely think of sending any more people here…Of the general opinion entertained here of the wretched prospect we have before us I cannot, I think, give you a more

convincing proof than that every person (except the two gentlemen already mentioned, whose sentiments I am perfectly unacquainted with) who came out with a design of remaining in the country are now most earnestly wishing to get away from it.

That in November 1788. Conditions would get worse. When in May 1789 the *Sirius* returned from the Cape, where it had made a dash for supplies, it brought stale flour and staler news. The colonists' letters had been handed on to a ship leaving the Cape for England, but they knew that months would pass before the letters could be delivered, if they ever were, and months more before they could hope for a reply. Through the empty weeks stores were depleting further and hunger was added to loneliness. By 1790 it seemed that, with no supplies arrived from England, the colony might very well starve. Punishments were escalating, so home places were increasingly marked with blood and anguish. Crimes were multiplying too. A man who had already suffered the first instalment of his 500-lash punishment for stealing food, and was being kept shackled in the hospital until he could endure the rest, managed to get an iron off one leg 'and in that situation was caught robbing a farm'. Collins grimly recorded that 'on being brought in, he received another portion of his punishment'. But the devoted guardian of law could see the paradox. He knew that such acts resulted from 'either the villainy of the people, or the necessities of the time'. He also knew the motive to be irrelevant: villainy or necessity had to be treated alike, as equally deliberate crimes. And he worried: 'Very little labour could be enforced from people who had nothing to eat.'

As the slow days passed, morale sagged further. Norfolk Island still enjoyed its reputation for natural bounty, a reputation based more on distance than reality, so with typical daring Phillip decided to split the colony. In March 1790 he sent the *Sirius* with almost half the convicts and an appropriate number of marines under Major Ross to the island to give each settlement its best chance of survival. Ross would replace King as commandant of the island; King would continue to England on the *Sirius*: and we are reminded how few pieces Phillip had to play in this desperate endgame.

A small event is caught in the amber of that last-ditch strategy. George Maxwell, third lieutenant on the *Sirius*, had fits of irritability even on the voyage out, thrashing sailors for slight cause and earning a public rebuke from Phillip, who would tolerate no unauthorised thrashings on ships under his command. Then in October 1788, with the *Sirius* off the Horn and bound for Capetown and essential supplies, Maxwell had ordered so dangerous an amount of sail clapped on that 'the ship lay down sufficient to heave the capt[ain] out of his cot on the cabin floor', and Hunter, 'finding he was delarious', had him taken off the watch.

So says Able Seaman Jacob Nagle, professionally concerned with the orders of officers, especially deranged ones. He also reports that after the *Sirius* returned to Sydney in May 1789, Maxwell 'got so raving he was sent to the hosptittel under the care of the docters', and, 'being leunatick', was kept in a house in the hospital gardens with a man to watch him. Collins puts Maxwell's condition more genteelly; the lieutenant, he writes, had over several weeks fallen into 'a melancholy and declining way', and had therefore been discharged from the *Sirius* before it embarked for Norfolk Island in March 1790.

Being sometimes allowed to go out alone, Maxwell managed to escape his keepers. Two days afterwards he was seen again, sighted in the lower harbour by a sergeant out fishing. Alone in a tiny boat he had been rowing from one side of the lower harbour to the other, back and forth, back and forth, for those two days, without rest or food or drink. Was he searching for his lost ship? Sent back to

England a year later in John Hunter's care ('laying in his cabin in a dreadful condition, constantly delerious and unsencible of anything whatever', Nagle tells us) Maxwell died off Batavia in April 1791, and was buried at sea 'in as genteel a maner as could be expected to see'. His story reminds us that these imperial adventures could cost officers, soldiers and sailors too their health, or life, or sanity.

With the *Sirius* and the *Supply* both gone to effect the great transplantation to Norfolk Island, the mother colony tasted the desolation which had been the island's sour diet from its inception. Collins commented that Sydney looked 'as if famine had already thinned it of half its numbers', which indirectly it had. Phillip himself surveyed the huts and gardens of those who had gone, re-allocated them, reduced the working hours for men now seriously weakened by hunger, cut the ration yet again, and settled to wait.

On 5 April 1790 the *Supply* came back with terrible news. The *Sirius* had been wrecked on the jagged reefs of Norfolk Island. The human cargo had been saved, and (as it was to turn out) a surprising amount of the provisions, but the colony's one big, fast ship, their pride and their security, was at that moment being pounded to pieces on a reef. Now they had only the battered little *Supply* between themselves and slow, unremarked death by famine.

Then on 3 June 1790—the day before their beloved King's Birthday—another ship appeared; not the longed-for supply ship but the *Lady Juliana,* carrying a cargo of female convicts and almost no supplies. It brought more bitter news. In the previous December the store-ship *Guardian*, stuffed with goods for the colony, was attempting a passage around the Horn when it struck an iceberg. The ship had been forced back to Capetown for repairs. No one knew how or when the supplies could be got to Sydney.

That was ill-fortune, but ill-fortune was compounded by neglect and stupidity. David Collins commented on the arrival of the *Juliana*: 'In the distressed circumstances of the colony, it was not a little mortifying to find on board the first ship that arrived, a cargo so unnecessary and unprofitable as two hundred and twenty-two females, instead of a cargo of provisions.' Worse, while the women were healthy most of them were not only female but old, 'a description of people utterly incapable of using any exertion to their own maintenance'.

Ten days after the *Lady Juliana* came the store-ship *Justinian* with essential supplies, and on its heels three more transports of the Second Fleet, with a quarter of their human cargo already dead, and most of the rest disease-ridden, debilitated or decrepit. David Collins was not tender to convicts, but he was appalled by what he saw. As the ships unloaded, 'several of these miserable people died in the boats as they were rowing inshore, or on the wharf when they were lifting out of the boats; both the living and the dead exhibiting more horrid spectacles than had ever been witnessed in this country'. And it had been wilfully done:

> All this was to be attributed to confinement, and that of the worst species, confinement in a small space and in irons, not put on singly, but many of them chained together...it was said that on the *Neptune* several had died in irons; and what added to the horror of such a circumstance was, that their deaths were concealed, for the purpose of sharing their allowance of provisions, until chance, and the offensiveness of a corpse, directed the surgeon, or someone who had authority in the ship, to the spot where it lay.

With that arrival Phillip knew that avarice had been added to the toll of neglect and stupidity. Britain's gaol-keepers had taken their chance to empty the hulks and dump Britain's detritus onto the struggling colony; greedy ship's masters had taken their fees, neglected their convict cargo, and compounded the tragedy. Now he knew his desperate enterprise was vulnerable not only to lethargic administrators and the vagaries of water and wind, but to rogues as well.

WHAT THE AUSTRALIANS SAW

How did the Australians see the British intruders? Clues litter the British accounts. Consider John White's observations on Australian attitudes to the British taking of fish. He records an incident soon after the British landfall at Botany Bay, when the Australians were still displaying what he diagnosed as 'a kind of cautious friendship'. The British lowered a net one evening and took a great haul of fish. Some local men were watching. They did not interfere, rather seeming astonished by this novel and efficient mode of fishing, and excited by it too. But White recalls that 'no sooner were the fish out of the water than they began to lay hold of them, as if they had a right to them, or as if they were their own; upon which the officer of the boat, I think very properly, restrained them, giving, however, to each his part'. White adds that at first the sharing-out did not appease the Australians, but they quietened after each had received his fish.

'As if they had a right to them, or as if they were their own'— and then peace as each man received his fish. Because immediate hunger could be satisfied? Or for some other reason? Why were fish a cause of conflict? Unlike Cook, who tended to call in the muskets when puzzled or affronted, Phillip was ready to be patient. He knew that Australian behaviour deserved careful watching and careful interpretation. He decided that in this case the raiders were driven by hunger, and sensibly ordered that natives always be given a share of the catch. Watching from our comfortable distance, we think that men restricted to fishing lines and spears would not easily tolerate such mass looting of their limited resources. It did not occur to Phillip that the Australians thought themselves owners of the fish; that they had been hospitable to these graceless, greedy visitors long enough; that the belated readiness of the British to share their fish was taken to be an (inadequate) recognition of local ownership and visitors' obligations. Fishing rights and fishing equipment were to become a constant theme in the developing contest between the two peoples, and between underlying understandings of 'ownership' and 'rights'.

With the move to Sydney Cove puzzles multiplied. Unarmed convicts wandering in the 'woods' who encountered parties of Australians might be treated gently, even guided back to the colony, while others, engaged in gathering herbs or the native 'tea' (sarsaparilla), or cutting rushes for roofing, were threatened with spears or even killed. For Phillip the victims had been innocently collecting the natural bounty of the forest. He therefore concluded that the attacks must have been acts of vengeance: that some convict had injured some Australian, and they had exacted a reasonable man's revenge. It did not occur to him that his men were pillaging the locals' larder with neither permission nor payment. He took it as a mark of trust and therefore teachability when Australians readily accepted what he thought of as free 'gifts' of fish or bread or trinkets. Remember too his famous 'circle in the sand' at his first meeting with the Port

Jackson people. Phillip did not and could not fathom the Australians' more subtle and comprehensive understanding of reciprocity.

The British also had the habit of appropriating any unattended objects which attracted them. They had been doing it for years. On Cook's second voyage in 1773 Captain Tobias Furneaux's ship the *Adventure*, separated from Cook's *Resolution*, made landfall on the coast of Van Diemen's Land. His people saw clear signs of native presence—piles of scallop shells, smoke from fires—but failed to make contact with them. Then they came upon several 'wigwams, or huts', where they found some net bags, and in one of those bags the stone used to strike fire, along with some tinder made of bark. Another hut yielded a slender spear. 'These things the *Adventure*'s people carried away, leaving, instead of them, medals, gun flints, a few nails, and an old empty barrel with iron hoops'—that is, metal items they thought the locals would covet. Was this thieving, 'collecting', or compulsory trade? Furneaux seems to have thought that what he saw as fair exchange could be no robbery.

Around Sydney, even as that first good-humoured 'romping' and dancing was going on, convicts and soldiers had begun to pick up the spears, spear-throwers, nets and paddles they found lying on the beach or tucked among the rocks to trade with home-bound sailors for the curiosity market at home. Payment was usually in spirits, an urgent need in that grim place. Did they think of this as theft? Might not these strangely feckless people have simply thrown the things away? The incomers could not know the value in hours and skill expended in the making of these objects, nor that they bore the signature of their maker in the detail of their making, and would never be appropriated by an Australian.

By the end of that first year Phillip reported 'the inhabitants of New South Wales to be among themselves perfectly honest. [They] often leave their spears and other implements upon the beach, in full confidence of finding them untouched'. Tench was equally clear, commenting, as formal trade was initiated late in 1790 (which was when he learnt how highly one warrior valued his spear): 'It is a painful consideration that every previous addition to the cabinet of the virtuosi from this country had wrung a tear from the plundered Indian.'

Despite such intuitions regarding the ownership of Australian objects and the sentiments stored within them, the British were less capable of analysing their own responses: when Australians in their turn picked up European objects they happened to want, like the metal spades or hatchets they saw lying about among the strangers, they risked being shot. Phillip himself tells of one old man, who within weeks of the British landfall had welcomed Phillip's second visit to his home territory, the southern branch of Broken Bay, 'with a song and a dance of joy'. On both visits he tended the wants of the British party with hostly warmth, and was accordingly rewarded with a hatchet and other small presents. Then he dared to pick up a spade. Phillip immediately gave him a couple of slaps on the shoulder, and pushed him away. He was astonished when the man flew into a rage, grabbed up his spear, and threatened his guest with it. Phillip remained steadfast; the old man lowered his spear—and Phillip was persuaded a valuable moral lesson regarding the sanctity of property had been learnt.

Phillip's usurpation of Sydney Cove with its small but reliable water supply and its grassy spaces, the features which had led him to select the site, had also excluded the Australians from reliably accessible water and good hunting grounds. Arthur Bowes Smyth had seen a mob of eleven kangaroos soon after the landing, but British stalking techniques, even aided by muskets, could not match the locals' hunting skills, and soon kangaroos were rarely seen. By July 1788 Phillip knew the Australians around the settlement to be 'much distressed for food'. They would appear whenever the boats went out to haul the nets, but now they lacked the strength to fight for a share in the catch, instead being 'very weak and anxious to get the small fish, of which they made no account in the summer'. They were still avoiding the settlement, and three convicts, one with four spears left in him, had already been killed in the bush, but they still accompanied the *Sirius* or any other boat going down the harbour in their canoes, presumably hoping for fish. But now, catching fewer fish themselves, and with so many sick men to feed, the British could offer them little.

So how did the Australians living around the harbour see the British intruders? The people who first came upon the British fishing or exploring the coves of the harbour seem to have accepted their presence with unnerving equanimity. This suggests that they thought they knew who the strangers were; that they could make adequate sense of their sudden appearance within their own cosmology. Did they think the British were visiting ghosts, changed in form but familiar in sensibility, who would in time go on their mysterious ghostly way? Would that explain their keen curiosity as to whether these pallid creatures were sexual beings? Tench tells us that in those first beach encounters the Australian women had usually been kept back, but that sometimes they seemed to be 'offered with every appearance of courteous hospitality'. Why? Were the local males merely indicating that, in this regard at least, they possessed enviable wealth? Or were they testing the newcomers' corporeality? It remains impossible to know, because no one took them up on the offer, if offer it really was.

I have two main worries about the popular 'ghosts returned' hypothesis. First, there seems to have been no abrupt change in attitude, which is what we would expect had there been a radical revision of identification; second, the funeral rites described by Collins suggest the recently dead were troubling, even malign, presences which the living were anxious to speed on their way. I would expect a mob of returned ghosts to generate more anxiety. Were the British perhaps seen as a distant tribe, ignorant of the finer local protocols, but to be tolerated for as long as they were transients, especially as they came bearing gifts? In time, of course, local attitude clarified when, having established through experiment that the British were certainly human, they realised that these humans intended to stay, and to make their alienation of land and resources permanent.

What would they have seen as the young settlement established itself? Tench gives a brisk description of the unloading of the ships and the setting-up of the encampment from the British point of view:

> Business now sat on every brow and the scene to an indifferent spectator, at leisure to contemplate it, would have been highly picturesque and amusing. In one place a party cutting down the woods, a second setting up a blacksmith's forge, a third dragging along a load of stones or provisions; here an officer pitching his marquee with a detachment of troops parading on one side of him and a cook's fire blazing upon the other. Through the unwearied diligence of those at the head of the different departments, regularity was, however, soon introduced, and as far as the unsettled state of matters would allow, confusion gave place to system.

There were other far from indifferent spectators of the scene, and I doubt they found it 'amusing'. What could they have made of all that scrambling activity? Then two days after the landing there was a stranger spectacle. The Reverend Johnson conducted his first Sunday service, with troops and convicts gathered around a great tree. What would the silent watchers have made of a man shouting and occasionally gesticulating at other men and some women, grouped by sex, drawn up in rigid rows, and maintaining rigid silence? This must have been at least as bewildering a spectacle as White's mysterious 'war-party or wedding'.

It is possible to construct some hypotheses. After all the initial exuberance between the British and local parties around the harbour, the encampment at Port Jackson saw only a few visits to its fringes before they fell away altogether some time after that courtesy visit from the two old men. There followed a prolonged silence. Phillip was disappointed: what had gone wrong? Neither he nor we can know, but my suspicion is that the secret watchers saw less and less of anything that made sense to them: that they saw men mindlessly attacking trees, including many useless for canoes or spears, and bringing them to the ground; shamefully demeaning themselves with women's work, digging in the ground where no yams grew while women sat idle; men dragging metal chains, carrying rocks, piling them up, while other men shouted and hit them; men decked in bright garments but quite unpainted, strutting and turning in the dullest dance ever seen. Meanwhile these peculiar people were feeding themselves on smelly dry stuff they tugged out of barrels and with the fish and greens they pilfered from the rightful owners, while marvellously edible animals were left to wander about on their own four legs, free to run away on a whim. The Australians were used to the wild wariness and dazzling speed of goannas and of absconding kangaroos. They knew nothing of the centuries of breeding which had produced the staid ways of domesticated flocking animals.

They also watched the strangers spread their dark airless habitations over the flats by the stream where the kangaroos came to graze and then frighten away the few which still came by outrageously inept stalking. Even with muskets the British could not approach the Australians' success. Later they would watch the newcomers unleash great dogs which would pull kangaroos down, at any season, in any numbers, with no thought of conserving supply. They would also see sick men lying untended, and other men seized, bound and punished by their fellows by that strange tool of civilisation, the whip. They would watch as men screamed or, worse, remained silent, as gobbets of bloody flesh flew. And they would see men strung up by their necks before silent companions in terrible isolation, with no intervention by kin, and then the bodies left to hang, their spirits uncomforted.

There are other episodes we are not told they saw, but have reason to believe they did. When the British made their expeditions around the harbour and into the bush they kept a wary watch for Australians, but seemed to think that they themselves were invisible. I doubt they were. I think the settlement was ringed by eyes, and all their sorties noted, discussed, puzzled over. Now consider the following story told by John Hunter.

The governor and most of his senior officials had been out on one of their expeditions, this time around Broken Bay and along the Hawkesbury, in June 1789. Now they were going home, and had arrived after a hard day's walk at the northern arm of Port Jackson. They had not arranged for a boat to meet them, and when a bonfire failed to attract attention from Sydney Cove they had to set off the next day on another long walk to reach Middle Harbour. Once there they still could not attract attention even by firing their muskets, so two of the rank and file, whether sailors or marines we don't know, offered to paddle a native canoe they found on the beach across the water to the cove where the *Sirius* was anchored. There was, however, a problem: the first man who tried to get into the canoe immediately overset it and had to swim ashore. Pooling their formidable nautical expertise, the party then set about making a catamaran 'of the lightest wood we could find'. When it was finally launched it could not carry the weight of a single man, quietly sinking beneath him.

It must have been an awkward situation, with the naval cream of the colony standing about defeated by a stretch of calm water, wondering what to do next. Some proposed making the tough two-day walk over the mountains and through the scrub to Sydney Cove. Hunter's shoes were already in shreds, so with the walk beyond him, he and his friend Collins decided to make the easier walk back to Broken Bay and wait for the boats there. Then two of 'the people we had with us' (after days of slogging and camping out, lesser ranks were still not worth mentioning by name), gallantly offered to swim across to a spur of land near the *Sirius*, a 400-metre swim achieved, as Hunter proudly tells us, in seven minutes: the first Bay-to-Bay in Sydney Harbour. Another triumph of British pluck, if not of British seamanship, entered the record.

What would watching Australians have made of so pathetic a performance from British males, when their own women would take their frail canoes out past the breakers with infants aboard? What Tench and his friends indirectly tell us is that these were a people who cultivated preternatural physical prowess to compensate for the necessary simplicity of their equipment. They were also a people who, living heroically hard, travelled heroically light. Travelling light is a necessity for all genuinely nomadic societies, where men and women must carry what they need as they travel between seasonal food sources, constantly moving on. They are not to be confused with the very different 'nomadic' pastoralists, who move through the land to favoured grazing, carting their supplies and equipment along with them in wagons or on pack animals, and doling food out for consumption at measured intervals. Such cautious travellers are not true nomads, who are rare creatures in the world.

To return to those astonishing canoes: a group called 'Tribal Warrior' has been working recently to restore the Aboriginal maritime presence on the waters of Sydney Harbour. They can take pride in their seafaring ancestors, the iron men and women of 1788.

The anthropologist W. E. H. Stanner directs us to another more elusive quality which might have infused the canoe contretemps for Australian watchers. He points out that traditional Australian societies achieved an enviable equilibrium of effort and return: they not only lived confidently and (usually) well in austere circumstances, but 'sweetened existence by spiritual pursuits of life in no way concerned with mere survival…The least-cost routines [of material and social life] left free time, energy and enthusiasm to be expended—as they were, without stint—on all the things for which life could be lived when basic needs had been met: the joys of leisure, rest, song, dance, fellowship, trade, stylised fighting and the perform-ance of religious rituals'. He sums up this complex as a talent for 'jollifying humdrum…it seemed to be a law of Aboriginal life to embroider the unavoidable'.

'Jollifying humdrum.' The ability to see the comedy lurking in human affairs. I think many British doings must have brought rich amusement to the Australians, along with the anxiety and the anger.

Too much emphasis on mutual misreadings can obscure a remark-able fact. There may have been an early assumption among the British that these Australian 'savages', who seemed barely able to cling to life in their natural state, would either withdraw or simply die out, now that a higher civilisation had arrived. But our white forefathers regarded themselves as convict-keepers rather than settlers, and as invaders not at all. There were no pitched battles between residents and incomers, but instead, as we have seen, rather touching performances of mutual good will and gift-giving, and a remarkably determined endeavour by Phillip to bring the Australians into regular contact with the settlement so they could experience the benefits of civilised life. These natives had no pigs or breadfruit to incite greed, they guarded their women well, and their spasmodic gestures of hostility posed no serious threat to the British. Phillip knew his enemy was not the Australians, but starvation.

Unusually in colonial situations, or at least the ones I know about, for most of his five-year rule Phillip pursued an energetic policy of amity with the local population. Even more remarkably he, like many of his officers, recognised that these skinny, naked creatures were not animals in vaguely human form, but men like himself. And the Australians returned the compliment: gross and bleached as they were, impossibly inept at the basic business of living, their probably defective bodies kept wrapped and hidden from sight, the strangers were human too.

We have seen that by the time he had dispatched his 'Narrative' to England in October 1788, Watkin Tench was regretfully deciding the natives of the new land were savages after all, and 'like all other savages, are either too indolent, too indifferent or too fearful to form an attachment on easy terms with those who differ in habits or manners so widely from them'. (He unsurprisingly failed to notice that the British were experiencing much the same difficulty.) But that was because he had lost the hope of continuing contact with these fascinating people. Over the coming months he was to prove, like his friend William Dawes, not the least 'indolent, indifferent or fearful' in pursuit of a better understanding.

Phillip had done his best to improve relations by trying to stamp out the trade in stolen Australian artefacts, forbidding the sale of native fishing tackle or weapons within the camp. But trouble continued: over that first year more than a dozen convicts 'unaccountably disappeared', others were found dead, often mutilated, while others again were found alive, but stripped and wounded as if in exemplary warning. Worse, the Australian responses were not predictable. In July 1788 two convicts had sneaked off to Botany Bay, 'gathering vegetables', they said, when they came upon a party of Australians, who signed to them to go back the way they had come. Instead they ran in different directions. Spears were thrown, and one man suffered two wounds. Nonetheless he plunged into the water and 'escaped' by swimming across a narrow arm of the bay—while 'the natives' (who could very easily have killed him) 'stood on the bank laughing at him'. Then yet another Australian found him, and helped him back to the settlement. Collins also reports that despite hostile incidents some Australians were reliably friendly, one 'family' living in an adjoining cove being 'visited by large parties of the convicts of both sexes on those days when they were not wanted for labour, where they danced and sung with apparent good humour, and received such presents as they could afford to make them', which reminds us that a great deal was going on that did not appear in the records.

Tench had first thought the Australians speared convicts in the woods for the fun of it—in 'a spirit of malignant levity', as he put it—but on longer reflection he came to share Phillip's view that it was 'the unprovoked outrages committed by unprincipled individuals' which had led to the change from cautious friendship to dangerous aggression.

The change had been slow, and sometimes ambiguous even to those who experienced it, but by late 1788 the situation was clear. Lieutenant Bradley regretfully reported:

> What has been experienced lately in several instanced meetings with the Natives, has occasioned me to alter those very favourable opinions I had formed of them, & however much I wished to encourage the idea of their being friendly disposed, I must

acknowledge now convinced that they are only so, when they suppose we have them in our power or are well prepared by being armed. Latterly they have attacked almost every person who has met with them that has not had a musquet & have sometimes endeavoured to surprise some who had.

Then the Australians went unequivocally on the offensive, mounting two well-executed raids canoe raids into British territory and making off with a succulent British goat each time, so showing, again in Bradley's opinion, 'great cunning'. The strategy was for two canoe-loads of men to swoop down on an edge of the settlement—the Observatory point in this particular case—and while one lot distracted the guard the others would spear a goat, toss the animal into a towed canoe, and make off at speed. The British could not catch them. Then a couple of weeks later, they did it again. Then a whole canoe fleet carrying more than thirty men barely failed to snatch some precious British sheep.

Just what was going on in these occasional acts of aggression against British men (attributed, as we see, to an undifferentiated collectivity called 'natives') might become clearer with time. As for the raids: I think that on the evidence we have, we cannot know whether the Australians' abduction of the animals was in retaliation for the disruption of their own hunting, or simply the taking of desirable meat from hopelessly incompetent hunters. The elegance of the strategy, however, clearly demonstrates malice aforethought, and some pleasure, too. Phillip regretfully decided that for the moment the Australians would have to be taught to keep their distance, and resorted to firearms to do the teaching.

With alienation increasingly dramatised in 'incidents', he also decided on a strategy of his own. He would kidnap a couple of local men, treat them kindly, teach them English, and so at last be able to communicate the benevolence of his intentions. In view of the frightening diminution in the colony's supplies, he also hoped to gain access to local food resources. A desperate strategy, to kidnap in order to make friends, but one with a long history in the annals of imperialism.

Accordingly, on the second-last day of 1788 a boat under the command of Lieutenant Ball of the *Supply* and Lieutenant George Johnston of the marines pulled into Manly Cove, and two men were lured within reach by the offer of gifts. Then they were grabbed, and wrestled into the boat. One managed to fight free, but the other was overpowered, bound, and taken to the settlement. He was to remain there until his death from smallpox in May 1789. His name was Arabanoo.

Arabanoo must have gone through pure terror on that first day, and then for days to come: seized, flung into the bottom of a huge canoe, surrounded by clamouring strangers, stripped, immersed in hot water, and his skin roughly scrubbed and his hair cropped before his whole body was trussed in some strange yielding stuff. But he was, his abductors decided, of a docile, even melancholy, temperament and quickly accustomed himself to captivity. He attracted a great deal of attention over those first days, but long after his novelty wore off for other officers Arabanoo continued to enthral Watkin Tench.

Up until now Tench had had to focus on mute material objects, like spears or bark shelters or canoes, in his quest for understanding. He had also learnt something of Australian social organisation: he had begun to identify 'wives' and to guess at tribal divisions or alliances from inflections of warmth or hostility between groups. But (like the rest of us) he was most hopeful of arriving at a deepened understanding through getting to know an individual.

Tench spent a great deal of time with Arabanoo, and he learnt a great deal from him. Initially he had the usual difficulty of distinguishing individual quirks from what we would call cultural practices. One example: he was astounded at Arabanoo's prodigious appetite for fish and meat—until he realised this was not peculiar to Arabanoo but an attribute of the nomad hunter, who cannot store what he catches. With the benefit of hindsight we can sometimes guess at things Tench could not see. For example, he knew nothing of levels of initiation or the hierarchy of knowledge in the male Australian world: he saw Arabanoo's patterned scars, and only wondered at their ugliness. He knew Arabanoo was eager to teach him his language. He therefore judged him to be slow-witted when he would suddenly fall silent. He did not consider that Arabanoo might not have been at liberty to answer certain questions or to speak of certain things. But despite opacities and misunderstanding, Tench came to love Arabanoo, recognising him as a gentle soul, and a remarkably patient one, being especially tender with the children who constantly clamoured around him—including, presumably, Tench's young friend from the beach—and we wonder if this warrior tolerance of children was a cultural habit, too.

Tench also noticed another quality: a high, even touchy, sense of self-worth.

> Although of a gentle and placable temper, we early discovered that he was impatient of indignity and allowed no superiority on our part. He knew he was in our power, but the independence of his mind never forsook him…If the slightest insult were offered him, he returned it with interest.

That is: he was gentle, but he was a man jealous of his dignity, and even in alien circumstances quick to respond to challenge. Phillip should have taken warning from that.

Arabanoo's capture failed to have the desired conciliatory effect.

Interracial relations continued to deteriorate. In March 1789 a party of convicts marched off in a body to plunder the people at Botany Bay of their fishing tackle and spears. Black warriors routed them, killing one and wounding seven. Phillip, furious at the flouting of his orders, had the survivors flogged, and insisted that Arabanoo watch this display of the splendid impartiality of British justice. Arabanoo was sickened by it, as he was sickened by the fetters and chains convicts dragged around with them. He seemed to think that men should not be subjected to such humiliations.

The education of Arabanoo in the ways of the British was interrupted by the eruption of diseases, first 'the venereal', and then, more alarmingly, smallpox—no one knew from where but they thought perhaps from the ships of La Pérouse, long since sailed away. The earnest labour of the British, especially White and his surgeons, in their seeking out and care for survivors, along with their frequent expressions of bafflement as to its origin, persuade me that the story of their deliberate infection of the locals by 'variolous matter' brought in by 'doctors' is a nonsense—especially as they had no physical access to individual natives at that early stage except for Arabanoo, who sickened only in the later stages of the epidemic. (Now it has been reasonably demonstrated that the smallpox probably came overland from the Macassan traders who cropped the trepang along the northern coasts of Australia.)

The dimensions of the catastrophe were horribly evident. Soon black corpses were littering the beaches and the bays, and piled in the caves. Of the handful of stricken people found alive and brought into the settlement for treatment, only two, a boy called Nanbaree, about nine years old, and a fourteen-year-old girl, first called Araboo, later corrected to Boorong, survived, and were adopted into the households of Surgeon White and the Reverend Johnson.

Arabanoo's tenderness towards his afflicted compatriots so touched Phillip that he had his remaining fetter struck off. He did not use his new liberty to return to his own people, perhaps because too many were dead. David Collins memorialised his anguish:

> On our taking him down to the harbour to look for his former companions, those who witnessed his expression and his agony can never forget either. He looked anxiously around him in the different coves we visited; not a vestige on the sand was to be found of human foot; the excavations in the rocks were filled with the putrid bones of those who had fallen victim to the disorder; not a living person was any where to be met with…He lifted up his hands and eyes in silent agony for some time; at last he exclaimed, 'All dead! All dead!'

The Australians traditionally explained what we would classify as natural human deaths as the fruit of malicious sorcery. They probably began by blaming sorcery for the smallpox, until the deaths multiplied beyond the possibility of individual malice or clan anger. As far as can be judged from biologists' analyses of skeletal remains, theirs was a society unacquainted with epidemic disease. It was also a society careful of human lives once past the vicissitudes of infancy and before the fatal dependency of extreme age. Food-getting had its risks, but not usually lethal ones, and while there were set-piece battles between rival groups and individuals where the risk of injury was high, the annihilation of the enemy was never the object: when courage had been adequately displayed on both sides and enough blood shed, the battle ended. The occasional massacre of whole campfire groups in retaliation for particular secret murders paradoxically only underlines the high value placed on the individual life. Even as late as the 1930s W. E. H. Stanner noticed that while the great battles he witnessed in the Northern Territory provided ample space for courage, skill and fortitude, and were genuinely terrifying to watch, few deaths resulted, because 'an invisible flag of prudence floated over the field'.

In the autumn of 1789 around Sydney Cove, deaths came in scores and hundreds. Baneelon, a later captive of Phillip's, told him that the smallpox had killed up to half the local population. We know his fellow captive Colbee had lost all but two of his band to the disease, and had to unite with another clan. What we do not know is the effect this massive loss had either on individual survivors, or on their social practices.

In mid-May 1789 Arabanoo died of the smallpox, and Tench and his British friends grieved for him.

John Hunter lamented the death of Arabanoo not only for personal reasons, but because it signalled the death of the hope of reconciliation. Had Arabanoo lived, 'he could have made [his people] perfectly understand that we wished to live with them on the most friendly footing, and that we wished to promote, as much as might be in our power, their comfort and happiness'—which indicates that the British as yet had no awareness of possible conflict over land. Now, despite the weakening effects of the smallpox, 'the same suspicious dread of our approach' and the same acts of vengeance taken on unfortunate stragglers continued unabated. With the colony facing the prospect of starvation, Phillip decided to kidnap again. In December 1789 two men were lured into waist-deep water by the offer of fish; then seized, bound, and taken to the settlement. Their pitted faces made clear that both had survived the smallpox. The child-survivors Nanbaree and Boorong, wildly excited to see them, greeted them by name, the older man as Colbee, and the younger as Baneelon.

In a double display of guile and athleticism Colbee managed to escape after a week's captivity, with an iron fetter on his leg as memento of his time among the British, but Baneelon was to remain a captive for the best part of five months. A very cheerful captive: John Hunter, with his informed interest in the effects of rank on behaviour, thought Baneelon 'much more chearful after *Co-al-by's* absence, which confirmed our conjecture, and the children's account, that he was a man more distinguished in his tribe than *Ba-na-lang*'.

Why 'Baneelon' instead of the familiar 'Bennelong'? The issue of correct naming across cultural boundaries is a painful one, and too often symptomatic of a wider incomprehension. Surgeon White noted that, at the time of his capture, 'this native had no less than five names, viz. "Baneelon, Wollewarre, Boinba, Bunde-bunda, Wogé trowey"'. He also noted that 'he likes best to be called by the second'. Tench confirms that at first the captured man called himself 'Wolarawaree', and bestowed that name on the governor. Years later David Collins would set down his patiently accumulated information on how Australian names were given, and how they might be taken away. Names might claim real or fictive kin relationships, as when Baneelon gave Phillip the name Be-anna, 'father', while having Phillip call him 'son'. Some names were temporary, marking transient states and statuses. Individuals might exchange names to express affection, and then call each other by yet another name to celebrate the exchange. After death the name of the deceased ceased to be spoken, so those who had shared the name took another. (Before you dismiss all this as ridiculous and unworkable, list the number of names you have gone by throughout the course of your life, beginning with your baby name or names.) The British outsiders had no understanding of the complex social meanings stored within their captive's array of names. 'Baneelon' or 'Bennilong' or 'Ba-na-lang' was what they chose to call him—an uncertain sequence of sounds designating an individual, stripped of kin and social and ritual relationships, stripped of gender, stripped of status. (We learn from Tench that Baneelon meant 'Great Fish'. He also tells us that Baneelon 'has been seen to kill more than twenty fish by this method [of spearing from a canoe] in an afternoon', so it is possible 'Baneelon' was a feat-name.)

I have chosen to call this man by the unfamiliar version 'Baneelon' (the spelling Watkin Tench bestowed on him) to help us keep in mind what was so casually swept away, and so that we might escape the freight of banalities time has placed on the word 'Bennelong'.

We have seen the temptation of confusing individual and cultural qualities in the matter of Arabanoo's prodigious appetite. Generalising from individuals to groups has similar perils. Baneelon was a very different character from the reflective and melancholy Arabanoo. Young (he was guessed to be about twenty-six), tough and touchy, he would have been flamboyant in any society. Stanner, always attracted to dignified characters, dismissed him as 'a mercurial upstart', which is a common judgment. I think most commentators have seriously underestimated him, and Colbee too.

I am puzzled by the relationship between these two men, and also by some oddities about the mode of their capture. Here is William Bradley's account of what happened, giving us not only a close account of the events, but some insight into Bradley himself.

Wednesday 25th [November 1789] Governor Phillip judging it necessary that a Native should be taken by force, (no endeavour to persuade them to come among us having succeeded) I was ordered on this service, having the Master, two petty officers & a Boat's crew with me in one of the Governor's boats: as we went down the harbour we got some fish from the boats that lay off the [?] arm fishing, I proceeded up that arm in which we saw a great number of Natives on both sides & several landed on the beach at the [sth?] Cove hauling their Canoes up after them; As we got near the upper part of the [?] cove, we held two large fish up to them & had the good luck to draw two of them away from a very large party by this bait, these people came round the rocks where they left their spears & met us on the beach near the boat and at a distance from their companions sufficient to promise success without losing any lives, they eagerly took the fish, four of the crew were kept in the boat which was…backed close to the beach where the natives and the rest of our people were, they were dancing together when the signal was given by me, and the two poor devils were seized & handed into the boat in an instant. The Natives who were very numerous all round us, on seeing us seize those two, immediately advanced with their spears and clubs, but we were too quick for them, being out of reach before they got to that point of the beach where the boat lay, they were entering on the beach just as everybody was in the boat and as she did not take the ground we pulled immediately out without having occasion to fire a musket. The noise of the men, crying & screaming of the women and the children together with the situation of the two miserable wretches in our possession was really a most distressing scene: they were much terrified, one of them particularly so, the other frequently called out to those on shore apparently very much enraged with them.

…It gave me great satisfaction to find by the children [Boorong and Nanbaree] that neither of them had Wife or Family, who would feel their loss, or to be distressed by their being taken away.

It was by far the most unpleasant service I ever was ordered to execute.

Bradley's generous distress is evident. But there are peculiarities about the events he describes so carefully. Arabanoo had been lured out to a British boat and seized, with his people horrified onlookers. What possessed Colbee and Baneelon to wade out to a British boat baited with grins and a couple of dangled fish? I do not suggest that they wanted to be captured, but were they perhaps playing a game of dare with the British, for the delectation of their fellows on the beach? Was this an act of competitive daring that went wrong? These two were always rivals. We will be looking at the capture in more detail in the next chapter, but we notice that Colbee made his escape with insulting ease, despite his fettered leg, within the week while Baneelon stayed put. For the last few weeks his captivity, with his own fetter removed, seems close to voluntary. He escaped with dispatch at a moment of his own choosing. Certainly Phillip did not expect him to run, and ordered his steward, Baneelon's keeper, flogged for neglect of duty.

At the least we have to accept that Baneelon adjusted to his captive state remarkably well. Quickly throwing off the wariness Watkin Tench thought natural for a man in his situation, he feasted without caution on unfamiliar foods and drank the strongest liquors 'with eager marks of delight and enjoyment'. For all of his stay with the British he remained exuberantly experimental, ready to tackle whatever these peculiar strangers had to offer.

Baneelon was also determined to communicate even without benefit of a shared language. There was none of Arabanoo's reserve: Tench reports that Baneelon 'sang, danced and capered, told us all the customs of his country and all the details of his family economy'. 'Very early' he bestowed on Governor Phillip his own tribal name and adopted his, and took to calling him 'father'. And whenever he thought of his enemies from the tribe of the Cameragal on the north shore of the harbour 'he never failed…to solicit the governor to accompany him, with a body of soldiers, in order that he might exterminate this hated name'.

He was also notably eager to impress. A man of fine physique, he brimmed with stories of his prowess in battle and of his sexual exploits, which to his listeners often sounded like another form of war. (Later we will hear the story behind a crescent scar on his hand.) At a later time his volatility would disquiet the British as they came to see him as alarmingly unpredictable, but it seems to have been tolerated, even relied on, by his fellows, and was rebuked by violence only when he went too far. I am reminded of the tolerance extended to restless, aggressive young males among the Plains Indians—for as long as these qualities served the group. Then, if the difficult individual accumulated too many transgressions, he would be abruptly exiled from the tribe.

Collins says Baneelon was a Wanghal. We do not know how his tribe fared during the smallpox epidemic. All we know is that both he and Colbee, who was a Cadigal, survived it and wore its scars on their skins. We can be sure that its ravages must have necessitated a radical redrawing of old political arrangements. Those relations had always been tense. As Tim Flannery crisply puts it, 'the relations between the groups seem to have alternated between feasting and fighting'. After the disruptions of the smallpox they must have been in disarray.

My guess is that Baneelon had decided on trying for an alliance with the strangers shortly after his capture. (He might have toyed with the idea even earlier.) Under this hypothesis most of his actions and reactions can be explained, not least that tireless boasting of his sexual and fighting prowess: if he aspired to prominence among his people in this time of dizzying change, where traditional wisdom seemed of little avail, it was the virtues of young manhood he would need to dramatise. In action he was both a fast learner and a highly conscious performer. During his captivity his swift adoption of British manners, especially his extravagant courtesies to the females in the colony, prove his quick eye for style. Later, when he sailed back to England with Phillip, one of the few things we know of his three lonely years there is that he was especially struck by the performance of one lordly old gentleman, who glanced up as Baneelon and his entourage swept into a room—and then turned aside in an exquisitely calculated display of indifference to take a pinch of snuff and call for the bottle. Baneelon appreciated social theatricality in all its forms.

Baneelon's use of clothing was to become an important indicator of his state of mind. Arabanoo had learnt the perils of clothing early. After his capture, after his bath, after he had been put into a shirt, he backed close to a fire for the reassurance of familiar warmth on his skin. His shirt-tail caught alight. He suffered terrifying seconds as the flames licked his back before they could be quenched. He was thereafter wary of clothing, but to please his hosts he learnt to tolerate it. Baneelon, with his sense of cultural styles, recognised the British use of different cloths and colours to mark status, and happily accepted the distinction lent his person by formal garments. He was especially proud of the bright red jacket with silver epaulettes he wore on dress occasions. John Hunter suggests Phillip's very different interest when he reports that while Phillip put Baneelon into genteel nankeen on Sundays, his everyday dress, however hot the weather, was trousers and jacket in thick red kersey, 'so he may be so sensible of the cold as not to be able to go without cloaths'. Phillip's very basic strategy was to develop a physical dependence on warmth—and then to inculcate psychological notions of modesty in a man who felt no 'natural' shame.

Baneelon's understanding of the language of dress was altogether more sophisticated.

Then in May 1790, after five months' captivity, Baneelon made off. Writing to Banks a couple of months after the escape, Phillip remarked that 'our native has left us…and that too is unlucky for we have all the ceremony to go over again with another'. He concluded that 'that Man's leaving us proves that nothing will make these people amends for the loss of their liberty'. Passion for freedom might have been fed by a more carnal motive. Baneelon's captivity had been celibate. He probably wanted a woman, and there were none available to him in the settlement. Boorong told Phillip 'he had gone after a Woman he had often mentioned'. She may have been the good-looking woman Bradley recalled exchanging words with Baneelon from a beach when they had been out on one of their boat expeditions together. Baneelon had tried to coax her into the boat with him; she had refused. Her name was Barangaroo.

Other appetites were also going unsatisfied. Food supplies even for this pampered prisoner, and even though supplemented by a special allowance of fish and corn, had dropped to famine levels. (For the next months, starvation would be a serious prospect for the colony.) Baneelon was not philosophical about being put on short rations. He presumably could not understand the perversity of doling out miserable allowances and leaving beasts uneaten while warriors, especially guests, were left to starve. Tench records that prior to his escape the want of food had been making Baneelon 'furious and melancholy'. Tench sums up: 'We knew not how to keep him and yet were unwilling to part with him.'

Then Baneelon resolved the dilemma by slipping away to rejoin his own people.

SPEARING THE GOVERNOR

The first serious steps towards reconciliation were taken, like earlier friendly meetings, on the relatively neutral setting of a beach, with exit lines for both parties open to sea and to land. They began with an apparent catastrophe: the spearing of Governor Phillip at Manly Cove on 7 September 1790.

The spearing has become an iconic moment in Australian history. The slim wooden spearhead which pierced the governor's flesh might still exist somewhere, and haunts the dreams of museum-keepers who long to display this object which magically unites our first British governor with the continent's original inhabitants. Not many years later the spearhead would speak to its interrogators in a double tongue: of the chronic flightiness of 'savages', but also of their 'natural' ability to recognise the moral authority of personal valour and of Christian blood spilt in voluntary sacrifice. Icons speak in many tongues, which is what makes them icons.

*

At the time, the mystery embodied in the bloodied spear point was that almost immediately after the spearing the Australians around Sydney Cove decided to 'come in' to the settlement to make their peace with the interlopers. David Collins, normally a sensibly sceptical fellow, cheerfully inscribed the astonishing *non sequitur* in his journal-of-record: 'This accident gave cause to the opening of communication between the natives of this country and the settlement, which, although attended by such an unpromising beginning, it was hoped would be followed by good consequences.' What Collins is offering us is a secular miracle, Enlightenment style: first the 'accidental' spearing, then the submission, then the beginning of the civilising process.

And there, effectively, the matter has been allowed to rest: we contemplate the spearhead, we wonder at the event, we marvel at the outcome. However psychologically incoherent, the story at the mythic level is a curiously satisfying one—and who, after all, looks for sense in icons or savages?

I prefer more coherent explanations, especially when they concern the actions of peoples who are being dismissed as savages. What was really going on? In this as in earlier encounters our British informants were like infants squinting through a keyhole: they could see only some of the action, and what they heard was largely unintelligible babble. They could not know what conversations and other, subtler communications were taking place before their eyes, much less offstage; they did not know where, whom and what to watch. The best we can hope to find in the British eye-witness reports, made before the events were subjected to the moulding pressures of myth-making, are join-the-dots narratives plotted in terms of British expectations of both themselves and the 'natives': 'We happened to notice the following events, which we think are probably connected in this way.' If we re-examine the dots in the several accounts of this famously enigmatic spearing, looking to see if they can be joined differently, we might establish a more satisfying account of Australian actions and reactions.

The first part of the story is uncontentious. Since Baneelon's escape four months before there had been no contact with the Australians beyond the occasional spearing of unarmed convict stragglers in the bush, and increasingly angry brushes over fishing catches. There is fair agreement between the British reports as to what happened next. A great party of Australians, numbering perhaps two hundred people, and therefore necessarily including people from several tribes (this is after the decimation of the smallpox epidemic) had gathered at Manly beach to feast on the putrefying flesh of a whale carcass washed ashore there. Baneelon and Colbee were among them. A boatload of British on a hunting expedition to Broken Bay, including John White and Nanbaree, saw the feasters and began to pull into the cove. Nanbaree had picked up some English during his eighteen months in the colony, how much we don't know. As the boat approached the beach, a number of Australians picked up their spears, but Nanbaree reassured them in their own tongue. Then John White called out Baneelon's name, and first Baneelon and then Colbee stepped forward from the ruck and genially welcomed their old friend. The oarsmen pulled the boat ashore, and White, Nanbaree and others of the British party joined the people on the beach, the men clustering around them while the women and children kept their usual cautious distance.

A conversation is about to start, so it is well to consider the likely accuracy of what we are about to hear. Any investigation into early cultural encounters is bedevilled by uncertainties as to the adequacy of communication. Initially each side can only interpret the actions and intentions of the other in accordance with their own dictionaries of gesture expressed in a kind of dumb-show (remember Morton's vocabulary of signs). Communication by spoken words is negligible, and typically even more defective than the hopeful speakers assume. It is difficult to keep in mind that strangers do not grasp the meaning of your own familiar words, especially when loudly, slowly spoken. Despite the fluent conversations unblushingly recorded in the British accounts, we have to accept that even after several years of association most communications between the races living cheek-by-jowl around Sydney were managed by sign language eked out with a kind of pidgin English. All the British were impressed by the Australian talent for word-mimicry, a talent probably developed from their diplomatic need to fake polite fluency in the tongues of neighbouring language groups, but even when they got the sounds right, we cannot know how much of the sense was comprehended. As the indispensable David Collins was to put it in September 1796, a full six years after the events on the beach:

> By slow degrees we began mutually to be pleased with, and to understand each other. Language, indeed, is out of the question; for at the time of writing this, nothing but a barbarous mixture of English with the Port Jackson dialect is spoken by either party, and it must be added, that even in this the natives have the advantage, comprehending, with much greater aptness than we can pretend to, everything they hear us say.

To return to Manly Cove, with Nanbaree translating: reminded of the governor, Baneelon spoke of Phillip affectionately. He was especially delighted to hear that Phillip was nearby on an expedition to South Head. Baneelon had clearly fallen on hard times, being 'greatly emaciated' and sporting a couple of new scars, one on the fleshy part of the arm and one above the left eye. He also seemed to have lost his favourite woman Barangaroo to Colbee, which might explain his emaciation, women supplying men with most of their fish diet. But Baneelon was quickly his old animated self, asking very earnestly for hatchets, and readily accepting shirts, knives and a few handkerchiefs. The only tense moment came when a convict gamekeeper or, more correctly, game-shooter called McEntire tried to help him don a shirt (during his months of freedom he seemed to have lost the knack), and Baneelon recoiled with extraordinary revulsion. But his loathing seemed to relate only to that individual; when Baneelon begged the use of a razor to shave his beard in the British way, and was offered scissors instead, he set to clipping his hair with every sign of happiness. Furthermore, when he was told that the governor was anxious to see him, Baneelon said he would wait for him for two days before seeking Phillip out, and when the British finally departed he insisted on giving them several chunks of the decomposing whale, with the biggest lump designated his personal gift to the governor.

To the amused British the whole incident appeared to be no more than Baneelon up to his old impulsive tricks, but if they were less than delighted with their chunks of decomposing whale, it was in Australian eyes a splendid gift: a rare windfall delicacy. My guess is that if these dots were joined just a little differently, they might picture Baneelon seizing the chance to initiate political negotiations with what he took to be a placatory British offering of gifts and the promise of more, followed by his own reciprocal gift signalling his readiness to meet with the governor to resolve their differences.

What happened next is told slightly differently in the several British reports. Historians of the episode have usually chosen to select one of the accounts—often that of Watkin Tench, who wasn't there but who reads beautifully—to rely on, or have cobbled together bits from several mildly conflicting versions to construct a sufficiently coherent narrative. The difficulty is that while the discrepancies may be trivial, they may not be. Discrepancies need not be sinister. Even honest witnesses can disagree as to actions and sequences, as any traffic cop will tell you. But only the reconstruction of actual action-sequences can bring us closer to Australian intentions, so I must tax the reader's patience by occasionally going into slow-motion comparisons and evaluations to get those actions and sequences straight.

By chance the governor, out on his expedition, met the boat bearing his odoriferous present along with the friendly message from Baneelon. Eager for a rendezvous, he went to South Head to pick up some small gifts and suitable weaponry—four muskets for the men, a pistol for himself—and then continued to Manly Cove attended by Collins and his aide Lieutenant Henry Waterhouse. They found the Australians still feasting and, at least in Phillip's account, strangely reserved: 'Several natives appeared on the beach as the governor's boat rowed into the bay, but on its nearer approach they retired among the trees.'

Their reticence seems not to have troubled Phillip because he had either been told, or had privately decided, that during the earlier encounter with the hunting party Baneelon 'seemed afraid of being retaken, and would not permit any one to come so near as to lay their hands on him', which is a notion difficult to reconcile with the intimacies of the hair-clipping and shirt-donning. Could Baneelon really have thought himself at risk? When he and Colbee had been kidnapped they were first lured into waist-deep water and close to the boat. Indeed we recall that William Bradley, in charge of the kidnapping enterprise, states that the two men were enticed to the very side of the boat and well away from their friends on the beach by the offer of fish. He reports that the rest of the Australians and some of his crew were doing some of that mysterious 'dancing together' when he gave the signal and 'the two poor devils were seized and handed into the boat in an instant', with the rest of the crew scrambling aboard amidst 'great crying and screaming' from the people left on the beach and the yells of the captives. It had been a classic 'snatch'. This time the British party was deep onshore, and Baneelon surrounded by armed tribesmen. So why the cool reception?

The normally modest Phillip was proud of his flair for handling 'natives'. Unlike some of his compatriots, Phillip discounted their nakedness and their unnerving exuberance because he knew them to be fully human, and therefore fully capable of recognising and reciprocating trust. As we have seen, his first encounters with the Botany Bay people had set his style: he would lay down his arms and advance alone, hands outstretched. Time and again this strategy had been rewarded when potentially hostile men had accepted his gifts, and—the epiphany—clasped his outstretched hand. After the exchange of what he took to be a universal gesture of trust he was confident that good relations, education and the beginnings of integration could follow.

On this occasion at Manly, Phillip was explicit in his belief that 'the best means of obtaining the confidence of a native was by example, and by placing confidence in him'. He therefore stepped ashore unarmed and alone, save for a seaman carrying beef, bread and a few other gifts, and walked forward, calling his old companion repeatedly 'by all his names': a nice touch of anthropological sensibility. Some men appeared in the distance, one came closer and, taking up the gifts Phillip laid on the ground, declared himself to be Baneelon. Given his sadly changed appearance, Phillip seems not to have believed him. But when the man responded to the sight of a brandished bottle of wine by calling out 'the King', echoing the once-familiar toast, Phillip knew that this sorry figure was indeed the once-glossy Baneelon.

Nonetheless, the strange little dance of advance and retreat continued until Phillip and the seaman, along with a knot of armed Australians, were drawn out of the sight of the anxious men in the boat. And only then, when 'eight or ten of the natives had placed themselves in a position to prevent Baneelon being carried off', Phillip says—only then did Baneelon extend his hand, and allow Phillip to grasp it. Baneelon's gesture told Phillip that his solo performance had worked, and that reconciliation had been effected. He therefore went back to the beach and fetched his two officers ashore.

Or so Phillip tells it. An agenda guided his telling, how consciously I do not know. Phillip was about to get himself speared, and he knew, writing after the event, that Secretary Collins and most of his officers judged that to have been his own damned fault, plunging in among a people untrustworthy by nature without taking the elementary precaution of deploying some muskets. Phillip therefore had an interest in dramatising Baneelon's mistrust first of the British hunting party, and then of Phillip himself—a mistrust only laid to rest by Phillip's intrepid peace-making.

Young Lieutenant Waterhouse told a different story. He said that Phillip had first parleyed with some of the Australians 'in the nativ [sic] language' from the boat after one identified himself as Baneelon, and that Phillip then landed alone and unarmed. Instructing Collins and Waterhouse to keep the muskets at the ready, he walked up the beach with 'his hands and his arms open' in hot pursuit of that symbolic handshake, calling out to the Australians who were retreating towards the line of trees. Then he too disappeared into the scrub. Later Phillip returned to the boat saying he had made contact with a man claiming to be Baneelon who 'repeatedly called him Father and Governor', and recruited a seaman to carry some 'wine, beef and bread' ashore for him, along with a couple of jackets stripped from the backs of the boat crew—gifts presumably intended to remind the runaways of the pleasures of the world they had fled. Then Phillip was back at the boat again asking Collins to come ashore to verify the men's identity, and then the seaman came back to tell Waterhouse that Baneelon was asking for him, and he was instructed to join his superiors on the beach. Waterhouse did so, and there was a further round of hand-shakings. These two officers, along with the seaman-messenger, were to be present throughout all that followed, while both muskets and crew remained in the boat, which was kept resting on its oars.

I take you through this little go-round to demonstrate how innocent sources can differ on apparently innocuous details, which might prove significant after all. For this sequence I choose to follow Waterhouse, not Phillip. Waterhouse was there, he had no investment in what happened, as a junior officer he was used to watching closely and getting orders straight, and (unlike Collins) he was not already antagonistic to Phillip's conciliatory enterprise. Waterhouse's description of Phillip's enthusiastic trottings to and fro is plausible in the light of Phillip's conviction that he had a particular talent for this kind of thing, which he was eager to display, especially under Collins' sardonic eye. We can therefore conclude that, in contrast to his ready intimacy with the hunting party, Baneelon kept at a deliberate distance when the governor first landed, and had to be pursued and wooed into communication.

Contact once made—hands once shaken—Baneelon's usual

high spirits seemed to assert themselves. Phillip reports that 'he was very chearful, and repeatedly shook hands with them, asking for hatchets and cloaths, which were promised to be brought to him in two days'. (Note that for Phillip the symbolic handshakes were much more significant than the material 'hatchets and cloaths'.)

Tench offers a careful hearsay report of what Baneelon did next: a startling performance-riff. Referring back to his time in captivity in happy mime, Baneelon drank wine with a flourish and gleefully recalled the names and the idiosyncrasies of every one of the people he had known in Sydney, 'all of which', Tench says, 'he again went through with his wonted exactness and drollery', even to re-enacting on the cheek of the startled Waterhouse the kiss he once snatched from a Sydney woman. On only one issue he was less forthcoming: 'On his wounds being noticed, he coldly said he had received them at Botany Bay, but went no further into their history.' And again he insistently demanded hatchets, with the demand again being met with promises and lesser gifts.

What is going on here? The trick is to cultivate deliberate double vision: to retrieve from British descriptions clues as to autonomous Australian action, not the simple reaction the British 'naturally' assumed. I begin by wondering at that prolonged performance. Was it naive exuberance, as the British took it to be? Or was it staged to demonstrate Baneelon's intimacy with the incomers before an attentive and possibly sceptical audience? My guess is that at this point Baneelon was pursuing a rapidly evolving political project of his own: to establish himself as the crucial hinge-man between the white men and the local tribes, and indeed as the only man capable of eliciting proper compensation for past wrongs from these ignorant intruders (remember those demands for hatchets). Baneelon's time in captivity, which had cost him both his warrior prestige and his woman, could thus be parlayed into advantage in the ongoing struggle for political precedence, especially in the disordered circumstances following the smallpox epidemic. His initial coyness with the governor then appears not as shyness, a quality not much associated with Baneelon, but the deliberate aloofness of a man with a formal role to perform, and the successful imposition of an Australian protocol, invisible to British eyes, which required a wrongdoer to seek absolution by humbly pursuing the aloof wronged party.

Waterhouse reports that at some stage the governor, presumably as a mark of *his* confidence, had asked for an unusual spear Baneelon had (in his hand? beside him?) but Baneelon 'would not or could not understand him' and, taking the spear, laid it down on the grass some distance away beside a warrior unknown to Phillip. He then offered the governor a throwing stick, which he accepted. As Waterhouse remembered it, it was only after Baneelon had laid the spear on the grass that the British noticed that 'the natives now seemed to be closing around us' ('nineteen armed men and more in great numbers that we could not see'), and 'the Governor said he thought we had better retreat as they formed a crescent with us at the centre'. Collins makes no mention of the business with the spear, merely sourly remarking that 'twenty or thirty [natives were] drawing themselves into a circle around the governor and his small unarmed party (for that was literally and most inexcusably their situation)', before the governor, belatedly awake to the danger, proposed 'retiring to the boat by degrees'. Accordingly the little party withdrew closer to the beach.

It was only as the governor was making his final farewells and promises of hatchets and clothing for Baneelon and Colbee— promises which Waterhouse says Baneelon 'oft repeated…that it should not be forgot'—that 'Baneelon pointed out and named several natives that were near, one in particular to whom the Governor presented his hand and advanced, at which he seemed frightened, seis'd the spear Baneelon had laid on the ground'—and threw it 'with great violence'. At least in retrospect David Collins refused to be much ruffled; he thought the 'savage' had simply panicked in the face of Phillip's foolish advance, and (slightly discordant, this) that the whole absurd affair would not have happened had 'the precaution of taking even a single musket on shore been attended to'.

Now to play my ace in this complicated game of retrieved intentions: the account of the spearing from Governor Phillip himself, which describes the action on the beach at Manly Cove from his own perspective in (as we have seen) faintly defensive detail. You will remember that his account omits the elaborate to-ing and fro-ing described by Waterhouse, and dramatises his solitary landing and his friendly pursuit of Baneelon and the rest of the Australians. He also emphasises how wary Baneelon was initially, and then how affable, with the implication that Phillip's own relentless good will had done the trick.

Phillip recorded the sequence of events leading up to his spearing in unwittingly revealing detail. He remembered that, after the genial meeting with Baneelon and Colbee, the British party had begun to retire to the beach when they were joined by a 'stout, corpulent' native who had been standing at a little distance, but who now approached them, obviously in a high state of fear, and showed them a spear wound in his back. Baneelon then displayed the two spear wounds he had received at Botany Bay, and pointed out a strange warrior standing twenty or thirty yards away. (Here we must switch to double-vision mode: what is the story being acted out here?) At some earlier point ('in the course of this interview') Baneelon had picked up a spear from the grass: a 'very curious' spear, being barbed and pointed with hard wood, not shell or stone. It excited Phillip's collecting zeal and he asked for it, but Baneelon refused, instead taking the spear to where the stranger was standing, and throwing it down beside him. According to Phillip, Baneelon then gave the governor a common short spear taken from a nearby warrior, together with a club. Meanwhile other warriors had deployed themselves around the British party, Phillip thought for Baneelon's security against being grabbed—but perhaps as formal witnesses to what was to follow.

As was his affable custom Phillip began to advance on the stranger, empty hands spread. As he advanced, the man picked up a spear from the grass—the spear Baneelon had earlier shown the governor—and fixed it into his throwing stick. Phillip, believing there was 'no reason to suppose he would throw it without the least provocation, and when he was so near those with whom our party was on such friendly terms', continued to advance despite the warrior's increasing agitation, shouting the words he hoped meant 'bad, bad'. And the warrior steadied himself, drew back his arm—and threw.

The spear took Phillip above the right collarbone, penetrated his body and, with the point glancing downwards, emerged lower down his back close to the backbone. Some of the Australians, including Baneelon, Colbee and the spearman, decamped. Others flung their spears. One spear grazed Waterhouse's hand as he struggled to break the long spear shaft which jammed agonisingly into the sand as Phillip tried to run. Waterhouse's fright helped him break it, they ran, and another spear landed at Collins' feet as he neared the boat. Phillip drew his pistol and fired, the men got to the boat and scrambled aboard, and with Phillip supported by the shocked

Waterhouse the boat pulled away fast on the two-hour trip to Sydney Cove. During the whole incident only one British musket could be persuaded to fire.

That is the story as constructed from the direct accounts of British participants. The co-ordinating assumption of all the authors, with the tentative exceptions of Tench and Phillip who are both prepared to acknowledge puzzlement, is twofold: 'natives' are irrational, and their actions are purely reactions to British actions. The implication is that the British have conscious agendas, and 'natives' do not. The 'panic/accident' hypothesis has been accepted by most historians, but its acceptance renders a great deal of the action unintelligible, unless, of course, we are content to invoke the 'irrational savage' stereotype. If we want to uncover the Australian strategic thinking buried in the British accounts we need first to identify the anomalies. Why had Baneelon been so genial with the hunting party, and then so aloof with Phillip, the man he had said he most wanted to see? Why the prolonged acting-out of the intimacies he had enjoyed with the Sydney whites? Why the careful public listing of the gifts he was to receive on the governor's return, and the frequent emphatic reiteration of that list? Was this a childish obsession with presents, as the British read it, or was Baneelon announcing to his attentive listeners a formal contract of recompense? When the governor had been summoned, he arrived much more quickly than expected. It was only as Phillip was readying himself to leave that Baneelon drew his attention to the warrior with the unusual spear. That protracted performance of intimacy would also have allowed time for a selected warrior among the many gathered for the whale-feast to prepare himself for ritual action. And why, on this occasion and this occasion only, did the Australian warriors, excepting only Baneelon and Colbee, have their spears in hand?

If we consider only the actions and edit out the authoritative British voice-overs interpreting those actions, the 'silent film' strategy, Baneelon begins to look very like a master of ceremonies, not an impulsive buffoon. My conclusion is that we are looking at a formal summons, arranged by Baneelon, to a possible contest between champions but much more probably a ritual spearing, swiftly organised over a couple of hours and with representatives from the local tribes already fortuitously gathered, where Phillip would face a single spear-throw in penance for his and his people's many offences. Having inquired into this and other events, I am coming to think that Australian politics was not tradition-bound, as sentimentalists choose to think, but flexible and opportunistic, as is often the case in societies where warrior and hunting prowess stands high.

We know that as the governor advanced the warrior with the spear became increasingly agitated. Could this really have been from fear of being seized, with three, possibly four unarmed British and close to twenty armed warriors around, and with the British boat so far away? Either of my scenarios—a contest of champions or a punitive spearing—would explain his agitation, because both those exercises pivoted not only on a warrior's ability to throw a spear hard and accurately, but on the recipient's ability to evade or deflect it. It is therefore unsurprising that the warrior should have been seriously disconcerted by the white man's steady advance. Why was he coming so close? Why didn't he stand at the proper distance and prepare to use his club to parry? When the governor continued to advance ever deeper into his zone of critical distance, the warrior threw. He watched the spear strike (if my hypothesis is correct, probably with some incredulity: why hadn't the white man tried to deflect it?) and withdrew, his duty done and the matter settled. And the three Britishers began their run for the boat.

The agitated Waterhouse believed they were under fatal threat during that frantic, stumbling run, with no cover from the muskets until the last few steps, and then ludicrously inadequate. I disagree, largely because not one spear after the first found its mark. To my mind that is clear evidence the spears were not thrown with intent to injure. Within a very few days of their landfall at Botany Bay the British had realised that Australian spears were alarmingly accurate over long distances. Later, showing off at South Head, Baneelon was to fling a spear a mighty ninety metres into a head wind, but lesser warriors routinely managed sixty or seventy metres with killing accuracy and force. Given that accuracy, given that force, why were none of the retreating British killed, or even wounded? It is true Waterhouse lost some skin from his hand, but that was when he was wrestling with the spear shaft, which could spoil the precision of anyone's aim. Another spear landed, close but harmlessly, at Collins' feet. One spear per Englishman. My view is that with the final little flurry of spears the Australians were simply celebrating their triumph in this ritual punishment, and perhaps also reminding the British of the killing power at their disposal, just as the British had fired their guns at innocent trees and propped shields to demonstrate theirs.

Now for my claim regarding the warrior's expectation that Phillip might well evade the spear. During that first earnest evaluation of native weaponry, John Hunter had noticed that, while warriors propelled spears accurately and with 'astonishing velocity', 'a man upon his guard may with much ease, either parry, or avoid them'— provided, we want to add, he had practised such skills from boyhood, as Australian children did. Hunter also examined some of the local bark shields and was impressed by their capacity to 'turn' a spear.

We also know from First Fleet observers, confirmed by anthropologists like W. E. H. Stanner a hundred and fifty years later, that in pitched battles between native groups injuries were always fewer than watching whites thought possible, because of the Australians' preternatural skill in dodging. We should further note that even at such short range (given Phillip's magnificently steadfast advance it cannot have been much more than fifteen metres), and remembering native spearmen's notorious accuracy, the spear did not skewer Phillip through the middle but struck him high on the right shoulder: that is, on the outer edge of the body. It was not a mortal wound, but he would carry the scar to his grave. My own guess is that the wound was in the event more dangerous than intended. That crazy remorseless advance would unnerve anyone.

It is easy to become over-ingenious in interpreting the intentions lurking in other minds, but I also want to consider the nature of the spear which passed through Governor Phillip's body. The spear ended in a sleek barbed wooden head which slipped easily through flesh, and once the barbed head had been broken off it could be withdrawn with equal ease, leaving a clean wound which would heal well. (White commented on the Australians' remarkable capacity to heal.) Any warrior shown the weapon would have realised that. Three months later when the governor's 'shooter' John McEntire—the man from whom Baneelon had recoiled—was ambushed and speared, a very different weapon was used. Was McEntire's spear designed as an instrument of execution, while the governor's spear was crafted for occasions when clean wounds and spillage of blood, not death, were required? Given the sophisticated differentiation of function in Australian equipment, I believe that is likely. (This triggers a memory of those four spears left in a murdered convict in the first year of contact. Given the ease of tribal and individual identification to Australian eyes, had the spears been left as a statement of responsibility and a coded explanation for the killing?)

As for that preliminary display of wounds: Phillip describes Baneelon displaying his two scars, saying he had received them at Botany Bay, and then pointing to the unnamed warrior. Had the warrior inflicted Baneelon's wounds? When Phillip inquired into the warrior's identity he was offered various tribal affiliations, Nanbaree saying he was from Broken Bay, while Baneelon said he was a *Kayyeemy* from around Manly. Later he was firmly identified as Willemerin, a curer-warrior from Botany Bay. The Botany Bay people had cause for grievance, from the early conduct of La Pérouse to depredations of convicts eager for loot and, I suspect, an escape from boredom. I conclude that the wounds Baneelon displayed so deliberately were indeed the result of ritual spearings, probably inflicted by this particular man; that what Baneelon was 'saying' to the governor in urgent mime was: 'Look, this is serious business, but while you'll be left with a formidable scar it won't kill you.'

The British accounts agree on the disparity of the weapons distributed to the combatants: the warrior with his long spear, the governor either with a short light spear and a club or a throwing stick. It is that disparity which persuades me that what happened on the beach was no contest of champions. On one side it was an impeccable, disastrous performance of British phlegm, and on the other a punitive ritual to settle grievances accumulated against the British, possibly initiated by a tribe other than Baneelon's, who believed themselves wronged or insulted or slighted by the whites, and who had identified Phillip as the leading warrior because of the deference accorded him, and also because of that famously absent right front tooth.

The matter was to be settled by a single spear-throw which might or might not draw blood, although it is likely that a blood flow would terminate the action more satisfactorily. Baneelon's organisation of the affair might indicate his and his people's acceptance of their role as Phillip's allies, and therefore as the appropriate mediator, or his tribe's view that they deserved reparation too. Later we will see Baneelon negotiating the return of stolen fishing gear, settling the number of hatchets and other goods required for compensation, and opening the way for his people to visit their new allies to enjoy their rightful access to coveted food supplies and other resources.

I think Baneelon believed he had fully instructed Phillip as to what was in store for him, first by holding aloof from the victim-to-be, as befits a man stage-managing so serious an event; then by showing Phillip those speaking scars; then by drawing his attention to the ceremonial spear; then setting it down beside his warrior nemesis. The attention Phillip gave the spear, his acquiescence in its being placed beside the strange warrior, and his own acceptance of a lesser weapon could well have been read as his acknowledgment and acceptance of what was to come. As any player of charades knows, the meaning of the dumb-show always seems crystal clear to the 'speaker', especially when the audience is as earnestly attentive as Phillip surely would have been. In the event things went slightly wrong, as they often do on ritual occasions, but the governor was successfully wounded, blood had flowed, and the way was opened for Baneelon's people's peaceable entry into their new allies' settlement.

How then ought we assess Phillip's performance? Stanner, commenting on Phillip's handling of another cross-cultural incident, writes that he displayed 'the mixture of calm, courage and wrong-headedness that was to characterise most of his dealings with [Australians]', but that is the wisdom of hindsight. Phillip's personal courage and his generous, even reckless, commitment to conciliation remain impressive. To his enduring credit, he also grasped in broad what had gone wrong at Manly Cove—that there had been a disastrous confusion of understandings—and refused to permit any punitive action. Instead he engaged in an admirably cool rethinking. What had happened?

After reflection he concluded that there had been no calculated hostility: that the spearman had acted merely from 'a momentary impulse of fear' when he was in terror of being seized. Only one thing puzzled him. Why had Baneelon done nothing? He 'never attempted to interfere when the man took the spear up, or said a single word to prevent him from throwing it'. Why? Finally Phillip decided that it had simply been a muddle: that '[Baneelon] possibly did not think the spear would be thrown'. After all, the spearing had been 'but the business of [a] moment'. Which is exactly what it was not, but rather a carefully planned ceremonial action to restore British–Australian relations to a viable equilibrium.

In his 1796 'Appendix' to his *Account*, Collins commented on another oddity regarding Australians: the 'friendship and alliance…known to subsist between several who were opposed to each other, who fought with all the ardour of the bitterest enemies, and who, though wounded, pronounced the party by whom they had been hurt to be good and brave, and their friends'.

In my view, the complex crosscutting of loyalties, combined with an ambitious leap for prominence to recover the status lost during his period of captivity, adequately explains Baneelon's apparent doubleness at Manly Cove, where he acted first as master of ceremonies and even as Phillip's second—and then very properly dissociated himself from any responsibility for the outcome. This was not Baneelon's quarrel. His concern was with the return of stolen goods and adequate material payment for the injuries his tribe had suffered. He later commiserated with Phillip, even claiming to have severely beaten the offending warrior, just as he had probably congratulated the surprised victor, whom he was later to acknowledge to Phillip as a 'friend'. The 'ritual spearing' hypothesis also explains the affable yet oddly detached tone of inquiries as to the governor's health made by a couple of Australians from the Rose Hill area who took the opportunity to say—now the whites had seen how very efficient Australian spears were, now that relations had been restored to a civilised balance by the bloodletting on the beach—how little they liked white men settling in their territory. Perhaps they hoped for a British withdrawal: after all, for them the score card read 'Australians 1, British nil'.

The British took the hint, and reinforced the Rose Hill guard.

We are fortunate to have another kind of text altogether which allows us to trace the usually invisible process of the transformation of story into social myth: two paintings by the as-yet-unidentified 'Port Jackson Painter'. Whoever he was, he was not present at Manly Cove.

The first painting is not much more than a coloured snapshot of the action as described, with Phillip well up the beach, Waterhouse wrestling with the shaft, Collins approaching the boat, a lone marine on the beach firing a musket, and the Australians in what looks like confused retreat. The second image (reproduced in the plate section) compresses time in cartoon style, which suggests iconic rather than representational intentions: for example, with the governor already speared and one of his men in the act of firing his musket in a great horizontal effusion of smoke, three male natives are still sitting around their barbecue fires with their spears on the ground beside them, two armed warriors are running away, while others peek from behind trees (in the painting the trees cluster thickly, while Phillip tells us they grew twelve to fifteen metres apart). Only one warrior, one of the peekers, has his spear in anything like a throwing position. Other dark, chubby figures are tiptoeing into the trees like guilty children. Meanwhile Phillip is less than halfway down the beach, quite unattended, with the spear shaft still unbroken, Collins is gesturing from close by the boat, and Waterhouse, who from the written texts stayed close by Phillip's side throughout, is well down the beach running towards Collins. What the painting looks like is an astute visual compromise between Phillip's own interpretation of 'What Happened at Manly Cove'—that there had been no settled malice and no plan; that the Australians were as shocked by the event as the British; that the whole unhappy business was an accident—and the painter's own preferred emphasis, which falls on the heroic figure of the governor isolated on the beach.

We have the received verbal version of the spearing as evolved in the salons of Sydney Cove preserved in the long letter Elizabeth Macarthur wrote to a woman friend in March 1791, where the 'irrational savage' myth is cosily evoked.

The Macarthurs, arrived on the *Scarborough* late in June 1790, had been in Sydney for only a couple of months when the governor was wounded, but Elizabeth's account demonstrates that by early 1791 Collins had decisively won the *sotto voce* contest regarding the events at Manly Cove. From the beginning the governor had 'left no means untried to effect an intimacy', she reports, but to no effect, because savages are childishly unpredictable: 'They accept his presents as do Children play things; just to amuse them for a moment and then throw them away, disregarded.' They are at once flighty and deceitful: Baneelon and Colbee had seemed to accept their captivity happily enough when Colbee 'in a very Artful manner' made his escape, and later Baneelon 'took himself off without any known reason' after having 'appeared highly pleased with our people, and Manners'.

Encountered by chance at Manly Cove, both men had been affable and had happily exchanged gifts with their old friends, although in Elizabeth's account stinking whale meat transforms into inoffensive whale bone. The governor had therefore landed 'by himself, unarm'd in order to show no violence was intended'. So far so good. Then, unlike all the accounts following close on the events, Elizabeth has Baneelon immediately advancing, shaking hands with the governor, and asking for presents, with other friendly Australians clustering around them as they 'continued to converse with much seeming friendliness'. As the governor, noticing they had walked rather far from the boat, began his leave-taking, Baneelon indicated 'an Old looking man' who was advancing. The governor approached the 'Old' man, and was speared. 'The reason why the mischeif [sic] was done,' Elizabeth says airily, 'could not be learnt.' Then, equally irrationally, the locals came swarming into the settlement, 'with many taking up their abode among us'.

Thus ends an intellectually incoherent but emotionally satisfying story which marvellously incorporates the attributes of 'the savage' European colonisers manage to find everywhere—deceitfulness, impulsiveness, and casual ferocity—while the only defects the British exhibit, at least in this telling, are to be too trusting and too brave, Elizabeth Macarthur reminding us that 'very imprudently none of the Gentlemen had the precaution to take a gun in their hand'. Nonetheless (and in the face of accumulating evidence) she remains comfortably convinced that 'the natives are still in such fear of our fire Arms, that a single armed Man would drive an hundred natives with their spears'. Thus is reality managed in a colonial situation.

The spearing of Governor Phillip occurred on 7 September. Collins tells us that a few days after the 'accident', as the British agreed it was, they happened to take a great catch of salmon, and Phillip sent thirty or forty fish to Baneelon and his party, still camped on the north shore, as 'a conciliatory gesture'. This can only have reinforced Baneelon's confidence in both his analysis and the success of his strategy. A week later another British party spotted a small fire, again on the north shore, and found Baneelon and a small party of Australians there. 'Much civility passed,' Tench reports, and the two groups agreed to meet again in the same place later in the day.

The (unarmed) British duly landed, Baneelon at last got the hatchet he had been asking for, along with another large fish, and there was an eerie return to the nervous merriment of those very first meetings at Botany Bay and around the harbour beaches. Tench tells us that Baneelon called loudly for beef, bread and wine, consumed them with gusto, and then subjected himself to the British ritual of being shaved, 'to the great admiration of his countrymen, who laughed and exclaimed at the operation'. Submitting to ordeal by froth and razor seems to have become a new-minted demonstration of trust for the Australians, as well as a neat compliment to their well-shaven friends. The men with Baneelon still flinched from the razor but allowed their beards to be scissor-clipped, and Baneelon's woman Barangaroo, with whom he was reconciled (another sign of restored prestige?) and whom he now proudly displayed to the British, suffered having her hair combed and cut at Baneelon's request: another pretty compliment to the British. The British even made an abortive attempt at matchmaking between Boorong, the girl raised in the pastor's house, and a fetching lad named Imeerawanyee (in some accounts spelt 'Yemmerrawanne') but Boorong indicated her feelings were engaged elsewhere.

And then, Tench says, 'we began to play and romp with them', this time not by dancing but in trials of strength, with men competing to lift each other off the ground, a contest which the British won hands down. Baneelon complained that spears and fishing gear had been stolen from some of his people; the next day the equipment was returned to him; and we wonder how the British officers knew where to find it.

At that frolicsome second meeting Tench recorded the presence of a stranger, an affable but aloof man who, while he readily shook hands with any Britisher who approached him, stood separate from the rest 'in a musing posture, contemplating what passed'. Tench, coveting a 'string of bits of dried reeds' the man was wearing around his neck, pleasantly offered his own black stock (a fashionably elaborate scarf) in exchange. The man, equally pleasantly, refused, and Tench was sufficiently impressed by his dignity to be nervous when young Imeerawanyee laughingly snatched the necklace from the man's neck and put it around Tench's. But the man bore the impudence with serenity, and accepted having Tench's stock tied around his own neck. It may be his tolerance is explained by Imeerawanyee's youth or a close kin relationship, or, just possibly, by Tench's sensitive uneasiness.

To the surprise of the British, despite his promises Baneelon was not there, but after an hour of amicable exchanges they were directed to the beach where they found him fishing—or pretending to fish—with Barangaroo. Again, Baneelon was initially shy; again this looks very like properly remote conduct from an offended party.

Was Baneelon especially cautious because his conduct of negotiation with these potential allies was being assessed by higher authorities, not known to the British but embodied in the person of the thoughtful stranger? Baneelon was young to claim political consequence, especially when his prominence was the result of the accident of his capture and captivity. We would expect his performance to be watched, even directed, by older, wiser heads. We are given a handful of hints as to the durability of such an invisible hierarchy. For example, the convict-artist Thomas Watling, arrived at Sydney late in 1792, casually mentions a 'poet' who passed through the settlement 'and held forth to several hundreds of his countrymen, who after kindly entreating, escorted him to some other bourne, to further promulgate his composition'. Who was this wandering bard, travelling so freely across clan boundaries? Later again David Collins remarked the respectful excitement which would be generated among youngsters in Sydney when some unremarkable old men happened to pass through the town: 'We have been immediately informed of their arrival, and they have been pointed out to our notice in a whisper, and with an eagerness of manner which... impressed us with the idea that we were looking at persons to whom some consequence was attached...'

The British party invited Baneelon to visit the governor, who he was assured was recovering, but Baneelon indicated that the governor must first come to him, presumably to mark Phillip's acceptance of the justice of his punishment and to conclude the episode without residue. Accordingly, a mere ten days after his spearing, Phillip painfully levered himself into a boat and went to attend on Baneelon. Then on 8 October the British again saw the signal fire, and a little fleet of British boats set out. They found what looks at this distance like a formal delegation of Baneelon, Barangaroo and another woman, and six Australian men, 'all of whom', Tench tells us, 'received us with welcome except the grave-looking gentleman before mentioned, who stood aloof in his former musing posture'. This time most of the men submitted to the ministrations of the barber brought specially for the purpose. Next came not gift-giving, but a flurry of trading exchanges in which the Australians drove unusually hard bargains with their new partners. (This was the occasion the warrior refused Tench's pleas for his spear for anything less than a hatchet.) Then, in exuberant good humour, Baneelon and three other natives, not including the grave gentleman, departed by British boat and Australian canoe to visit the governor. Given the British penchant for kidnapping, they sensibly left a hostage behind in the person of Parson Richard Johnson.

Baneelon had been especially eager for Barangaroo to come with him, but she wrathfully refused. She 'violently opposed Baneelon's departure', Tench tells us, and 'when she found persuasion vain, she had recourse to tears, scoldings and threats, stamping the ground and tearing her hair'. Then, when Baneelon remained unmoved, she furiously smashed one of his fishing spears. Presumably she disagreed with the politics of conciliation. Barangaroo was always a woman with attitude.

Arrived at Sydney, Baneelon led his little party confidently through the settlement, running happily from room to room in the governor's house, discoursing knowledgeably on mysterious objects like candle-snuffers, and fondly kissing Phillip's orderly sergeant— although we should note that he still recoiled when the gamekeeper McEntire tried to approach him. From that time onwards there were always Australians around the settlement, calling in at the governor's yard for fish and bread; coveting British possessions, particularly metal ones, and occasionally making off with them; and diverting themselves watching the peculiar doings of their new allies.

Their presence rapidly became a mixed blessing. Even Tench admitted that 'sometimes by their clamour for bread and meat (of which they now all eat very greedily) [they] are become very trouble-some', especially as the British themselves were still on painfully short rations. (The risk of famine was decisively alleviated only towards the end of June 1792.) Within a month of the reconciliation 'every gentleman's house [had] become a resting or sleeping place for some of them every night', a pressure not much alleviated when the governor built Baneelon a substantial brick house at Baneelon's earnest request and at a site of his own choosing, out on the beautiful point which now bears his name and the Opera House.

The building was completed by the end of November. In his reports Phillip was always careful to refer to this grace-and-favour dwelling as a 'hut', but Collins makes clear that the 'hut' was 'a brick one twelve feet square, covered with tiles', and this at a time when British soldiers and officers at Rose Hill were camping in decaying wattle-and-daub structures which offered scant protection from the weather. 'To occupy a brick house put together with mortar formed of clay of the country and covered with tiles, became, in point of comparative comfort and convenience, an object of some importance,' as Collins rather prissily put it.

For Phillip the house was important in binding Baneelon and his friends to the new alliance, and to give them a specified secure place. Now they could come freely to the settlement in their canoes and lounge about watching the marines drilling and convicts working as stage one in Phillip's great experiment of civilising the nomads.

We cannot know precisely what shifts of mind or circumstance persuaded particular Australian groups to 'come in'. It looks like a frogs-in-a-pond process as families came, saw and decided to stay for a while. Colbee made his separate peace with Phillip on 18 October in what we can now recognise as the correct way. Obligingly placing himself with his few surviving kin in an adjacent cove, he summoned the governor to him. The governor, equally obligingly, came, 'a hatchet was, as usual, desired and given, and Colebe [sic] promised to come to dinner the next day'. Phillip was beginning to get the hang of the protocol. Early in the New Year the first corroboree for presentation before a white audience was arranged by Baneelon and Colbee, as befitted their new prominence, to celebrate and consolidate the alliance—and Britishers discovered how difficult it was to vibrate the knees at will.

Why did reconciliation come out of violence and catastrophe? I think we have been looking at a performance of conscientious magnanimity from the governor and a ceremonially ordered settlement of grievances from the Australians, played simultaneously on the same stage. I also believe that the great fact of British blood spilt on the sand extinguished accumulated native grievances, and initiated an alliance between subordinate incomers and ordinate possessors— from, of course, the Australians' point of view.

We are indebted for the possibility of this kind of reconstruction largely to Tench, who was always ready to report everything he saw, including actions he did not understand, in detail and in scrupulous sequence. Unlike some of his colleagues, and minor inconveniences aside, he was delighted by the influx and by the new opportunities offered by intimacy: 'During the intervals of duty our greatest source of entertainment now lay in cultivating the acquaintance of our new friends, the natives.' By nature hopeful, he was sanguine as to outcomes. Now good will and proximity would conquer all: 'Ever liberal of communication, no difficulty but of understanding each other subsisted between us.'

Even Tench soon had to admit that 'inexplicable contradictions arose to bewilder our researches'. As the British got to know the Australians better, it sometimes seemed they understood them less.

Within two months of the spearing Baneelon was dining again at the governor's house, just as he had in the days of his captivity. At his first dinner he was promised a custom-made leather shield covered with the best tin, a gracious bending of British technology to savage purposes, to celebrate the renewed friendship. The next day a boisterous party of Australians came over to see if the shield was ready (it wasn't), and Boorong took the opportunity to ask for the usual hatchet for each of her two brothers, also members of the party. After all, some payment was due, the British having kept her from the service of her family for the eighteen months she had spent in the household of the Reverend Johnson.

From the Australians' point of view things were going excellently well, with compensation duly paid to the appropriate people and a decent hospitality displayed towards their kin and friends. Phillip was also happy. He had been gratified that Baneelon chose to linger with him until late in the afternoon of that first visit, when some of his family came to fetch him. At last his hope was being realised: 'No doubt could be entertained but that they would visit the settlement as frequently as could be wished.'

Or, as it turned out, rather more often and in greater numbers than their hosts might have chosen. Provisions were depleting; there was no sign of the promised store ships; drought was withering the young crops. The settlement was also increasingly burdened by convicts too weak, old or ill to work. Collins estimated that 1790 had cost 159 lives: 143 from sickness, three absconded or lost, four executed, and nine drowned. That is a lot of deaths for so small a community to absorb.

With material and psychological strains multiplying, their new guests were making themselves rather too much at home. John Harris, arriving with the Second Fleet in June 1790 as surgeon to the New South Wales Corps, expressed a newcomer's fierce intolerance: 'The Whole Tribe with their Visitors have plagued us ever since [Phillip's wounding] nor can we get rid of them. They come and go at pleasure They are very Fond of our Bread, Beef etc.' Baneelon's house on the point failed to relieve the pressure. When it overflowed with visitors (and more and more seemed to be coming) they simply spilled into the governor's yard and waited cheerfully to be fed. Two youths in full ceremonial fig chose to stay in the yard to prepare for a tooth-drawing ceremony, and came back afterwards to recover; children were parked there under the governor's care while their parents went off on essential travels unimpeded; and at least one redundant wife fetched up in the governor's charge when her husband dumped her for another woman. Such unsought responsibilities could lead to undesired revelations: in the last case the abandoned wife left the governor's protection after little more than a week to rejoin her husband, while the other woman, having taken up with another man, became a frequent visitor to Sydney, where, as

Phillip glumly notes, 'she was said to have granted her favours to several of the convicts'.

This was not the moral-reformation-by-example Phillip had envisioned. Australian interactions seen at close quarters could only erode his hopes for their quick integration into proper British ways of thinking and doing. Worst, and despite British disapproval, men continued to beat their women as of right, and then nonchalantly took them off to the hospital and Surgeon White to have their wounds and bruises dressed. Some women seemed to prefer this treatment to the sedate pleasures available in the colony. At the end of December a young girl had begged to be allowed to live among Phillip's servants and under his protection, but she stayed for only a few days before, curiosity satisfied, she returned to her old life. Before she left she stripped off all her clothing, retaining only the woollen nightcap she had been given to keep her newly shaven head warm. Phillip drew the unavoidable inference: 'She had never been under any kind of restraint, so that her going away could only proceed from a preference to the manner of life in which she had been brought up.' Even young Boorong could not be kept within the settlement, however brutally she might be treated outside it. One day in the new year she came paddling in with another girl who had also enjoyed a spell under British protection, both of them hungry, both of them beaten around the head and shoulders. They said two men known in the colony had beaten them because they refused to sleep with them. And yet, after a couple of days of food and Surgeon White's care, they paddled away again.

Both the girls' freedom and their vulnerability were probably the consequence of the disruptions effected by the smallpox epidemic, exacerbated by the proximity of the British camp as an alternative resource and refuge. But Phillip was in no mood for sociological analysis, gloomily commenting, 'Making love in this country is always prefaced by a beating, which the female seems to receive as a matter of course.' His comment does not illuminate the case—the girls were beaten precisely because they said no—but it captures his increasing despondency.

Meanwhile, Baneelon was visiting the settlement and the governor daily, along with 'his wife, several children' (orphaned by the smallpox disaster?) 'and half a dozen of their friends', and Baneelon and Barangaroo together proved notably more trying guests than Baneelon alone. Barangaroo showed none of her husband's sensitivity to alien protocols. A stormy soul, she expressed herself freely and, despite expressed British concern regarding modesty, insisted on going naked save for a slim bone in her nose even to the governor's table, except once, when, fresh from a grand ceremonial occasion, she appeared in the glory of body paint. Even Baneelon, who had gone meekly clothed throughout his captivity, now often seemed to have mislaid most of his garments, or simply chose to carry them in a net around his neck.

Phillip was also to discover that the couple's displays of affectionate concern were almost as trying as their flares of violence. When Barangaroo sat herself down by the governor's fire and complained of a pain in her belly, Baneelon proceeded to a prolonged curing ceremony, warming his hand with his breath and applying it to the affected part while sustaining a monotonous chant occasionally interrupted by episodes of barking like a dog. The ceremony had gone on for a very long time when Phillip intervened, sent for the surgeon, and persuaded Barangaroo to take 'a little tincture of rhubarb, which gave her relief, and so put an end to the business'—to the even greater relief, one imagines, of the governor's household.

The governor's yard continued to overflow with Baneelon's

friends. Outdoor livers, they were uninhibited guests. Here we have less information on some matters than I would like: for example, could they have been persuaded to use the governor's privy? To the Australians, used to depositing natural wastes at a decent distance from the group campfires and then moving on, British privies must have seemed pestilential places, and from a genteel sniff and curl-of-the-lip in Elizabeth Macarthur's letter to her friend Bridget Kingdon, I rather doubt they did.

David Collins, exemplary chronicler though he was, fails to record any of these disturbances and disruptions, presumably judging them to be trivial. We know of most of them only because Phillip, deep in his sea of troubles, nonetheless took the time to report them in fine detail to his bemused superiors—because they pressed upon him, but also, I think, because he intuited that these matters could be significant in their later implications.

Now I offer an account, put together from Phillip's own recounting, of six weeks in the life of a colonial governor committed to tolerance and conciliation, from mid-November 1790, when the 'coming in' was fully effected, to the end of that year.

On the morning of 13 November, a Sunday, Baneelon arrived at the governor's house accompanied by a small swarm of Australians, sixteen altogether, some of them strangers. He had been away for a couple of days visiting the tribe at Botany Bay, until recently his enemies and now, it seemed, his friends, so the strangers were probably Botany Bay people he had invited to make their first visit to the settlement, with this a guided tour of the new amenities.

It was a success, Phillip tells us. 'Appear[ing] highly delighted with the novelties,' the visitors settled down, lit a fire in the governor's yard to cook their handouts of fish, and 'sat down to breakfast in great good humour'. Barangaroo was one of the group, and Phillip was distressed to see she looked 'very ill' from a bad scalp wound she had just received from Baneelon for having (deliberately) broken a fish spear and a throwing stick. Phillip took his opportunity publicly to remonstrate with Baneelon for injuring this woman he clearly loved, but to no effect: Baneelon simply said she deserved it, and when Phillip continued to press him he repeated she was bad, and therefore he had beaten her. Phillip could get no more sense from him, 'for Baneelon either did not understand the questions put to him or was unwilling to answer them'—a not unusual experience for investigators into domestic sexual politics.

Breakfast done, the whole troupe set off to take Barangaroo and another woman whose scalp had also been laid open to the hospital, where John White obligingly dressed their wounds. Then they all trooped back to the governor's yard.

So much for the morning. Tench was to concoct an amusing story out of what happened next, but Phillip was not amused at all. He gave a detailed report to his superiors, presumably because he sensed there were matters of consequence at stake. I have therefore resorted to some more slow-motion narrative and analysis.

Leaving his friends in the yard, Baneelon marched into the house, found the governor writing at his desk, sat down beside him, and began talking. This would be a great liberty in an Englishman, but not to Baneelon, who had no notion of the sanctity of doors, or desks, or privacy, or writing. He needed to talk with the governor on an important matter, so in he came.

He was out of sorts. As he talked he fingered a hatchet—a British-made hatchet, which adds piquancy to the scene to follow—which he said he was going to use to 'kill' a woman who had offended him. This was a seriously provocative statement given their very recent conversation about the beating of Barangaroo, and the governor expostulated. But Baneelon was not to be moved: after more talk he got up, remarked that he couldn't stay for dinner because he was off to beat the woman, and strode towards his house, with the governor, the governor's secretary Collins and a sergeant trailing anxiously in his wake.

A handful of people—youths, men, women and children—were lounging on the grass outside the hut, with the girl in question lying among them, either asleep or already shielding her head. On the way the governor had contrived to substitute his own walking cane for the hatchet, and then to retrieve the walking stick too, so he must have been reasonably confident that Baneelon would not be able to do any real damage, but before the sergeant and the shocked Collins could intervene (and with the muscular speed which marked him as a warrior) Baneelon snatched up a 'sword of the country' and dealt the girl two savage blows on the head and shoulders.

He seemed deranged with rage, shouting and roaring. When the whites grabbed him, his followers snatched up their spears, but then were content to watch as Baneelon screamed threats, brandished a spear at the governor, and yelled for a hatchet to finish the job on the girl. (Tench, who was not present, provides Baneelon with a splendidly melodramatic speech: 'She is now...my property: I have ravished her by force from her tribe: and I will part with her to no person whatever, until my vengeance shall be glutted...')

Some sailors from the *Supply*, alerted by the hubbub, hastily pulled their boat ashore, picked up the unconscious girl and carried her to the boat, and thence to the hospital. Despite the uproar Phillip was cool enough to note that, with the exception of two youths, who protested, none of the Australians present tried to interfere with her removal. Nor did they seem concerned about her injury—except for one young man. He had watched the assault without making any attempt to intervene, but now he said he was her husband, and asked and was given permission to go in the boat with her. His name was Boladeree.

With the girl whisked to safety, Baneelon and the British party, attended by an escort of Australian males of various ages, walked back to the governor's house while the governor forcefully explained to Baneelon that if he should try to kill the girl again, or even to beat her, he would pay with his life. Baneelon, maintaining his rage, kept insisting on his right to kill her: she was, he shouted, both the child of his enemy and had herself once dared to take unfair advantage of him in battle. When chided by David Collins he dramatically mimed just where he was going to wound the girl before he cut off her head. Then he stalked off, breathing fire.

The governor was naturally outraged by a performance which had managed to violate most British notions of proper conduct. He was also shocked that Baneelon's followers had reached for their arms on what he thought of as British territory. He had the girl taken to his house and so under his direct protection, and when young Boladeree begged permission to stay with her, Phillip agreed— although he also noted disapprovingly that the young man had not stirred a muscle while Baneelon was making his attack. Phillip also posted an armed guard on their door, a sensible precaution given that soon afterwards a mob of Baneelon's adherents appeared in the hospital garden demanding their victim, to be driven away only after a shouting match and a show of force from the guard. Meanwhile 'several of the natives', presumably better informed as to the girl's whereabouts, came to visit her at the governor's house, and urged she be returned to Baneelon and to Baneelon's house. This Phillip refused to do, being persuaded she would surely be murdered.

Baneelon sulked for two days before he appeared at the governor's door. He responded furiously when the guard prevented him entering, but then regained his temper, and when asked he promised not to beat the girl again. He also needed the surgeon. He had beaten Barangaroo again in the interim, and she, in defiance of all protocols of proper female behaviour, had grabbed a club and whacked him back, so now both their heads needed dressing. But the thought of going to White's hospital made him nervous: he told Phillip he was even reluctant to sleep in his own house because he feared the surgeon would come and shoot him, and he kept dashing back to the room where Phillip had persuaded him to leave his spears to demonstrate his own readiness to spear him back. Perhaps Baneelon realised that John White had a hair-trigger temper too.

With truly astonishing patience, Phillip called the surgeon to his house, made peace between the two men, escorted them back to the hospital where the desired dressings were applied, and then went on to the surgeon's house where the girl now lay. Baneelon spoke to her gently—upon which Barangaroo, instantly jealous, snatched up a club and made a determined effort to bash the girl herself. She desisted only when Baneelon, begged by the governor to control her, gave her a hard slap in the face. This was not what the governor had in mind, but it had the desired effect.

The girl was then taken back to the governor's house and, with Baneelon's approval, was installed along with Boladeree in a maid's room. Baneelon had realised that Phillip was seriously angry. Having got his own temper back, he offered his spears to Phillip as he entered the governor's yard, and laid them down. Thereupon Barangaroo, infuriated by his submission, and displaying her usual magnificent disregard for political niceties, staged a demonstration of her own, sitting down on the spears and refusing to budge until she was dragged off, shrieking wildly, by an embarrassed guard. Taking away a warrior's arms was a serious business, and Barangaroo was determined to defend her husband's honour. Then, in a delicate gesture of trust, Baneelon himself asked the soldier for them, and handed them directly to the governor—although his men, still in possession of their own arms, still looked dangerously ready to use them.

Then Phillip turned the whole lot of them, including the raucous Barangaroo, out of the yard, excepting only Baneelon, who took his dinner at the governor's table with his usual good humour. He was on the point of leaving when the girl begged to be allowed to leave with him. So great was her distress that when Baneelon gave his personal guarantee she would not be hurt Phillip allowed her to go, and so eager was she to rejoin her friends that she ran ahead towards Baneelon's house: a poor return for Phillip's compassionate interventions.

It had been a long few days, packed with unpredictable events and incomprehensible excitements. Even Watkin Tench's acuity failed when he tried to fathom what had been going on. He finally classified the 'singular circumstance' of the girl's wounding and its aftermath as one of those 'inexplicable contradictions [which] arose to bewilder our researches which no ingenuity could unravel and no credulity reconcile'.

Let us see if we can do better.

Coolly considered, Baneelon's violence against the girl, together with his readiness to use violence against any Britisher who got in the way, was a political disaster. It cost him the governor's confidence, already shaken by evidence of what he saw as Baneelon's political flightiness, with the Botany Bay enemies of yesterday become the friends of today. Why did he behave so wildly in this instance? What had happened to the quick-study mime who in captivity had picked up nuances of gesture and expression with such acuity, and responded with such flair?

The first thing to note is that, if the British accounts make Baneelon's behaviour sound reckless to the point of psychosis, there is nothing in his compatriots' response to suggest that they found anything remarkable in it at all. On the contrary: they stayed out of the affair between Baneelon and the girl, and were ready to fight only when the British intervened. This looks like another cultural misunderstanding—or a whole knot of them. My guess is that, having taken possession of his house within the colony, and (reasonably) believing that Phillip recognised his and his people's territorial autonomy—remember he had freely chosen his own house site— Baneelon had been inviting both friends and foes to view his newly acquired land rights and his privileged relationship with the British, and also to exploit the governor's reliable hospitality. His political influence was accordingly expanding, with even the Botany Bay people so eager to evaluate his claims and to share in his good fortune that they travelled the ten kilometres to Sydney Cove to do so. The British colony could supply both food and diversion, which were scarce commodities in their tough lives.

I think the 'singular circumstance' of the girl's near-fatal and very public wounding was triggered by Phillip's equally public nagging in the yard that morning when he took Baneelon to task on what was, for Australians, a domestic matter. Baneelon, having brooded on that improper and insistent questioning, decided to make a public display before the British, his own people, and also the people from Botany Bay, of his autonomy, which extended in this particular matter to power over life and death. Phillip had demonstrated his own power to inflict extreme violence, with regular floggings and four hangings within the year, two in February 1790, when Baneelon had been a prisoner, and two more in late October, after the 'coming in'. The girl, child of a personal enemy, a member of an enemy tribe, and a female who had dared to harass him during a male-to-male combat, was a legitimate target for vengeance. While Baneelon could not muster the pomp which framed Phillip's displays of violence, he could summon both the audience and the authenticating passion to carry the scene through. I think he was saying, in that furious, staged event: 'These are my people; this is my territory; and this is my law. I defy you to impede me.' And when he was finally coaxed into magnanimity, he wanted that recognised too. Cross-cultural contests are not limited to dancing and wrestling matches.

I would also like to take a moment to consider that earlier tableau when Baneelon burst in on Phillip as he wrote at his desk. Phillip was using the magic of literacy to communicate with physically remote superiors in highly abstract terms, like 'good government', or 'law', which he knew would be understood. Baneelon addressed his issues of proper conduct directly by spoken words and exemplary action, fully adequate within his face-to-face system of kin and clan. The two men might sit side by side, they might talk together—but they nonetheless inhabited quite different worlds.

The performance with the girl pivoted on Baneelon's understanding of warrior protocols and their relationship to the sexual politics of the Australians, which themes must now be explored. But first we need to remind ourselves of sexual politics as practised by the British.

The offering of women for sexual use to cement friendship or political or economic alliance was standard practice among Australians. There is no clear evidence of that privilege being extended to the British, although as early as 1791 some women were selling their favours to convicts, presumably with the permission of their men. By 1796 the practice was common enough for David Collins, always prone to exaggeration in moral matters, to claim that more than a few Australian women were ready to exchange their 'chastity' for 'a loaf of bread, a blanket, or a shirt', and that 'several girls who were protected in the settlement, had not any objection to passing the night on board ships, although some had learnt shame enough…to conceal, on their landing, the spoils they had procured during their stay'. Whether this was indeed 'shame' or a sensible precaution against robbery by Australian or British males we do not know. Or had these particular girls responded to new opportunities under the new regime by emancipating themselves from male control? I remember those fisherwomen in their canoes, keeping their first catches for themselves and their youngest children by consuming them on the spot.

What was not at all standard was the British response to sexual encounters or, more correctly, their lack of response. While they might be ready to pay in rum or goods for the use of a woman's body, they recognised no obligation to her male kin, finding it both more convenient and more 'natural' to trade directly with the women. Australian males could find themselves abruptly outside the loop, with their women likely to suffer their anger.

As for convict women: the sexual doings which marked the disembarkation of the female convicts at Port Jackson on 6 February 1788 have become as legendary as the wild electrical storm which accompanied them. For once, and briefly, Phillip seems to have been reconciled to letting anarchy prevail, as women shrieked and men pursued them into the shadows. Remembering the determined efforts of some convict women to get into the men's quarters during the voyage out, and the near-conjugal relationships others established with sailors, the women may have been less victimised than my phrasing suggests. The truth is that we do not know what happened during that wild night, our usually reliable informants like Tench choosing to remain discreetly silent.

Even with a semblance of propriety restored, and despite Phillip's best efforts, unprotected convict women could fall prey to men of all ranks. Some escaped from the melée by entering into a permanent liaison with a free man or, failing that, a convict of steady temperament or, best of all, a free man of rank of steady temperament. As we have seen, only Chaplain Johnson among the First Fleet officials had been allowed to bring his wife with him, poor lonely soul as she must have been. While Hunter and Phillip himself abstained, most senior officers (like David Collins and John White) entered into long-term relationships with convict women. The first child born into the tiny community at Norfolk Island and proudly baptised 'Norfolk' was the son of its commandant Philip Gidley King and a convict woman, Anne Inett, who bore him a daughter in the following year. Even the uxorious Ralph Clark acquired a convict woman and a daughter during his time on the island, and brought them back to Sydney with him.

Such irregular children were acknowledged in the colony by being baptised under their fathers' names, and, as with Surgeon White, some were taken back to England by their fathers for integration into polite society. I confess I find the early colony's smooth techniques of managing sexual matters among its elite at least as opaque as the Australians'. For example: how did those delinquent officers manage their courtly duties of squiring the growing band of colonial ladies to the picnics on the harbour's islands and inlets described by Elizabeth Macarthur? Presumably such arrangements were simply designated unspeakable and therefore invisible. Social myopia has always been a British virtue.

Not all the officers succumbed, or not publicly. Watkin Tench was either unusually disciplined or unusually discreet in matters sexual. Tench had never been in Tahiti. His dreams were not haunted by coffee-coloured girls 'performing a thousand lewd tricks', as were the dreams of comrades who had visited the enchanted island, and who were accordingly deeply disappointed by Australian girls. At first Tench thought Australian girls unattractive and the old women positively alarming. He also disapproved of the convict solution, as far as we know having no truck with convict women, who were in any case too forward for his taste. What he found pleasing in women was a bashful shyness—which he was to discover, to his own and to our surprise, among some of the young women of the local tribes.

One in particular enchanted him. She was about eighteen; she was, like handsome Barangaroo, a daughter of the Cameragal; her name was Gooreedeeana. One day she had come to his hut 'to complain of hunger'. A married woman, she presumably was under instruction to do whatever was required to acquire provisions. Instead Tench talked gently with her, and then memorialised her as 'excel[ling] in beauty all their females I ever saw'. He acknowledged he was moved by 'the firmness, symmetry and the luxuriancy of her bosom', but even more by her expression, 'distinguished by a softness and sensibility unequalled in the rest of her countrywomen'. (We can glimpse something of what he means by looking at the photographs of four softly smiling young women in Stanner's *White Man Got No Dreaming*.) Smitten, he was anxious to see if her beauty had protected her from violence. Gently examining her head, 'with grief I found it covered by contusions and mangled by scars'. She also pointed to a scar on her leg, sustained when 'a man had lately dragged her by force from her home to gratify his lust'. Tench chivalrously loaded her with all the bread and salt pork he could spare, and apparently sought no more reward than being allowed to measure her. She was, he recorded, exactly five feet one and three-quarter inches tall. (We are told that Baneelon at five feet eight inches 'towered' over his fellows.) Tench would see her only once more, this time in a canoe with other women, 'painted for a ball, with broad stripes of white from head to foot'. Painted, she was his lovely Gooreedeeana no more. But perhaps she visited his waking dreams and made his exile easier to bear.

Tench's friend William Dawes, an introspective, scholarly type, was in his fellow-lieutenant Daniel Southwell's judgment 'a truly religious' young man who was nonetheless 'without any appearance of formal sanctity'. (The Reverend Johnson was an earnest Evangelical.) Dawes, the colony's most adept student of the physical sciences and entrusted with its astronomical observations, had chosen to take up solitary residence in the new Observatory. From his first days in the colony he had been eager to make a formal study of the local tongue and the local religion. He had done his best to teach Boorong something of his religion in the hope she would reciprocate with information regarding hers, but 'her levity and love of play in great measure defeated his efforts'. There was another young girl with whom he established a more rewarding relationship, or so we assume from the tender passages recording their attempts at communication he stored in his language notebook. The exchanges have a pleasantly domestic and sometimes an erotic flavour. The girl Patyegarang says she is very warm: 'I will cool myself in the rain.' She stands naked by the fire, he desires her to put on some clothes, she replies: 'I will get warmer quicker this way.' Sometimes she sounds downright coquettish: in answer to the question, 'Why don't you learn to speak like a white man?' she answers, 'Because you give me everything I want without my having to ask.' She says: 'We will sleep separate.' But she also teaches him a word which means 'to warm one's hand by the fire and then to squeeze gently the fingers of another person'. And, finally: 'Why don't you sleep?' 'Because of the candle.'

We don't know what arrangements Dawes made with Patyegarang's kin, but there can be no doubt that during his time in the colony Dawes' sympathies swung from the British and towards the Australians. When Phillip ordered him out on a punitive expedition against the Australians after an ambush-murder, Dawes refused until this 'truly religious' young man was coaxed into submission by the chaplain. Dawes then formally notified Phillip that he would never obey such an order again. Phillip, who had no patience with recalcitrant junior officers, forced him to quit the colony in

December 1791 with the marines who had opted to go home. Dawes had applied to stay for three more years. Left to himself, I wonder if he would ever have left.

His departure cost us access to the local language as it was spoken at the time of contact. It possibly also cost us a brilliant ethnography, although his tender conscience might not have allowed him to open the local people to easier communication, and so to more disruptive exploitations.

Dawes must have been an attractive fellow, as these brooding, solitary types often are. Tench cheerfully acknowledged his intellectual superiority, loved him wholeheartedly, and did his best to coax him out on exploring trips with him. Young, bored Mrs Elizabeth Macarthur, for a time the only lady in the settlement except for dull Mrs Johnson, frequently found herself walking the distance to his observatory to seek his instruction, first in astronomy, his particular passion, and then, when that proved beyond her capacities, in the less taxing science of botany. She lamented in a letter to a friend that 'he is so much engaged by the stars that to mortal eyes he is not always visible'. We note that the scraps of his tender little vocabulary have mainly to do with the night or times of rain, when officers' wives were unlikely to drop by.

Now for an example of the kind of enigmatic episode which keeps historians modest. Two convicts attempted to hide on the *Gorgon*, the ship which would take Tench and his fellows home at the end of 1791. They were detected before it sailed and brought back to the settlement. Such escape attempts were common. But Collins notes that a convict woman was also thought to have concealed herself on the ship. She was not there. Instead she 'was found disguised in men's apparel in the native's hut on the east point of the cove'—that is, at Baneelon's house. We can understand the 'men's apparel', a sensible disguise where a British woman could not move around without attracting notice. But what was she doing at Baneelon's house? Until I read this meek little sentence I had thought of both the house and the point as effectively Australian territory, unfrequented even by British males except by invitation. So why had she taken refuge there, so dressed? Could she have had a liaison with an Australian man? A conspiratorial friendship with an Australian woman? This time I can't even guess what might have been going on.

How violent were Australian men toward their women? The answer has to be: 'Very.' When Baneelon was boasting of his exploits in 'love and war' soon after his capture he vividly enacted the various histories of his many battle scars, but failed to explain one on the back of his hand. When he was asked about it he laughed, and said, Tench reports, that he had suffered it when he was 'carrying off a lady of another tribe by force'. She bit him, he 'knocked her down, and beat her until she was insensible, and covered in blood'. And then he took his pleasure. We might think Baneelon was choosing to embroider reality, but too many other accounts report violent rape as common-place. Collins came to believe that the usual way to get 'wives' was to steal them: to seize them, beat them, and then drag them home and rape them. This kind of conduct towards the enemy is not unusual in warrior societies, where the seizing and raping of enemy women seems to be an established male sport. But sexual assaults could happen even within the group: the split lip Baneelon wore not long after his return from England was a gift from his friend Colbee when, lacking a woman of his own, Baneelon assaulted Colbee's wife. What is more puzzling to us and more shocking to the British was the violence men directed against women within the immediate family, particularly their wives.

Trying to penetrate the dynamics of the sexual politics of a different society is a risky enterprise for the outsider, especially when the society is in demographic upheaval and political flux. We are also always more sensitive to 'disreputable' conduct between others than the taken-for-granted interactions in our own social world. The Spaniard Malaspina, visiting the Sydney colony in the autumn of 1793, when early licence had been increasingly replaced by law, was nonetheless shocked by British males' ferocity both to each other and to their women—whom he also thought 'great whores', save for the wives of a few respectable officials. It is true that some British men beat, raped, even killed women, especially convict women. Even the meagre sources we have yield a formidable list of reported and prosecuted sexual and physical assaults. But British violence was typically expressed by fists and feet, and tended to happen when the perpetrator, and the victim too, were in private and in drink.

What the newcomers saw as remarkable—what I think would be remarkable anywhere—were the blows Australian men publicly, casually, dealt their women for trivial offences, and their ready resort to weapons. Their women were, literally, browbeaten. Tench, who was not given to jumping to conclusions, reported that 'the women are in all respects treated with savage barbarity…When an Indian is provoked by a woman, he either spears her or knocks her down on the spot. On this occasion he always strikes on the head, using indiscriminately a hatchet, a club or any other weapon which may chance to be in his hand.' The provocation could be so slight as to be invisible to the alien eye, and ill-treatment seemed to have little to do with the victim's temperament. Tench quickly identified Baneelon's Barangaroo as a shrew, and the beatings she received did not much trouble him, but Colbee, 'in other respects a good-tempered merry fellow', treated his sweet-natured Daringa with equal brutality, and showed off her scars with pride. Nor was the brutality tempered by circumstance: Colbee beat Daringa savagely when she was big with child, and Baneelon gave Barangaroo a severe beating on the very morning she gave birth.

We might have expected such displays to be muted inside the newcomers' settlement, and that women known to the colonists would enjoy some immunity, especially in view of the Australians' general courtesy in respecting British sensibilities. That did not happen. Even when Baneelon and his friends had taken up near-permanent residence within the settlement, spending a large part of each week there, men would casually club their wives, and as casually take them to the hospital for White and his assistants to dress their wounds. As we have seen, remonstrance had no effect: when Phillip chided Baneelon for laying Barangaroo's head open because she had in fury broken a fish-gig and a throwing stick, he replied firmly that 'she was bad, and therefore he had beat her'. And that was that. In September 1794, after six years of contact, Collins noted that Baneelon's sister and the wife of Imeerawanyee, after both men had sailed away to England with Phillip, 'wish[ed] to withdraw from the cruelty which they, along with others of their sex, experienced from their countrymen'. They were granted permission to sail to Norfolk Island on the *Daedalus* to live under the protection of the island's lieutenant-governor. After enduring close to a year without the protection of their men, withdrawal from their home society must have seemed their only remedy.

As for female violence: while women sometimes mimicked their menfolk in tribal fights, even throwing the occasional feeble spear, their role was to lend vocal, not physical support. There was a strong social inhibition against a female striking any male, while boys were encouraged to hit little girls and even their own mothers with impunity. Occasionally the sources mention women fighting between themselves. Certainly women of different tribes were thought to use witchcraft against each other: when the girl Boorong returned from her own people, she explained that she was ill because Cameragal women had deliberately urinated on a path she had to cross. Women inflicted punitive beatings on females who offended them, as when young girls unlucky enough to have attracted the attention of husbands were drubbed by jealous wives. Consider again the conduct of the girl first assaulted by Baneelon in front of Phillip, and then by Barangaroo. She made no attempt to protect herself from either attack. Her main concern seemed to be to take her punishment—and then be allowed to rejoin the group.

Of course all was not blood and tears. David Collins records a pretty picnic scene or, as he put it, 'a family party' on a beach, with one of Baneelon's sisters and his younger wife paddling their canoes back to shore, singing in rhythm with their paddles as they came, and presenting Baneelon, who had been looking after his sister's child while she fished, with their catch, which he set about cooking. As he cooked, 'his pretty sister War-re-weer [lay] asleep in the sun' and the successful fisherwomen sat at their ease, one eating oysters, the other suckling the baby she had retrieved from its uncle's care.

It is indeed a charming scene, and it is tempting to sentimentalise it. But Collins also tells us in another passage that women were compelled 'to sit in their canoe, exposed to the fervour of the midday sun, hour after hour, chanting their little song, and inviting the fish beneath them to take their bait; for without a sufficient quantity to make a meal for their tyrants, who were lying asleep at their ease, they would meet but a rude reception at their landing'. Had Baneelon's women returned empty-handed, we have to assume that the scene would have been less pretty.

We know a little about Warreweer. She had either not married 'out' or her husband had chosen to come to live with her kin, where her irascible brother's company might have afforded her unusual security. She was fortunate in her husband 'Collins', a man the British considered both braver and more gentle than most of his compatriots. These two seem to have loved each other with explicit tenderness; British observers were touched by Warreweer's devoted care during her husband's slow recovery from a particularly dangerous spear wound. In August 1798 pretty, loving Warreweer was murdered in what looked like a payback killing. Revenge killings always fell most conveniently on women and children.

How to explain so much violence against women? Feminists would remind us that these women were essential to the family economy, and worked longer hours than the men. The glamour surrounding hunting and its attendant physical skills might contribute to female suppression, but the people living around the harbour were coast-dwelling fisherfolk; while the larger animals were hunted, they were not a major food source. Women, as collectors of vegetables and the most persistent fish-seekers, were the most reliable providers. Couples also fished co-operatively. The husband and his wives (he usually had two, one senior, one junior) could seem happily inter-dependent, spending whole days together in what looked to lonely Britishers like enviable family harmony. Tench could identify couples long before he fathomed other Australian relationships. Baneelon and Barangaroo seemed close to inseparable. They clearly enjoyed each other's company: Collins reports he often saw them together 'feasting and enjoying themselves' on the island the Australians called Me-mel, and the British Goat Island. Collins also tells us that husbands had a small but essential role to play in the woman-dominated business of childbirth. Although they were never present at the event, it was their job to shape the little 'knife' used to cut the umbilical cord.

Furthermore, however thoroughly the metaphor of subduing an enemy suffused warrior accounts of sexual encounters, and however subdued most women (excepting always Barangaroo) appeared in the company of their husbands, the glimpses we have of their behaviour as a group show them to be anything but reticent. In their first encounters with the British their lively, not to say provocative, behaviour when they were at a distance contrasts with their timidity when coaxed to approach one by one. As we have seen, after the 'coming in' some women moved independently through the settlement, and some came to exchange sexual favours with soldiers, sailors and convicts for goods, without any visible intervention from their men. Collins also gives us reason to think that at least some women after contact were ready to treat men's business lightly: when he expressed a desire for some of the teeth he had seen knocked out at the climax of the great four-yearly male puberty ceremony, Baneelon's sister and Colbee's Daringa secretly gave him the three which had been entrusted to them, and which they should have handed over to the Cameragal. Why? We do not know—except that Daringa was eager that one of the teeth, Nanbaree's, should be sent to Surgeon White, who had raised the boy and had quit the colony the previous year. Furthermore the women seemed to fear only physical, not supernatural, retribution.

The Australians tended to exogamy, usually finding their wives

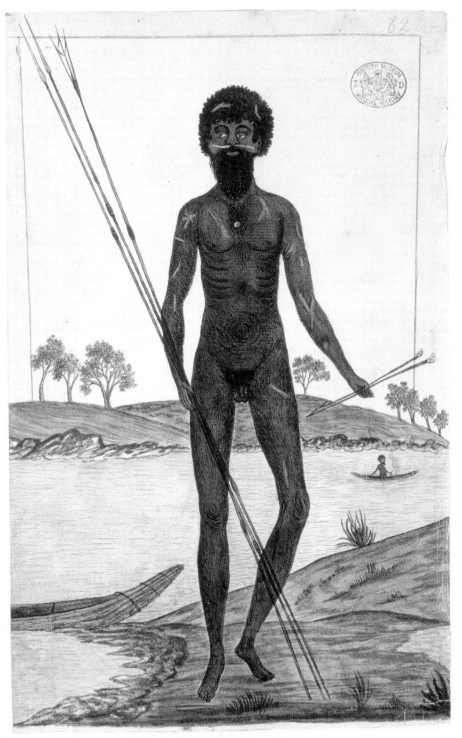

Cameragal warrior. Port Jackson Painter.

'…their confidence and manly behaviour made me give the name of Manly Cove to this place.' Governor Phillip to Lord Sydney, May 15 1788.

'Arthur Phillip, Esq.,
Captain General and
Commander in Chief
in & over the
Territory of New
South Wales.'

Frontispiece to
*The Voyage of
Governor Phillip to
Botany Bay*,
engraving by
William Sherwin
from an original
painting by
Francis Wheatley.

'Native name
Ben-nel-long.
As painted when
angry after
Botany Bay
Colebee was
wounded.'
Port Jackson
Painter.

'Baneelon
Wolarawaree'
Wanghal warrior.

View in Broken Bay New South Wales March 1788. William Bradley

'View in
Broken Bay
New South
Wales
March 1788.'
Lieutenant
William
Bradley.

'These people
mixed with ours
and all hands
danced together.'

'Sydney Cove, Port Jackson 1788.' William Bradley.

From a sketch by John Hunter dated 20 August 1788. The ships were the *Golden Grove* and the *Fishburn*.

'The Governor's House at Sydney, Port Jackson, 1791.' William Bradley.

Taking of Colbee & Benalon 25 Novr. 1789

'Taking of Colbee & Benalon 25 Novr. 1789.' William Bradley.

'By far the most unpleasant service I was ever ordered to execute.'

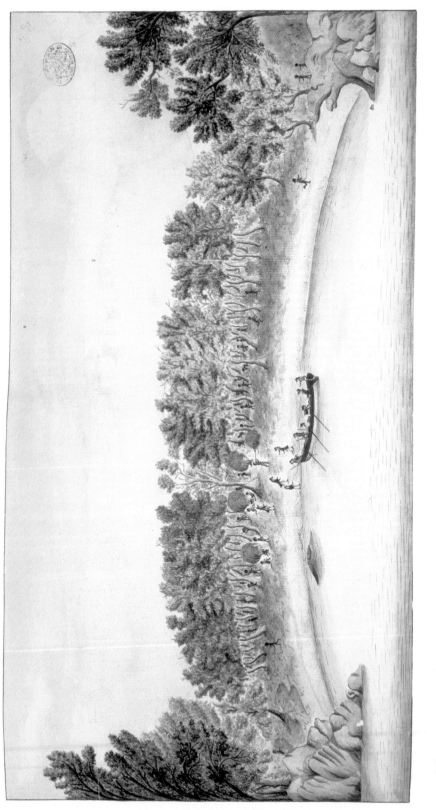

'The Governor making the best of his way to the Boat after being wounded with the spear sticking in his shoulder.' Port Jackson Painter.

The spearing of Governor Phillip, 7 September 1790

'Mr White, Harris and Laing with a party of soldiers visiting Botany Bay Colebee—at that place, when wounded near Botony Bay.'
Port Jackson Painter.

A handwritten note identifies the figure seated on the log as 'Colebee'.

'Portrait of Bungaree, a native of New South Wales, with Fort Macquarie, Sydney Harbour, in the background.' Augustus Earle, c. 1826.

outside their own group. That is rarely healthy for women, so being removed from the protection of their kin. But, on the evidence we have, even kinsfolk did not intervene in husbands' brutality. Wives under sexual assault might scream for their husbands, but Boladeree, husband of the girl clubbed by Baneelon in the display of 'justice' which so shocked Phillip, was a silent onlooker during the attack, despite his evident tenderness for the victim. Note, too, that the victim did not cry out. She only tried to shield her head. Given such silences, I think we have to assume a compelling, shared under-standing of a network of rights, liberties and infringements simply invisible to us.

Despite some British talk about their gentle, even passive, natures, Australians around the harbour sustained a tough warrior culture. British eye-witness accounts are thick with descriptions of pre-planned battles between antagonistic groups, with hard blows given and received and much blood shed. Through time, and as his own fascination grew, Collins gives us deepening access to the protocols of the warrior culture. Baneelon's British-made leather-and-tin shield had pleased him deeply, but on his next meeting with Phillip he claimed to have lost it. Collins tells us that 'in fact it had been taken from him by the people of the North Shore district', presumably the Cameragal, who seem to have had jurisdiction in these matters, and who destroyed it, 'it being deemed unfair to cover himself with such a guard'. Such were the rules governing what could look to the British like homicidal free-for-alls.

After years of absorbed watching, Collins concluded that combat was the single most important activity in Australian men's lives:

> The procuring of food really seems to be but a secondary business with…men. The management of the spear and shield, dexterity in

throwing the various clubs they have in use among them, agility in either attacking or defending, and a display of the constancy with which they endure pain, appearing to rank first among their concerns in life.

We might be among the Plains Indians. As if he sensed a connection, Collins went directly on to describe the pitiable condition of women, who 'are accustomed to bear on their heads the traces of the superiority of the males, with which they dignify them almost as soon as they find strength in the arm to imprint the mark'. He described some women with 'more scars upon their shorn heads, cut in every direction, than could well be distinguished and counted'.

He also acknowledged, with some puzzlement, that women had their particular roles in men's battles, proceeding to a detailed account of the opening ceremony of a well-advertised combat between the Sydney clans and clans from the southern side of Botany Bay. Before an invited European audience, the two sides seated themselves opposite each other at the appointed place, and each warrior drank a palmful of water. After this symbolic refreshment combat was initiated by an old woman from the Botany Bay side who, 'uttering much abusive language at the time' ran up to Colbee (whose priority marks him as a major warrior) and struck him savagely on the head—which he had obligingly bowed for her. She then worked her way down the Sydney line, bashing each bent head, with no resistance until she came to the lad Yeranibie, who struggled with her. The old woman seemed to be getting the best of him; she'd wrenched his spear away from him when their individual struggle was engulfed in the general melée.

Had the mature warriors been demonstrating their iron self-discipline by publicly enduring a hard blow, on the head, from a woman—three insults in a row—without retaliation? Had young

Yeranibie cracked under intolerable provocation? Or had some other cue been given which Collins simply failed to see? Collins sensibly refrained from comment, being content to describe, but his description implies that the dramatisation of sexual difference penetrated deep into the theatre of warrior power.

Within the groups, reputations for toughness, for swift-rising aggression, for determination in vengeance, brought respect. Baneelon's radiant rages indicate that; so, we will see, does Colbee's more deadly anger. It is calmer, gentler men like 'Collins' who appear unusual, and who attract British comment.

This suggests we may be looking at a familiar, depressing phenomenon. In societies where physical competition between males was habitual, flamboyant, and frequently tested in one-to-one combat and formalised battle, a man could most conveniently show how tough he was by publicly beating his wife.

My conclusion: contest cultures are uncomfortable places for both sexes.

BOAT TRIP TO ROSE HILL

Phillip was trying to run a fragile convict colony by a distinctive mix of material equity and draconian discipline. He was also expending a great amount of time and scarce food in keeping his new friends happy. A week after the affair of the wounded girl, he feared another eruption. He had been told that the Cameragal had killed one of Baneelon's kinsmen and Phillip assumed, with some trepidation, that Baneelon would seek revenge. Mysteriously, he did not. Instead he was seen out with a Cameragal party, peaceably collecting wild fruits. Equally mysteriously, a man from Botany Bay he had often declared to be his enemy was sleeping at his house, and seemed to have been there for a fortnight. Phillip thought something was brewing.

Then one night long after dinner Baneelon and Barangaroo appeared at the governor's house asking to be allowed to sleep there, and offering the lame excuse that they could not sleep in their own house because there were too many people there. Baneelon, in a highly excited state, also spoke of the kinsman killed by the Cameragal, and urged Phillip to take his soldiers and kill every one of them. When he and Barangaroo finally retired to sleep in a back room, he begged Phillip to lock them in, and to keep the key in his pocket.

Nothing more happened during the night, but I doubt Phillip slept well, wondering what tribal broils he was importing into the heart of a colony where survival depended on the maintenance of strict social order.

By the last months of 1790 Phillip was in full educational mode. He was far from well. A man of fifty, he had taken a bad fall on an early expedition out from the settlement which seems to have brought on a chronic illness, probably of the kidneys, because afterwards he was prone to crippling pains in the side, lower back and loins. He had also been speared, grievously, and his daily harassments were multiple. Nonetheless, ailing as he was, harassed as he was, he remained intent on displaying the beauty of the principles of natural justice enshrined in British law, and the security they would surely bring all who embraced them. He also believed that, given time, the natives would come to cherish what he thought of as British ways: to shun impulsive violence, to act honourably and justly; to value the comfort, elegance and modesty embodied in clothing; and above all to relinquish their harsh and socially untidy hand-to-mouth existence in the bush.

Over those weeks of late spring evidence was accumulating that his hopes were utopian. He had watched while the girl Boorong chose to exchange her easy life in the settlement for, as it seemed to him, sexual assaults, beatings and hunger. Men and women alike could be given clothing one day and return naked the next. And now Baneelon stripped before he went into the bush.

Even more disturbingly for Phillip, a man who prized his word, he was coming to recognise Baneelon was an easy liar, lying sometimes for advantage, sometimes to please, and sometimes, it seemed, for no reason at all, or none that Phillip could fathom. Domestic proximity had also taught him that these cheerful, ebullient, likeable people were alarmingly violent in words and deeds, and yet eerily resilient, with the violence seeming to leave no residue of resentment.

But despite disappointments he retained his faith in his new friends' humanity, and continued to believe that, given enough time and care, they could be soothed and smoothed into civility. That determined indulgence would sorely tax his patience.

For example: in late November, with a small house built for his accommodation at Rose Hill completed, Phillip decided to stay there overnight. Baneelon, Colbee and two other Australian men made clear they very much wanted to go with him. Phillip was probably using one of his small six-oared cutters to make the trip to Rose Hill, so there was little space for passengers, but he agreed—only to find himself entangled in yet another marital squabble. With the boat and its all-male passengers already embarked, Baneelon had run to get his cloak from his house, but was 'delayed by his wife', as Phillip demurely puts it. It was only as the boat was pulling out of the cove that he came scrambling back over the rocks of the point under a barrage of abuse from the pursuing Barangaroo. As he swung into the boat, shouting he would be gone for only one night, she ran to her new canoe, drove the paddles through the bottom, flung them into the water, and headed back at a run to Baneelon's house, 'presumably to do more damage', as the startled Phillip put it.

Barangaroo's fury was not to be trifled with. Phillip tactfully offered to put Baneelon back on shore, Baneelon gratefully accepted, and as he ran to rescue the rest of his possessions the trip at last got under way. Phillip, recording that the three other Australians in the boat had kept their mouths firmly shut throughout the entire performance, commented that 'none of these people have ever been seen to interfere with what did not immediately concern them'.

The three visitors dined lavishly at Rose Hill, but were so insistent that they had to go home that Phillip had his boatmen row them to Sydney the next morning. When the boat came back he was astonished to see that Barangaroo and Baneelon had somehow got themselves aboard. Both were in the highest of spirits, and Barangaroo's head was miraculously intact. Again they dined long and festively. Then Barangaroo said she wanted to go home, Baneelon said she'd cry if he didn't take her, and the governor felt obliged to order the boat down again that evening, to return for him the next day. Six journeys back and forth instead of two, purely to indulge his new friends. There is no record of how the boatmen felt about all those extra hours of hard rowing.

Then on 10 December 1790 there came a seriously sinister event. Phillip's convict gamekeeper John McEntire was badly wounded in a surprise attack in the bush.

In pursuit of his heroic policy of conciliation Phillip had demonstrated himself time and again to be a singularly level-headed man, but when McEntire was half-carried, half-dragged by his two companions into the settlement, he seemed level-headed no longer.

McEntire had been out hunting twenty kilometres from the settlement with three other men. They had been sleeping through the heat of the afternoon in a bough hut (an interesting accommodation to local conditions) when they were woken by a noise, and when they investigated four Australian men leapt up and ran away. McEntire, recognising one of them, told his companions to wait, laid his own gun aside, called out to the men, and began walking after them. Then one of the Australians turned, jumped onto a log, coolly scanned the (now unarmed) whites, and hurled his spear at the gamekeeper, with terrible effect. His three friends barely managed to drag him, bleeding heavily with the spear buried in his chest, back to the settlement.

It was, transparently, an ambush. If the sleek wooden spear used for spearing the governor had done little internal damage, this spear was murderous. It penetrated deeply into McEntire's body before the point jammed into a rib, but it would never emerge cleanly. Heavily barbed, with sharp fragments of red stone attached to the barbs by resin, it was designed to shatter inside the body. This spearhead could not be withdrawn without massive injury, infection and death. Colbee, having examined the wound, told the surgeons not to try to remove it. He also declared that the gamekeeper would surely die; which, after lingering for miserable weeks and after a phantom recovery, he did.

Phillip was persuaded that this killing was political, not personal, largely because McEntire, a Catholic, swore on what was to be his deathbed that he had never wronged an Australian. Recalling Baneelon's loathing of the man, I think he had done something, and something Australians regarded as deeply vile. As gamekeeper, McEntire was free to move through the bush and could offer insult as he chose. He was also constantly poaching game, using a gun, that most unsporting weapon, to compensate for his lack of stalking skills, and so driving game away from more skilled hunters.

Australians around the settlement immediately identified the tribe by the spear, and named the culprit: a man called Pemulwuy, from the Botany Bay tribe.

Phillip was puzzled by the identification. He knew the Botany Bay people had been dangerous ever since the days of La Pérouse, but Baneelon had assured him that during his recent visit to Botany Bay he had effected a reconciliation: that 'they had danced, and that one of the tribe had sung a song, the subject of which was his house, the governor, and the white men of Sydney'. He also told Phillip that both the Botany Bay tribe and the Cameragal had agreed to throw no more spears at the white men. Phillip also knew there had been men and women from Botany Bay among the visitors to the governor's yard on the day of Baneelon's attack on the girl. Had Baneelon simply overestimated or exaggerated his influence? Or was Pemulwuy leading a break-away movement committed to a policy of confrontation? Phillip did not know. Even more disquietingly, while Colbee and Baneelon had both earnestly promised to deliver up the assassin, neither showed the least inclination to do so. Within a day of the ambush Colbee was off amusing himself at South Head, while Baneelon vanished for more than a week on ritual business among the Cameragal.

This time Phillip had the name of the individual perpetrator, but this time he abandoned his determination to punish only individuals. This time the whole tribe would pay. The policy change was due in part to an authentic anthropological insight. It was tribal strength these warriors cared about, and diminution in tribal strength would shake them as nothing else would: 'Nothing but a severe example, and the fear of having all the tribes who resided near the settlement destroyed, would have the desired effect.' Phillip also knew that the British would not discriminate between either individuals or tribes if any more whites were attacked. And he was weary of the increasing number of unprovoked assaults on inoffensive people moving through the bush. He had hoped the 'coming in' had put an end to the violence. Now, after months of tolerance, he thought it 'absolutely necessary' to put a stop to it.

He therefore decided to send out a punitive expedition against the Botany Bay tribe, identified as the 'principal aggressors' against the whites largely because Baneelon had told him so. Two men were to be captured and brought back for public execution. The expedition was also to bring back the heads of ten men—any ten men—in the sacks provided, presumably for public display. All spears seized were to be broken, and left on the ground. Phillip was adamant that women, children and other possessions were not to be tampered with. He seems not to have wondered how the women and children would survive, with their hunters and protectors dead.

The man he chose to lead the expedition was Captain Watkin Tench.

Tench was somehow able to persuade Phillip to reduce the punitive levy to six heads or six captives taken, with two to be hanged on delivery, and set off at the front of what he calls, with fine deadpan humour, a 'terrific procession' of more than fifty men at 4 a.m. on the morning of 14 December. The men were in their heavy woollen uniforms (remember Sydney's climate in December), and draped with provisions and muskets and ropes for the prisoners, along with bags for the heads and hatchets for the head-taking. Tench continues, still gloriously solemn: 'After having walked in various directions until four o'clock in the afternoon without seeing a native, we halted for the night.' The next morning they got lost, got found again by stumbling onto the sea-shore, and sighted five 'Indians' 'whom we attempted to surround'—and who promptly ran away. Tench reports that 'we' (all fifty of them?) 'pursued, but a contest between heavily-armed Europeans, fettered by ligatures, and naked unencumbered Indians, was too unequal to last long'. True, but it is a pleasure to contemplate. The weary men then tried to creep up on 'a little village' of five huts, only to see its occupants leaving at speed by canoe.

Tench had been instructed to refrain from all conversation with Australians, even friendly ones: this was to be a terrific expedition indeed, with its punitive purpose grimly evident. He was accordingly embarrassed when the soldiery got back to their baggage to spot a solitary man tranquilly spear-fishing in shallow water about 300 metres from the beach. Tench decided to ignore him—after all, the man was too far away to kill or capture—but the Australian hallooed cheerfully and came loping up to the troop. It was their old friend Colbee, who 'joined us at once with his wonted familiarity and unconcern'. When they asked where Pemulwuy was, Colbee waved vaguely towards the south, and said he was long gone.

Colbee then ate, drank and snoozed along with his friends until they set off in the early afternoon for the trek back to the settlement, spending another tormented night beside a sandfly- and mosquito-ridden swamp on the way, while he, presumably, went back to his fishing.

Or perhaps not. Tench informs us that this was Colbee's second meal in twenty-four hours at British expense. Back in the settlement the day before he had announced his intention of pursuing the punitive expedition, to see what fell out. Failing to dissuade him, anxious that he not be embroiled, but unwilling to use force to restrain him now that trust was the order of the day, Phillip decided to nobble him: despite the shortage of rations he would feed him so gargantuan a meal he would be put safely to post-prandial sleep. Colbee ate hugely (a whole large snapper), called for more ('at least five pounds of bread and beef'), leapt up, rubbed his stomach, and strode away to catch up with the fun. Again we see black laughter rising like smoke from the page.

The hot, weary and well-bitten expedition trudged back to Sydney, only to be ordered out again a week later with the unfortunate Tench again in command. This time a slightly smaller force began the march in moonlight, to avoid the worst heat of the day, with the aim of surprising the same village they had failed to surprise the week before. Leaving their heavy knapsacks behind and with their cartouche boxes tied on the tops of their heads to keep them dry, they managed to cross the fords of the northern arm of Botany Bay. Then they came upon a creek. It was wide, but with the tide out it looked reasonably dry—until they were well embarked on the crossing, when the stuff under their feet turned to quicksand, or, more correctly, to slow mud. It was only after terrifying struggles and the real threat of drowning that a soldier cried out for those not yet stuck to cut boughs from trees and throw them to the men (now including Tench) who were sinking. They pulled the last of the men free with the ropes brought to bind their intended captives. Immersion in the mud had rendered half of their weapons unserviceable.

Undefeated, they divided into three parties, and half an hour before dawn rushed the target 'village'—to find it uninhabited. It looked to have been abandoned for a long time. And then, with some of the men exhausted and barely able to keep up, they had to make a dash back to their knapsacks and provisions to beat the incoming tide. They wandered about through another dawn before returning, muddy and grumpy, to Sydney. This time they had not sighted a single Australian.

The punitive expedition displayed a large element of farce. But a dangerous step had been taken. Phillip had been told by witnesses he knew to be less than reliable that a Botany Bay warrior called Pemulwuy had speared the unsavoury McEntire. He had proceeded to convert an unproven individual charge into a collective capital offence—for Australians. In time settlers would seize on his example. From now on, Australians suspected of anti-social acts would be outside the protection of British law. Are we then looking (as is often claimed) at the birth of a racist policy?

I doubt it. If we look closely we notice several odd things about that famous expedition. First, the formally authorised violence was hedged about by a bristle of restrictions. The orders made clear that soldiers alone were permitted to fire on Australians, and then only if directly ordered to do so or in self-defence. Phillip had no intention of tolerating, much less encouraging, white vigilantism. The soldiers were also instructed that at all times the specific reason for the punitive action had to be made clear, which, given the state of verbal communication at this stage of contact, was a tall order. He also reminded everyone within earshot that all Australian property, so often pilfered by convicts and soldiers for sale back in Britain, was sacrosanct, and enjoyed the full protection of British law.

The expedition was also out of character. Phillip had borne his own spearing three months before with admirable anthropological cool. While he had not the least doubt that he and his compatriots were the legitimate new lords of the soil, he was ready to gamble a great deal of time, patience and personal suffering to bring about friendship with the local tribes. He had been anxious to persuade the people to come into the settlement, to live under British law, and to absorb the benefits of British civilisation: indeed he twice resorted to kidnapping to secure a go-between to bring about a peaceful outcome, and against the odds the extreme gamble worked: he had bagged the wily Baneelon. He had also hoped a rapprochement would put an end to the Australians' apparently casual spearing of convicts. Seventeen Britishers, nearly all of them unarmed, had been speared since first contact, some of them fatally, yet to this point Phillip had steadfastly refused to retaliate, insisting that the attacks must have been provoked by convict misconduct.

With the McEntire spearing he knew his strategy had failed. A friendly accommodation had been reached with the local Australians only a handful of weeks before, yet that friendship had not put an end to the violence. And this attack was notably more sinister than those before it, being a deliberate and murderous assault on a man skilled in the bush, and who normally carried a gun. (The British took comfort in believing that Australians were terrified of guns.) McEntire had also been acting under Phillip's orders when he was attacked: he was 'his' man. Furthermore, in Phillip's thinking the gamekeeper had a perfect right to be where he was, hunting game in the bush. Phillip's Australian friends had named the spearman, made soothing noises about bringing him in—and shown not the least inclination to do so. Justice had to be done; and both Australians and British had to be brought to respect the rule of law. So what to do?

What Phillip did was order out the expedition—and select Watkin Tench to lead it. Tench was famously sympathetic to the local people. Phillip also condescended to ask Tench's advice regarding the reprisals. As we would expect, Tench softened the terms, urging that the British should content themselves with capturing six men, some of whom would suffer exemplary capital punishment in public, while others could be released when their lesson in British justice was well-learnt. Phillip refined Tench's suggestions further: if the agreed tally of six men could not be captured, six were to be shot, while if six were captured he would hang two and send the rest to Norfolk Island. The sum was straightforward. If Tench used muskets six men might die; if he refrained from using muskets—if the focus was on capture, not killing—only two. Phillip knew his man. Tench would be loath to shoot.

In the event, the 'terrific procession' of fifty-two men which came stumbling back to the colony after three days' hard slogging through December heat brought not a single captive with them. They had sighted some, they had chatted with Colbee, and that was the total of their success. What did Phillip do next? He sent out a smaller but still formidable expedition of thirty-nine men on the same mission. This time they were ordered to march at night, as Tench says with a carefully straight face, 'both for the sake of secrecy and to avoid the heat of the day'; this time they saw not a single Australian. As we have seen, the main excitement was when several men, including Tench, came perilously close to drowning as they floundered in an unexpected patch of quicksand. When I first read that passage I kept expecting Colbee and a few grinning companions to step from behind the trees to rescue them. The British might have seen no Australians, but the Australians had surely seen them.

Throughout, Tench's attitude to these excursions was one of irony. He knew that a mob of British soldiers crashing through the bush had minimal chance of sighting, much less seizing, Australian men on their home ground. Phillip must have known that too. He also knew he would have to endure some local ridicule, especially after the second weary, muddy expedition came straggling in. So what was he up to?

I suggest Phillip's primary concern was to stage a histrionic performance of the terror of British law, in accordance with the fine late-eighteenth-century theatrical tradition of formal floggings, elaborate death rites and breathless last-minute reprieves and repentances. I think the performance was designed to impress both the increasingly restive convicts and soldiers within the settlement, and the Australians inside and around it. Certainly Collins, writing soon after the events and never one to mince his words, declared there had been no expectation of taking any prisoners or shedding any blood on Tench's two expeditions: that they were, simply, theatrical statements about the new order—or, as we might say, performative acts, the governor being 'well-convinced that nothing but a severe example, and the fear of having all the tribes who resided near the settlement destroyed...[would] put a stop to the natives throwing spears'.

In sum: my view is that Phillip sent out the troops and then sent them out again to remind the British that violence towards Australians was the monopoly of the soldiery and the prerogative of the state, while the tribes were given the opportunity to reflect on Phillip's capacity for military action—if he were tried too far. He threatened them with collective punishment, in defiance of British protocols, not because he had a taste for racist terror but because he had a good anthropological eye. What the tribes cared about was their fighting strength, individual injuries being simply shrugged off. Phillip knew that if he could not teach the tribesmen to refrain from all violence against whites, he would not be able to protect them, and the wolves would be loosed upon them. Racist terror would come soon enough. But not in Phillip's time.

Arthur Phillip, being committed to strenuous reasonableness, was an intrepid thinker, especially in matters of discipline. Preparing for his governorship of a convict colony—pondering how hard men could be terrified into docility—he had hit on the interesting notion of marooning condemned murderers and sodomites (both offences carried mandatory capital sentences) on the coast of New Zealand, where the resident cannibals could be relied on to finish them off at their leisure: an economical if doubtfully Christian way to maximise dread. He also considered, briefly, more tender uses for Polynesians, proposing that Polynesian women 'may be brought from the Friendly and other islands to a proper place [in the settlement] prepared to receive them, and where they will be supported for a time, and lots of land assigned to such as marry with the soldiers of the garrison'—a brisk route to an instant yeomanry. (Convicts, excluded from this government-funded largesse, would have to content themselves with convict women.) A daring thinker indeed, but also a pragmatist: recognising potential difficulties, he dropped the plans.

John Dann, the distinguished editor of Joseph Nagle's journal, tells us that Phillip 'came from a very humble background, was educated at the charity school at Greenwich hospital, and was one of the relatively rare individuals to achieve the rank of captain in spite of having begun his life at sea at the very bottom, as cabin boy and seaman, before becoming a midshipman'. That rough apprenticeship served Phillip well when it came to handling seamen. He began his rule on the *Sirius* by dividing the watches into three instead of the usual two as being 'much more comfortable for the seaman', as sailor Nagle reports approvingly. Nagle also reveals Phillip's quick resolution of a shipboard incident which could have generated long-term disaffection. About halfway to Tenerife on the voyage out, Third Lieutenant Maxwell, already on his way to insanity, called the men of both watches onto the deck, and had the boatswain's mate 'thrash them all around, one by one, and told them he would soon have them south of the line' (that is, beyond civilisation and at his mercy) 'and he would then work their hides up'. Captain Hunter, alerted by the racket, came up on deck, gave Maxwell 'a severe setting down', and went below to report to Phillip. Who 'ordred every officer on board the ship to appear in the cabin, even to a boatswain's mate, and told them all that if he new any officer to strike a man on board, he would brake him amediately', Nagle reports smugly. Then Nagle—writing from memory late in life, having lost his Australian diary in the course of his colourful career—provides Phillip with a marvellously vehement speech to his officers, further enlivened by Nagle's adventurous spelling, which reads like a seaman's manifesto:

> He said, 'Those men are all we have to depend on, and if we abuse those men that we have to trust to, the convicts will rise and massecree us all. Those men are our support. We have a long and severe station to go through in settleing this collona, at least we

cannot expect to return in less than five years. This ship and her crew is to protect and support the country, and if they are ill-treated by their own officers, what support can you expect of them? They will be all dead, before the voige is half out, and who is to bring us back again?'

The expression and spelling might be Nagle's, but the sentiments were Phillip's, as attested by his later interventions in several shipboard brushes. On land, as governor of a convict colony, he was to be altogether harsher.

First, with soldiers, whom we might have thought equally important to the 'collona' as guardians against anarchy. In March 1789 (while Arabanoo was still a captive) six marines were discovered to have been looting the provision shed by the elegant expedient of having three keys forged to three essential doors, and then plundering at will whenever one of their number happened to be on guard duty. All six were hanged before their weeping comrades. In his account of the hanging Tench gulps, dubs them, implausibly, 'the flower of our battalion', and leaves it at that. David Collins characteristically points to a larger moral: 'From the peculiarity of our situation, there was a sort of sacredness about our store, and its preservation pure and undefiled was deemed as necessary as the chastity of Caesar's wife.'

Jonathan Easty, a private marine who somehow continued to keep a neat, careful journal throughout all his time in the settlement, took a different view of this public act of justice: 'thare was hardley a marine Present but what Shed tears offacers and men...' Even Collins acknowledged that while some of these men were rogues, 'some of these unhappy men were held in high estimation by their officers'. Six useful lives forfeit to Phillip's reading of priorities within a highly precarious colony when the sailors were elsewhere, the *Sirius* off securing supplementary rations, and the *Supply* investigating a reef.

These men hanged for robbing the provision shed. We can see the hard reason for that. But there was also a seventh man, the confessed ringleader. He escaped punishment because he turned king's evidence, and we wonder how he could continue to live among his fellows. This is not a society we will easily understand.

Above all, there is the issue of flogging, huge to us, apparently commonplace to those who practised it. Some of the six marines had previously been punished for drunkenness and brawling, probably inspired by that stolen rum. Collins mentions in passing that the seventh man, Joseph Hunt, he who turned king's evidence, had received 700 lashes in two allotments, separated by three weeks for healing, for being absent from his post. Not many days before the public hangings, a party of sixteen convicts set off, armed with staves, to take vengeance for the killing of a fellow convict by the people of Botany Bay. They were worsted, leaving several wounded and a man and a boy dead. Phillip, intolerant of all unofficial vendettas, 'directed that those who were not wounded should receive each one hundred and fifty lashes and wear a fetter for a twelvemonth'. The same punishment was to be inflicted upon those in the hospital as soon as their wounds healed. 'In pursuance of [this] order,' Collins tells us, 'seven of them were tied up in front of the provision store, and punished (for example's sake) in the presence of all the convicts.' These were the floggings which horrified Arabanoo.

'For example's sake.' Phillip believed in examples. Discreet by temperament and training, he exercised his remarkable authority with minimal consultation, in part to avoid disruptive jealousies, more because he recognised the ultimate responsibility to be his. Much of the law's ferocity in the convict colony was a distillation and intensification of British practices in the British homeland. The work of E. P. Thompson and his associates on late-eighteenth-century Britain has become famous for its analysis of the class motivations behind the savagery of the law's penalties, and also its dramatic last-minute pardons, the arbitrariness of mercy serving to dramatise the awful terror of the law. We would expect colonial law to mimic that harshness. But Sydney law had its peculiarities. Phillip was, profoundly, a naval man. We need to investigate the influence navy protocols and practice had over him.

Historians have taken different views of British shipboard discipline. For example, Marcus Rediker characterises the imposition of order on merchant ships as 'a system of authority best described as violent, personal and arbitrary', and provides hair-raising examples to prove it, while N. A. M. Rodgers reconstructs a more human and consensual bundle of formal and informal law from evidence of punishments on board ships of the Royal Navy in his *The Wooden World: An Anatomy of the Georgian Navy*. He emphasises the negotiability of the seaman's lot—for example, a sailor could always make a run for it when his ship made port, and find another master ready to take him on. That liberty was not available to the men who manned the ships to Sydney. They had some protection: naval officers, unlike merchant shipmasters, were vulnerable to legal challenge if they exceeded their proper authority, with the upper limit for immediate punishment being officially set at a dozen lashes. More serious crimes required the time-consuming business of a court-martial—but also carried the risk of more formidable punishment at the end of it. Rodgers concludes that both men and officers accepted *de facto* escalations of informal floggings as the best solution in a situation in which other forms of punishment—prolonged imprisonment, deprivation of rations—were simply not viable.

Drunkenness, a common offence, was treated indulgently. 'What will we do with the drunken sailor?' had it about right with its 'Put him in a longboat 'til he's sober'. But theft from one's mates was a major crime in the enclosed territory of a ship, with no secure hiding places for treasured possessions. Charges of theft would usually go to court-martial, and risked sentences of up to five hundred lashes. On occasion the culprit's shipmates' anger was utilised directly in the ceremony of 'running (in fact, and more cruelly, slow-marching) the gauntlet' between the men, who struck the offender at will. Should he fall, would he be allowed to get back on his feet? His shipmates would decide.

Knowing this, we can make more sense of the stunningly tough sentences Phillip handed down for the theft of food and personal property at Sydney Cove. With years of naval discipline behind him and the little colony his present command, Phillip knew that for a man to take more than his rightful ration was both to imperil his comrades and to threaten an order at once artificial, fragile and essential.

Which leaves the largest issue: the emotional and political sediment left by those floggings. We hear from Rediker about the pride some men took in their scarred backs, and in their silence under the lash. Greg Dening, who has counted the lashes officially recorded on all fifteen British naval vessels sailing in the central Pacific between the years 1767 and 1795, tells us that 21 per cent of sailors received a flogging. How were they regarded? As heroes? Villains? Fools? How did they regard themselves? Jonathan Easty was stiff-lipped about his occasional ten or fifteen lashes. Was that the silence of pride, or shame, or anger? Did convicts respond differently from seamen? We know that some convicts stood silent, or their cries went unrecorded, while others screamed; that some remained unreconciled to every aspect of their servitude, and wore their ravined backs as badges of defiance. These were nonetheless extreme principles to be so vigorously asserted within a tiny, mutually dependent society, where daily intimacy was inescapable. What were the psychological consequences, for officers, for marines, for convicts, of such visible, dreadful harshness?

As the hunger worsened and thefts multiplied, Phillip did not flinch. A convict found guilty of pilfering potatoes from a garden was sentenced to 300 lashes. The shredded wreck was then to be chained for six months—six months!—to two other felons serving out their sentences, and for the duration of his sentence to have his allowance of flour stopped. He would have to survive, if he survived at all, on two pounds of salt pork and two pounds of rice a week. Watkin Tench was a member of the court which arrived at this decision.

It is worth imagining our way through this particular horror, the fruit of such principled thought, and the physical anguish and slow, shackled death by starvation it proposed. (In actuality the man's flour ration was restored after a few days, but the dramatic point had been made.) We also remember that in Dening's count of the 'cliometrics of violence' on those sailing ships in the central Pacific, the man who received the most stripes, a German armourer on Vancouver's *Discovery*, 'received a total of 252 lashes on nine different occasions'.

Phillip had his reasons for the Boschian escalation of punishments over those desperate months. He knew that the crimes, overwhelmingly thefts of food and essential clothing, were the fruits of necessity, which was the inevitable result of the failure of the state to provide for its dependants. Later he was to say as much: in a letter to Lord Dundas in October 1792, two months before he would quit the colony forever, he acknowledged that he could 'recollect very few crimes during the last three years but what have been committed to procure the necessaries of life'. But he also believed that to respond sympathetically to that awareness would unloose anarchy, with every man at another's throat and social bonds dissolved.

So he did his duty, flogging and starving with exemplary ferocity. How did the Australians respond to that?

We remember that when a man offended against Arabanoo Phillip took the opportunity to demonstrate the supra-racial majesty of British law by having him flogged before him, and that Arabanoo was horrified. Later, after the 'coming in', when a convict stole fishing gear from Colbee's wife Daringa, Phillip rounded up his Australian friends and had the offender flogged before their eyes. This time the response was more active: Daringa wept, and Barangaroo, always one for direct action, leapt up, seized a stick, and made to wallop the flogger.

There is an enduring fascination about such scenes of calculation miscalculated. Where Phillip saw right order made visible, with God and King behind whipping post and gibbet, the Australians saw disgusting, wanton cruelty. We know the intentions of one side; we see the responses; there can be no doubt as to their emotional import—but the 'why' eludes us. What precisely was it that the Australians found so intolerable about flogging? They could watch a man stand with no more than his shield to receive the spears of punishment; to bleed; to fall. They could not endure to see a man bound and helpless, while other men set about him with a whip. Because he was deprived of the choice to endure the pain, or to try to evade it? Was it the punishments' remorselessness, giving the designated victim no room for amends or negotiation, no hope of the interventions of kin? It seems that the impersonality which Phillip saw as the glory of the law was to Australians profoundly anti-social, and therefore inhuman.

There was also the nature of the wounds inflicted. Flogging meant the pulping and shredding of flesh and the laying bare of bone, producing a meaningless mat of scarring which marked a man as shamed. A spear wound healed clean, and its scar carried a permanent message of transgression purged by challenge and pain courageously borne.

We cannot read the exact meanings behind the Australians' revulsion, but I am reminded of certain passages of a recent television documentary about the return of one-time inmates to the Benedictine orphanage at New Norcia in Western Australia. (Most of the children were not orphans, of course, but the issue of black–white unions.) The returnees were to my mind remarkably generous to their erstwhile guardians, forgiving them their childhood hunger and the misery of separation from siblings. Then one previously calm man began to weep on camera—to weep with a kind of horrified bewilderment—as he had wept as a child years before when a friend of his guilty of some trivial infringement had his hands tied to the head of the bed, and was flogged as he lay. After all the deprivations and cruelties of his childhood, it was this the adult man could not forget. 'He wouldn't cry,' he said: 'He wouldn't cry.' And cried himself.

It seems that what is judged reprehensible violence is a cultural matter. We are disconcerted that men like Watkin Tench or John White—men we judge to be kind, men we have come to like, men who in some sense we think of as forebears—could watch those hangings and floggings unmoved. Australians were horrified, too.

All we can be sure of is that after such sanctioned displays, whether of flogging or wife-bashing, both sides were left goggling at each other across a cultural chasm. Every society is adept at looking past its own forms of violence, and reserving its outrage for the violence of others.

20 JANUARY–FEBRUARY 1791
POTATO THIEVES

I have taken time investigating the likely thinking behind Phillip's two punitive expeditions because a man's reputation depends on it, and reputation is all the dead possess. However, while I have little doubt that his actions were calculated to achieve the outcomes I have suggested, they may have had a psychological dimension as well.

By 'coming in' the Australians had lost both mystery and status. They could no longer be considered even potentially useful to the colony's well-being: instead they were a present burden on it. Over the last few weeks Phillip had suffered them as engaging but unruly guests who had disappointed his early hopes. They were also taking up altogether too much of his time, and intruding in the well-guarded quiet of his house. And, with increased familiarity, their behaviour only seemed more baffling.

We have all felt the exhaustion which can suddenly invade when we are navigating the uncertainties of living among foreigners. Phillip had a talent for careful watching, reflection and (even more unusual) a degree of self-scrutiny, as when he realised that his own inept persistence had contributed to his near-fatal spearing. But now he was a sick man, often in pain. The cruel December heat was made crueller by the fires the Australians had set to burn all around. The British were running out of food: there was no sign of the longed-for ships; as supplies ran out his people were being forced into native ways, making fishing lines from the stringy bark of trees, and the soldiers sometimes drilled barefoot. The colony for which he was uniquely responsible seemed to have been abandoned by those people at home duty-bound to sustain it. The emptiness of the harbour bore heavily on everyone, but it must have borne heaviest on Phillip.

He sustained a professional calm in public, as he had been trained to do, but we cannot infer from this man's public performance the dynamics of his inner life. Given his situation, given his isolation, it is possible he was suddenly disgusted with the whole tense business of studying alien actions, and the struggle to interpret alien intentions. The calculation of the gamekeeper's ambush may have liberated him into violence: a violence which would obliterate those exhausting ambiguities and the endless puzzling over motives. We have seen the refraction of a similar frustration in Baneelon's outbreaks of fury at Phillip's refusal to respond to what Baneelon saw as clear obligations owed between friends and allies: the swift and unequivocal lending of direct physical aid against enemies coupled with a respectful appreciation of one's ally's autonomous authority. Why should Phillip not have grown weary too? And the summer had barely begun.

What happened next might have been trivial anywhere except in the famished colony. One night in late December three Australians who had been 'pretty constant visitors at Sydney for some weeks', and who should therefore have known better, were caught pilfering potatoes from a settler's garden. Worse, when the irate owner tried to chase them away one of them hurled a fish spear at him. The convict crime of garden-robbing, punished by major floggings, deprivations of rations and, if accompanied by violence, by death, was now being practised by Australians on British territory. Phillip was also informed that some of the Australians frequenting the settlement area had turned from begging to extortion; that they might burst in on anyone who happened to be alone in a hut, and demand food. This was not what Phillip had had in mind.

Accordingly he sent a sergeant and six soldiers to apprehend the potato-stealers; then rounded up a few officers and followed himself, which suggests the depth of his concern. Soon they came upon a fire with the two men and a couple of women and a child sitting around it (roasting the purloined potatoes?). There was a flurry of confused action, a club, thought at the time to be a spear, was thrown; muskets were fired. Both men, one of them bleeding, escaped, but the women and the child were captured and brought back to the governor's house. There, to Phillip's distaste (he had hoped for more sensibility), the captives settled down comfortably in a shed to sleep, and went off next morning after their breakfast of bread and fish.

Throughout these events the heat was killing. We know that on 27 December the mercury stood at 32 degrees Celsius in the shade.

The governor's feelings were further abraded when Baneelon, just back from a tooth-evulsion initiation ceremony with the Cameragals, his sworn enemies on the night of the locked door only a fortnight before, but now his best friends, cheerfully acknowledged that he had slept alongside the very warrior who had speared the governor. He seemed to have no recollection of his promises to avenge the spearing. Phillip must have felt himself wounded afresh, especially as this amnesia was being displayed by a man he needed to trust. This was also the night that Barangaroo appeared at the governor's table in her ceremonial paint, and the girl who had placed herself under his protection chose to take her worsted nightcap and rejoin her people.

With the New Year came worse news. Baneelon, chancing upon two colonists fishing from their boat, had confiscated their catch. He did not use violence, but he had his spears in his canoe along with his wife and sister, while the anglers were unarmed. Yet when Phillip charged Baneelon with the fish shakedown, he blandly denied it. Australians denied guilt as a matter of course, because both the degree of guilt and the limits of responsibility in the particular case were matters to be settled by negotiation, or, if sufficiently serious, by ordeal, but those routine denials, made even when 'guilt' seemed transparent, were shocking to the British, who placed a high value on honesty and oaths. Phillip must have been outraged by that flat denial. When he confronted Baneelon with his victims he thought that Baneelon merely blustered, but fortunately for us he was careful to report just what was said. Baneelon, said Phillip,

> entered into a long conversation, the purpose of which was an endeavour to justify himself, and this he did with an insolence which explained itself very clearly. He frequently mentioned the man who had been wounded, and threatened revenge; but, appearing to recollect himself, he offered the governor his hand. When it was not accepted, he grew violent, and seemed inclined to make use of his stick.

The governor responded by calling a guard into the room.

We think we hear Baneelon the clan warrior speaking here, possibly even placatingly. He knew, as Phillip at this point did not, that the wounded potato-stealer had died of his wound. A warrior was dead: there was therefore a right to compensation, on which the catch of fish was a down-payment. But the man had provoked the wound which killed him, so further compensation would be a matter of negotiation. Unsurprisingly, Phillip heard Baneelon's explosion of angry, urgent speech as 'the height of savage insolence' which would have been 'immediately punished in any other person'.

Not only Baneelon's anger but his distress was clear. He would threaten violence one moment and make to shake the governor's hand the next, calling him Be-anna, 'Father', as he had in the innocent days when neither man saw the cultural chasm yawning at their feet. Phillip, touched by the recurrence of that Be-anna— shouted from some distance, as was customary in Australian public statements of grievance—responded as an Englishman desiring conciliation would. He beckoned him closer. And Baneelon reacted as if mortally insulted—because his formal recitation of legitimate wrongs had been discourteously interrupted? He turned, left at a furious run, and as he passed the (unattended) wheelwright's shop he dashed in, snatched up a hatchet, and made off with it.

Was this last gesture the wanton insult, the direct blow to the face, Phillip took it to be? Or was the hatchet the second instalment of compensation due for the death of a man, and taken by right and by force? Their poor shared words were inadequate to sustain discussions of moral and legal maters at this level of delicacy. It was only after Baneelon had made his furious exit that the governor learnt that this had indeed been a matter of death. John White, accompanied by Nanbaree and Imeerawanyee, had gone out to look for the wounded man. They found his corpse instead. It had not been buried or burnt, but lay with the face carefully concealed but the body covered only by a few branches, perhaps because the spirit had not yet been avenged. A fire burned nearby.

With Baneelon's flight the tragedy of mistaken meanings was, for the moment, over; but the affectionate bonds forged between the two men during Baneelon's captivity, when each could act out his own understanding of right and proper conduct under the benevolent, uncomprehending gaze of the other, were shredded. From now on both men would remain persuaded of the righteousness of their own cause, and despair at the wilful opacity of the other. From now on, negotiation on seriously divisive political issues would surely fail.

There were immediate consequences. Henceforth no Australian was to be permitted to go to the western point of the cove, where the potato thefts had occurred. Now the colony would be demarcated on racial lines, with the appearance of an Australian on what had previously been shared ground defined as a defiance of British law.

Meanwhile John McEntire, after a momentary 'recovery', died, just as the Australians said he would, the autopsy revealing the full malevolence of the spear which had killed him. Water was dangerously short; the weather continued close and sultry. The Australians were firing the scrub for miles around, so that men coughed and wept in the smoke, and parakeets and fruit bats fell from the choking sky. Worry over depleting provisions had forced Phillip into a bad bargain with the rapacious master of a Dutch vessel who was to ferry the men of the shipwrecked *Sirius* back to England, which would mean the loss of their company, but a saving on supplies.

A month later, after inquiring anxiously at the fishing boats as to the governor's mood—and after earnestly swearing another man had taken the hatchet, which was as close as he could come to an apology—Baneelon returned to the governor's yard, apparently chastened. He was given the usual bread and fish, but he was not permitted to enter the house. Phillip tells us that he 'appeared to feel his degradation', although he 'repeated his visits very often', probably through need. The British had been providing most of his and his family's food for the best part of three months. With mutual trust perhaps terminally damaged, a potentially fatal dependency had been born.

Baneelon's fall from grace appeared not to trouble his friends. During his disappearance Australians had continued to make themselves at home in the governor's yard. In atomistic Australian politics, quarrels of this kind were personal matters. His rival Colbee, who might have thought to replace him as hinge-man with the British, brought his wife and a baby not more than two or three days old the ten kilometres from Botany Bay, where Daringa had borne her, to present the child to the governor at Government House two days before Christmas 1790. Daringa commandeered a hair from an English officer's head to wrap around the little finger on the baby's left hand to effect its amputation through attrition, and when the traditional method worked too slowly, she called upon the surgeon to finish the job with a knife.

There are other glimpses of the casual mingling of British and local lives during that long summer. On 28 February 1791 an English cutter was hit by a rain squall when out fishing. It filled with water and listed, the crew members who could swim made their escape, and one who could not was saved by a few Australians, Baneelon prominent among them. The Australians then salvaged the boat and its gear. We are casually told that Baneelon's sister, also in the fishing boat, 'had [her] two children on her shoulders in a moment, and swam on shore with them', while a young girl companion made it on her own.

What was this little band of females doing in the British working boat in the first place? This was a specialist fishing boat, skippered by the convict William Bryant, a fisherman by trade, who had been appointed full-time fisherman to the hungry settlement. He lost that position early in 1789 for selling fish on his own account, being rewarded for his enterprise with a hundred lashes and his and his family's eviction from their comfortable hut, but he continued to work in the boat and was soon in charge again. There can only be one boss in a fishing boat: a wisdom which transcends place, time and the dictates of justice. Why did he clutter valuable space with a native woman and three children, two of them infants? I suspect he had formed a fisherman's alliance with Baneelon's sister, who exchanged her local knowledge regarding fish movements and local habits in return for transport to the less accessible fishing spots. Naturally she took her children with her, along with a young girl learning this essential female craft. There must have been many such trans-cultural arrangements inside the colony, all of which we miss if we keep our eyes too firmly fixed on the governor's yard.

(Bryant was accustomed to having young children around, having two of his own. He was also a man of resource: a month after the swamping he, his wife, his children and four other convicts escaped in a six-oared boat, well provisioned by systematic theft, and set out for Batavia sixteen or seventeen hundred leagues away. They made it to Timor, where the Dutch arrested them. Bryant had good cause to risk so desperate a remedy. He was convinced he had served out his term, but Phillip, lacking the papers necessary to authenticate his claim, refused to acknowledge his change of status.)

Baneelon's rescue work after the capsize brought him back into favour, or at least through the governor's door and into his house. But now I suspect a new, if subterranean, political contest was emerging. Phillip noted, wryly, that 'in consequence of this reconciliation, the number of visitors greatly increased, the governor's yard being their head quarters'. This suggests Baneelon was making an all-out effort to consolidate his position. It was essential that he continue to demonstrate that he could extract special privileges from the whites, which could then be deployed to his own and his compatriots' advantage—that he had the governor in his pocket. He was about to make another determined effort to inveigle Phillip more deeply into a kin relationship and possibly to establish a more secure claim to land. Barangaroo was at last pregnant, and to him. He would involve the governor in the birth of his first child.

So the slow days passed. Coping with the Australians might absorb a great deal of Phillip's time, but it constituted only a fraction of his work and worries. Rations had to be reduced yet again; the sudden downpour which let us glimpse native women and children together with British convicts in the same sinking boat had no more than mitigated the drought. He had little leisure, and less privacy. We have only a few glimpses of how he spent his few moments of relaxation during those hot months, and they are touching. Phillip had chosen to take other local guests into his house. He was already caring for a dingo pup and three spoilt baby kangaroos; later he would manage to keep a tribe of baby emus alive for five weeks. Now a female fruit bat, another victim of the unnatural summer heat, had joined his household. It would 'hang by one leg a whole day without changing its position', he tells us, 'with its breast neatly covered by one of its wings, [and] it ate whatever was offered to it, lapping out of the hand like a cat'. Phillip remarks that it was especially partial to boiled rice. Feeling his quiet little bat softly lapping his palm must have been one of the governor's few reliable pleasures.

There was also the possibility of legitimate respite from domestic eruptions and the determined criminality of settlers and convicts. It was part of the governor's duty to map new areas for possible settlement. He could always escape domestic troubles, and go out on an expedition.

One of Phillip's officers' most cherished duties was to explore 'into the interior parts of the country', and the governor, despite his age, despite the burdens of office, despite his uncertain health, usually chose to go with them, along with most of the colony's senior men. The expeditions were tough going, with every man save the governor having to lug his own provisions, the land baffling to the eye and punishing underfoot and the outcomes always less than impressive, but compared with the anxious tedium of life within the settlement they were fine adventures. The left-at-homes were accordingly resentful.

Arthur Bowes Smyth, the chronically disaffected surgeon of the *Lady Penrhyn*, recorded his vehement disapproval of one 'excursion up the country' Phillip chose to take a mere five weeks after landfall, when 'Anarchy & Confusion' prevailed in the infant settlement, with the chaplain sick and a sailor gone missing, the natives brewing mischief, and the 'Audacity of the Convicts both Men & Women arrived at such a pitch as…not to be equalled, I believe, by any set of Villains in any other Spot upon the Globe'. This is Bowes Smyth's curt entry for Sunday, 2 April 1788: 'This morning. Early the Governor set out in a Boat wt. his Aid de Camp [sic] &ca. upon another Excurtion up the Country, & means to stay 4 or 5 days.' On the 9th: 'The Governor return'd in perfect health, and as wise as he set out, having made no discovery of the smallest importance.'

Less than a week later, on 15 April 1788, Phillip was off again to explore the rivers and lagoons behind Manly Cove. He arrived home on the evening of the eighteenth only to be off again on the twenty-second, this time provisioned for seven days out, with 'every individual carrying his own allowance of bread, beef, rum, and water', along with 'the additional weight of spare shoes, shirts, trowsers, together with a great coat, or scotch plaid, for the purpose of sleeping in'. The six soldiers in the entourage were left to shoulder the tents and poles and the two camp kettles. Assistant Surgeon Worgan, who much enjoyed his own less ambitious excursions, commented: 'Had you seen them, they would put you in Mind of a Gang of Travelling Gypsies.' And this raggle-taggle crew was parading itself within a house-of-cards hierarchy which set high value on genteel appearances, gentlemen's exemption from sweaty labour, and high-minded devotion to local duty. Worgan and Bowes Smyth were possibly the more disaffected because Surgeon White was often a happy member of such sorties, fleeing cramped misery and rotting bodies to wander about potting exotic birds, 'for science', he would have said. (It turned out to be a particularly arduous venture, with the governor suffering his first attack of the acute pains in the lower body which would disable him before he left the colony.)

As the colony's circumstances deteriorated, exploration became not a pleasant if arduous duty, but a necessity, undertaken in the hope of finding food for immediate survival. Tench reports that on 2 April 1791, with the gardens 'destitute of vegetables' after a long drought, rations were reduced to 'three pounds of rice, three pounds of flour and three pounds of pork per week' per man. In mid-April, Phillip led a large expedition out from Rose Hill to explore the land around the Hawkesbury.

The plan was to cross the Hawkesbury River opposite Richmond Hill and settle once and for all the question of whether the 'Hawkesbury' and the 'Nepean' were the one river. This time, fortunately for us, Tench was a member of the team, which comprised the three senior officials in the colony, Phillip, Collins and White; Collins' servant; three gamekeepers; Tench and Tench's friend and expert navigator William Dawes; two sergeants, eight privates and two Australians: Colbee and young Boladeree, husband to the rescued girl, and a likeable, easy-going fellow who was now more or less living at the governor's house. (Baneelon, returned to qualified favour, had been anxious to come, but Tench tells us 'his wife would not permit it'.) The British wanted the Australians along for their local knowledge, their bushcraft and their hunting skills, and they cheerfully agreed when they were promised plentiful provisions and that the expedition would not stay out too long. The two enjoyed special privileges. Every man except the governor was burdened with a full knapsack with provisions, a gun, blanket and canteen. So heavy were the packs that on the first day out a soldier collapsed under the hard going, and a friend 'strong as a packhorse' had to carry his knapsack for him. Meanwhile the Australians skipped merrily along with their little knapsacks, 'laughing to excess' when an unhappy Britisher stumbled or fell, as they very often did. 'Our perplexities,' Tench dourly observed, 'afforded them an endless fund of merriment and derision.'

Expectations regarding the Australians' dazzling bushcraft were disappointed early. When only a very short distance out from Rose

Hill they confessed themselves hopelessly lost, and if asked for 'Rose Hill' would unerringly point in the wrong direction. As the days passed they clung ever closer to Dawes, because only Dawes, with his compass and his step-counter, seemed to know where he was. Neither did they fulfil their intended role as hunters enriching the explorers' diet with fresh meat. Initially they had been ready to swim for the ducks the British guns occasionally brought down, but then they went on strike, pointing out that the British ate the ducks while they had to content themselves with the odd crow. If the British wanted ducks, they could swim for them.

Nor were they accomplished campers. Tench noted that on arrival at a chosen camp site the Australians were as lilies of the field. 'Their laziness appeared strongly when we halted, for they refused to draw water or cleave wood to make a fire; but as soon as it was kindled (having first well stuffed themselves) they lay down before it and fell asleep.' Meanwhile the British, having made and fed the fire, broken out the rations, cooked and cleaned up afterwards, had to set about the business of erecting their shelters for the night. A nomad's streamlined travelling style has its advantages.

On the third day out, with the British exhausted and their enthusiasm well blunted, they were supremely irritated when after a particularly gruelling march their 'sable companions' on no grounds whatever exploded into a wild fit of high spirits, eating hugely, staging imaginary fights, hunting imaginary kangaroos, dancing and leaping about, and taking special delight in miming the more spectacular British slips and stumbles of the day 'with inimitable drollery'. We hear Stanner's sepulchral murmur of the Australian talent for 'jollifying humdrum'.

And they complained, quietly at first, then more vociferously as the days passed, as they were taken further and further away from their home territory. They also showed themselves to be completely lacking in British-style fortitude. 'Where's Rose Hill? Where?' they wailed, as the deprivations of the camp diet and the terror of alien country depressed them ever more darkly. They had expected the expedition to turn up opportunities for serious hunting, especially the ducks and kangaroos they rarely tasted at home. They had not allowed for British single-mindedness: Phillip reported that while 'ducks were seen in great numbers…the party seldom got a shot' as they kept up their gruelling pace. Both Australians kept warning of the dangerous hostility of local natives, and were confounded when the people encountered were unfailingly friendly. One genial old man paddling his canoe upstream to the best site for collecting hatchet stones, and already known to Colbee, went so far as to quit his canoe to guide the travellers to an easier walking track. Then he and his son camped snugly beside them with his little family just over the river, probably because, having to pass through other people's territory, they felt safer in the company of the powerful strangers. His tribe specialised in possum-hunting, with the men thinking nothing of shinning up trees which rose twenty metres or more before they began to branch, and the old man provided an impromptu demonstration of his tree-climbing skills in exchange for a biscuit. Tench remembers him 'laughing immoderately' as he leapt up the sleek straight trunk, chopping toe-holds as he went.

That night the old man and his son performed a ritual 'curing' on Colbee, drawing out the pain of an old wound, with the senior man rewarded with Colbee's worsted nightcap and a good part of his supper. Then, after most of the party except the watchful Phillip had fallen asleep, Colbee gave the old man a detailed account of Sydney Cove and Rose Hill. Phillip noted that 'in this history, names were as particularly attended to as if their hearers had been intimately acquainted with every person who was mentioned', and we wonder whether this information was part of a political transaction. (Was the 'curing' indeed impromptu, or had the apparently fortuitous meeting somehow been arranged?)

In his account Tench transformed hardships and confusions into a comedy of human foibles, white and black. The more analytic Phillip told the same story, but he noticed quite different elements within it, and again took the opportunity to reflect on what he saw as disturbing anomalies in the Australians' conduct. Why had Colbee and Boladeree insisted that every one of the tribes through whose territory they passed was 'bad'? Why had they set about demolishing a little hunting hut they came upon, and why were they 'much displeased' when he stopped them? Phillip could understand the caution—but why the aggression? When he had asked them to make contact with a solitary hunter heard hallooing for his dog—a hunter whose small son bravely approached the whites while the father stood watching from the trees—they urgently requested 'the serjeant, in whom they always placed great confidence, to take his gun and go with them'; a request Phillip naturally rejected. Why would they want a man with a gun?

He was also puzzled by the affability, even the generosity, of Australians once met with and properly 'introduced'—the affability, we might assume, of good hosts whose proprietary rights had been acknowledged by passing guests. Phillip could not be expected to infer the strict territoriality of these apparently casual wanderers, any more than he could have comprehended the contrary pulls of the pleasures and the dangers of travel, as when his Australian friends who had been so eager to make the boat trip with him to Rose Hill then fretted to go home. To his credit, he did not dismiss their fluctuating moods as simply foolish or feckless, but carefully recorded the apparent anomalies in their conduct with the patience of the anthropologist he was learning to be.

Phillip was also learning that 'reliable' Australians might have their own agendas. Baneelon's furious outbursts continued to bewilder him, but he was ready to risk an interpretation of what Colbee and Boladeree were up to on this wearisome expedition. The pair:

> had at first supposed that Governor Phillip and his party came from the settlement to kill ducks and patagarongs [kangaroos]; but finding they did not stop at the places where those animals were seen in any numbers, they were at a loss to know why the journey was taken; and though they had hitherto behaved exceedingly well, yet, as they now began to be tired of a journey which yielded them no sort of advantage, they endeavoured to persuade the governor to return, saying it was a great way to the place where the stone hatchets were to be procured, and that they must come in a boat.

The detail Phillip provides lets us develop his interpretation a little further. These fish-eaters had looked forward not only to great hunting, but possibly great fighting, too, as they pushed into unfamiliar territory with the armed whites at their side. But if neither fresh meat nor raiding was the object, then these most peculiar people must surely be after hatchet stones. Why else walk your feet off and risk ambush blundering around in someone else's territory?

The haze of confusions attending this expedition have allowed us to glimpse something of a crucial matter normally veiled from us: the nature of Australian attachment to the land. Let me offer another accidental fragment from the record. In February 1791 the *Supply* had gone to Norfolk Island carrying a detachment of the New South Wales Corps. They took with them a little Australian boy called

Bondel. He was an orphan: his father 'had been killed in battle and his mother bitten in two by a shark', Tench tells us, and the child had become deeply attached to Captain Hill, commander of the detachment. When the *Supply* returned a few weeks later Tench reports that his kinfolk eagerly asked after him, 'and on being told that the place he had gone to afforded plenty of birds and other good fare, innumerable volunteers presented themselves to follow him, so great was their confidence in us and so little hold on them had the *amor patriae*'.

'So little hold on them had the *amor patriae*.' So little love for their homeland. A tempting conclusion, but a false one. These were a people accustomed to journeying, especially when food was short—and then returning, as Baneelon would later return from distant England. His Australian companion would die there—distant places were known to be dangerous, and rife with sorcery—but their allure was powerful, so long as ultimate return was guaranteed.

To return to the expedition. Again, two quite different ways of understanding the world had walked side by side, had amused and annoyed each other, had eaten, talked and slept alongside each other, each having only the slightest comprehension of the other's motives and expectations.

On one issue, however, the Australians' views were transparent. They were tired of the hardships of the journey, and deeply aware of the novel comforts waiting them back in Sydney. When it began to rain their disaffection was complete: Colbee said his wife and child would be crying for him, and Boladeree 'lost all patience when the rain began, telling the governor that there were good houses at Sydney and Rose Hill, but that they had no house now, no fish, no melon, of which fruit the natives were very fond'. Phillip believed they would have abandoned the expedition altogether had they been sure they could have found their way home alone. They were vastly relieved when the weary party turned back after only five days out (they had carried provisions for ten), and with the mystery of the rivers still unsolved. So ended British fantasies of exploiting intrepid Australian bushmanship.

A month later Tench and Dawes, accompanied only by a 'trusty sergeant' and a private soldier, set off again and settled the matter of the rivers once and for all. The two turned out to be one.

Phillip returned from his expedition refreshed, but with his problems
unsolved. With the colony still hovering dangerously close to famine
and the drought continuing, rations had to be reduced yet again, and
while a sudden abundance of fish at the head of the harbour drew
some Australians away from the settlement, their broils continued to
disturb Phillip's peace.

On 8 May 1791 Baneelon and Colbee and their wives had taken
their usual wine and dishes of tea at the governor's house, and were
thought to have retired to Baneelon's house at the point. Then in the
dead of night Phillip was woken by the screams of the girl he had
rescued from Baneelon's vengeance, who was sleeping in a shed in
the governor's yard. Baneelon, Colbee and two other men had hidden
in the yard before the gate was locked for the night, and now were
trying to break into the shed, with the intention, the girl said to her
rescuers, of raping her. To avoid more trouble the guard had sensibly
let the would-be kidnappers escape over the fence, but Phillip was,
understandably, furious, both about the deliberate deception and the

disgraceful motive. 'These men,' he coldly observed, 'had left their own wives by their fires.'

When the pair next came to the governor's house Colbee blamed Baneelon; when the governor rebuked Baneelon, he sulked. Nor was he in the least penitent: when Phillip told him that 'the soldiers would shoot him if he ever came again to take any woman away', Baneelon angrily replied that if they tried he would spear them.

Bewilderingly, Baneelon seemed to think he had right on his side. He also said he was hungry, indicating his growing dependence on British supplies. The governor, not wanting him taking revenge for any further humiliation, ordered him fed. He also warned him that if he tried to invade the house or yard in the night again he would be shot, and in his hearing ordered his guard to fire on anyone attempting to scale the palings at night. From that time on Phillip also discouraged women from sleeping in the yard without their husbands, so closing the first women's refuge in Sydney.

What had Baneelon been up to? He and Colbee had not heedlessly tumbled back in lust and in their cups: Phillip kept an abstemious house, except for remarkable occasions like King's Birthdays. Baneelon had also recruited those two extra men. I think Colbee was telling no more than the truth when he 'blamed Baneelon'. In my view this was a raid organised by Baneelon to demonstrate his continuing authority over the person of the girl improperly removed from his jurisdiction. (Did he also expect her to be so conscious of her transgressions that she would submit to being hoisted over the wall in silence?) Her abduction by night from under the governor's nose and her subsequent gang-rape would also have economically demonstrated the autonomy of Australian law, and would have won Baneelon significant prestige in the concealed world of tribal politics. Had it come off it would have been a warrior feat worthy of being memorialised in song, or even by the award of a special name. The 'deception' which so upset Phillip, then the silent slither through the night and over the fence, would only have added lustre in Australian eyes, where stealth and courage were celebrated, especially when demonstrated in the dangerous dark. In failure Baneelon remained unapologetic, and, as his confused, angry conversation with Phillip suggests, intransigent regarding his authority over the girl.

There had been another odd incident a couple of months before which might or might not have had political meaning. In February 1791, not long after the consolidation of the alliance between Baneelon's clan and the British, the signal colours at the flagpole at South Head, which had been flying unmolested for more than a year, were stolen, cut up, and used to bedeck some of the canoes darting about the harbour. Had the tribes come to realise these fragments of cloth were dear to the British, and their taking an act of defiance of the accommodations reached across the water? Did they simply covet the bright cloth as decoration? The meaning of the action, transparent to them, remained opaque to the British, as it does to us, but it makes me wonder if Baneelon's abduction attempt might not have been designed to demonstrate his independence within the broad terms of the British alliance.

Whatever his intentions, Baneelon's actions had unhappy consequences. Now Phillip drew his first permanent domestic boundary. Henceforth the governor's yard would be closed to unauthorised visitors at night; henceforth Baneelon would enter the governor's house only by invitation.

The most formidable challenge to Phillip's authority over what he saw as British territory was to come from an unexpected direction. Phillip enjoyed Boladeree's company sufficiently to take him on the expedition out from Rose Hill. Indeed he liked him so well he was planning to take back him back to England with him. He was especially pleased by a trade Boladeree had initiated, peddling the fish he took in the harbour to the settlers at Rose Hill in exchange for vegetables, rice and bread. This was exactly the kind of mutually advantageous interaction Phillip had dreamt of. Then in June 1791 a little mob of convicts put an end to the trade by destroying Boladeree's new, cherished canoe, and he began his helpless slide in the nets of British law.

After finding his canoe wrecked Boladeree appeared at the governor's house at Rose Hill incandescent with rage, armed and painted for war, and (courteously, properly) proclaiming his determination to take revenge on white men, even up to their leader. Phillip, seeing the depth of his anger, undertook to kill the offenders himself, and when they were seized had Boladeree watch them flogged. He also assured him, falsely, that one had been hanged. (Honesty is an early casualty in trans-cultural exchanges.) With justice done to his own satisfaction, he gave Boladeree a few small gifts, and thought the matter ended. He also thought he had exacted Boladeree's promise that he would not spear anyone in revenge, which reminds us of the inadequacies still bedevilling language communications.

Boladeree watched Phillip punish the men to Phillip's satisfaction, accepted the gifts—and then, when he happened upon an unarmed convict in the bush, speared him twice. The wounds were not mortal; he did not plunder the man's possessions. He exchanged two wounds for a ruined canoe.

Phillip immediately understood that 'the canoe being destroyed was the cause of the attack', especially when Boladeree's companions readily identified him as the spearman. Meanwhile Boladeree sensibly went into hiding, as one did when tribal justice was being bruited, to give everyone time to calm down.

The governor was chagrined at the stop put to the barter trade between white and black at Rose Hill, but he knew the real problem lay deeper. It was not, as he had first thought, that Australians had no law. After three years of watching he had come to realise the rigour of Australian law, and the passion behind its defence of individual male dignity: he commented, 'These people set little value on their lives, and never fail to repay you in kind, whether you praise or threaten… whenever a blow is given them, be it gentle or with force, they always return in the same manner.' The first response, prior to talk of compensation, was retaliatory physical injury. A tribe would take direct action against an offending tribe; within the tribe there would be violence between families; within the family violence between individuals. He knew that under Australian law Boladeree had done what he had to do: that despite the offenders' punishment under British law, 'he thought it belonged to him to punish the injury he had received'. But if in his own terms Boladeree had done the necessary and honourable thing, Phillip also knew that as governor he could not tolerate coexistence with this other law. In the territories under his administration, British law and only British law must prevail. Boladeree was accordingly declared a felon, to be captured or shot on sight.

There followed a sequence of alarums and excursions around the harbour as Boladeree played a daring game of catch-as-catch-can with Phillip and his soldiers. Late in August 1791 the game turned serious. A retinue of Australians, some of them strangers and all en route to a dance at Botany Bay, called at the settlement, and 'six men, with seven or eight and twenty women and children came to Governor Phillip's house' to be fed. They were sharing out the bread they had been given when Phillip was told 'that [Boladeree] was on the opposite side of the cove, and that he was armed, as were most of his companions'.

Phillip was in a dilemma. This was clearly an act of provocation. But if Boladeree and his supporters were seized while the bevy of visitors, some of them new to Sydney, were still in the yard, they might panic, and some of the men had spears. So he waited until they were fed, gave them some fishhooks, and at last they went on their way. Then he sent out a sergeant and a few armed men to apprehend the outlaw. The British party fell in with some apparently friendly Australians, one of whom suddenly tried to wrest a flintlock from a soldier. A tussle broke out, and in the ensuing fracas a warrior took a musket ball in the leg. When British reinforcements went out they found the Australians had vanished. Young Nanbaree, overhearing the soldiers' orders, had stripped and run naked through the bush to warn his compatriots.

The episode was troubling in every way. Violence had been offered on the fringe of the settlement by armed men, to armed men. A spear had been thrown, which was an utterly forbidden act. Phillip might also have thought he was being played with; that Boladeree's challenge had been timed to increase the excitement of the strangers' visit to the town. Baneelon meanwhile was displaying an impenetrable unconcern: on being told that 'the soldiers were gone out to punish Boladeree for wounding a white man…this intelligence did not prevent him from enjoying a hearty dinner; and when he was going away he left a large bundle of spears, fiz-gigs, [fish spears] and various other articles under Governor Phillip's care'. The next day the party of Australians who had been at the Botany Bay dance passed through again, still confident of their welcome. These people refused to generalise from the individual quarrel even to tribal politics, much less to what Phillip saw as universal principles of law. Their response to the pursuit of Boladeree demonstrated that they understood enough of British law to know that 'nothing more was intended than to punish the person who wounded the white man, and that they would not have been fired on had not a spear been thrown at the party'. But the real lesson had not been learnt. They were treating this important affair as if it were one of their own petty feuds between individuals, not a matter of legal principle and rightful territorial authority.

There was no solution in sight. The pursuit went on, with Boladeree always warned in time by local sympathisers, including Baneelon. And the boy Nanbaree, who had lived in Surgeon White's house since he was nine, who had enjoyed a thousand kindnesses, now showed where his loyalties lay, gleefully skidding off to warn his compatriots of any movement by the soldiers. When he was scolded, he laughed.

There was also a humiliating element of taunt in all this. Boladeree and his canoe would turn up in the cove, and then churn away at speed when his supporters yelled that the soldiers were coming after him as he played his daring public games with this highly unreasonable man, making visible nonsense of his preposterous claim to total authority and exclusive possession of territory he and his followers had usurped.

And throughout all the drama Australians continued to visit the governor's house for food and relaxation 'with the same freedom as if nothing had happened'. Phillip must have had the unpleasant sense that he was being laughed at.

Then, Tench tells us, '[Boladeree] prudently dropped all connection with us and was for a long time not seen'. He reappeared only on the eve of Tench and his fellow marines' departure for England in December 1791. He was dangerously ill, with Baneelon and Colbee in anxious attendance. Baneelon secretly fetched John White to the 'outlaw' as he lay in the bush, and again we see the colour-blind compassion of White, and the depth of Australian confidence in him as a man, and as a curer. Then Baneelon begged Phillip to allow Boladeree into the hospital for treatment. And Phillip relented, 'taking [Boladeree] by the hand, and promising that when he was recovered he should reside with him again'. In the end Phillip found the matter was personal, too.

Boladeree entered the hospital under White's special care on 14 December 1791. We happen to know the number of patients in the surgeon's charge that week. David Collins tells us there were 403— plus one privileged Australian. Collins also tells us that during Boladeree's illness Baneelon sang over him in healing ceremonies in the hospital until he was supplanted by a more senior curer hastily brought from the north shore, and again we salute White for his easy acceptance of pagan curers into his own hospital, and his recognition of their legitimate authority over their own.

During the night Boladeree's fever worsened, and Collins reports that 'his friends, thinking he would be better with them, put him into a canoe', again with no attempt at officious intervention by White. They intended to take him to the north shore, his home territory, Collins said, but 'he died as they were carrying him over'.

The Englishmen learnt of the death 'by a violent clamour among the women and children'. It was confirmed by Baneelon when he came back to the town. He and the governor agreed 'that the body should be buried in the governor's garden'. In the afternoon of 16 December the corpse was brought over in a canoe, and deposited in a hut at the bottom of the garden. Phillip forgot his prohibition against the use of Australian arms in 'his' territory as warriors and a handful of women fought the ritual combats expressive of mourning. Boladeree's body was buried with full Australian warrior honours.

*

Phillip had learnt a great deal through those stormy months. Now he knew that offences between Australian groups were understood as collective, not individual, and that vengeance could be legitimately pursued against any member of the other party, including the women and children. It took him longer to realise that not all punishments had to be violent; that material compensation could sometimes resolve disputes between groups or individuals, without resort to physical vengeance. Increased understanding need not entail acceptance, but it does allow pragmatic adjustments. When in October 1791, four months after the Boladeree eruption, and with Boladeree still at large, a newly arrived seaman not yet trained to the local policy of conciliation destroyed the canoe of a native who had been invited on board his ship, he was punished for his vandalism in accordance with British law. This time, however, Phillip was careful to present the injured Australian not with the trivial gifts he had given Boladeree, but with 'a complete set of wearing apparel as satisfaction for the injury he had done him, as well as to induce him to abandon any design of revenge...' Earlier, he had used the local idiom of collective punishment with Tench's abortive expedition after McEntire's spearing. By the spring of 1791 this reflective man had come to recognise the need for compensation even in cases he would judge to be criminal, not civil. He had taken another unwilling step towards conciliation with the Australian system of justice.

Could he have continued that process of adjustment, negotiating crises as they happened, responding to experience, adjusting the law to special cases? Perhaps. After he left in December 1792 all accommodations ended as the British adopted a simpler solution: two independent systems of law, one to regulate the subjects of the King, the other to settle Australians' differences in accordance with their own notions of justice. Whites flocked to watch intertribal battles as a favoured entertainment, and could choose whether to be amused or scandalised by Australian intra-tribal and domestic violence. Meanwhile they visited ferocious collective punishments, often murderous, on Australians suspected of offences against whites, especially any challenge to exclusive British possession of the land. White offences against blacks would increasingly go unnoticed, and unpunished.

Meanwhile, the colony was beginning to do rather better than Tench allowed. If most of the livestock had been eaten during the great hunger of 1790, if prices for grain remained horribly inflated, agricultural yields were increasing as farmers came to understand the local soils, the vagaries of local weather and the most productive crops. Phillip had also sustained his determined egalitarianism: despite mutterings, especially from newly arrived officers unready to yield their customary privileges to feed a pack of convicts, he could say, with justified pride, that 'the daily ration of provisions issued from the public stores was the same to the convict as it was to the governor'. It is true that officers could supplement their diets from their private gardens if they could keep marauding convicts out, but Phillip's naval commitment to the physical welfare of his people, whatever their rank or status, remains impressive.

Phillip also contrived to sustain his hospitality to the Australians, with the governor's yard figuring as a reliable station on the food circuit, especially in times of dearth or personal emergency. Over the tense weeks of Boladeree's exploits Baneelon had been moving to re-establish his old primacy. Despite misunderstandings, despite misdemeanours, he was accepted once again among the inner circle of Phillip's Australian friends—although now there were other contenders for the governor's particular favour.

In the spring of 1791 Barangaroo was nearing her time. Her friends among the British had watched the developing pregnancy with interest. She seemed ready to incorporate British objects into her layette: Baneelon asked the governor for a British blanket for the baby, which was given to him, and when the governor coveted a fine net Barangaroo wore slung on her shoulder, she readily exchanged it for an English substitute crocheted for her on Phillip's orders by a convict woman.

One of Baneelon's schemes pivoted on the unborn baby. Daringa had dutifully returned to her family and Botany Bay to bear her first child, but Barangaroo did not make the easy trip across the water to Cameragal territory. Such orthodox behaviour was no part of Baneelon's plan—nor, as we shall see, of Barangaroo's, either. Baneelon announced to the governor that Barangaroo would bear their first child inside the governor's house.

Phillip demurred. Baneelon insisted. It was only after extended discussions that Baneelon could be persuaded to agree that his baby would be born in the hospital—which, if not as desirable a birth site as the governor's house, still represented a sturdy claim. Baneelon was determined that his child (whom he confidently predicted would be a boy) would have birth rights within the settlement, and a closer-than-fictive kin relationship with the governor.

These interesting discussions appear to have taken place exclusively between the two men. There is no indication that Barangaroo took either part or interest in them. When her time came she bore her baby not in the governor's house, not in the hospital, not even in or beside Baneelon's house on the point, but alone, at a secluded place of her own choosing. David Collins happened upon her a few hours after the birth. The baby—a little reddish creature, he reported—was lying on the traditional paperbark blanket (no crocheted net, no British blanket), and the mother was gathering sticks to mend her little fire in preparation for shortening the baby's umbilical cord. Under Collins' fascinated gaze (which seems to have abashed her not at all) Barangaroo heated the end of a bone covered in punk, applied it again and again to the baby's dangling cord until she judged it 'sufficiently deadened', and then neatly severed it with a sharp shell.

There are peculiarities about this birth scene. We happen to have a good account of what happened when Warreweer, Baneelon's sister, bore her first child. Warreweer's labour came upon her in the town, where she was quickly attended by a flock of local women and some British women as well (another glimpse of informal trans-cultural mixing). Childbirth among the Australians was an all-female affair, but the British women reported to Collins exactly what happened. There were practised midwives present, they said, massaging and encouraging the mother-to-be while other women looked on. After the baby was safely delivered one of the British women was allowed to intervene. She cut the umbilical cord with scissors, and then washed the baby, to the consternation of the traditionalists, but with the mother's consent.

No scissors for Barangaroo, and no interference from other women either, white or black. It seems she regarded birthing as a private matter. We might think her, as an older mother, to have been as much in need of care as young Warreweer, but Barangaroo chose solitude.

She was to die soon after the birth, either in consequence of it, or because of the beating inflicted by Baneelon which preceded it. She was a formidable woman, one of those personages who command attention at their every appearance, and she deserves an obituary, not least because her vivid personal style sheds a unique if angled light on Australian male–female relations.

Barangaroo was a Cameragal, a daughter of the largest, toughest and most dominant tribe in the region, but I suspect her notable independence was more personal style and political decision than tribal heritage. Remember her energetic intervention when Phillip had the convict who had stolen Daringa's fishing gear flogged before their eyes to demonstrate the muscular beauty of British justice. Daringa had wept, a fitting response in an Australian woman. Barangaroo had leapt up and proceeded to belabour the flogger. Of all the women we watch being hit by men, only Barangaroo hit back, and with a club, too. And when Baneelon offended or defied her, as in the Rose Hill boating episode, she took direct action, trashing as much of his property as she could lay her hands on. It was never wise to rouse Barangaroo. Time and again we see the tough and touchy Baneelon bow before the threat of her temper.

She could not have been young. Phillip tells us she had two children from a previous husband before she took up with Baneelon, and that both had died. (The two children often seen with the couple were not their issue, but adoptees.) The normally reliable Collins claimed she was close to fifty when she died late in 1791, but he inferred that from the fact that she was cremated, not buried; given that she had just borne a child, I think he must have been mistaken. She was clearly sexually charismatic, compelling to British and

Australian males alike, and wore the scars of unauthorised desire, having been twice speared, once through the thigh. Even the abstemious Phillip recorded her beauty at some length: '[Barangaroo] is very strait and exceedingly well-made; her features are good. And though she goes naked, yet there is such an air of innocence about her that cloathing scarcely appears necessary.' (Was this indeed 'innocence'? Or pride?) We also notice that Barangaroo was the only woman he always named, with Boroong, 'the girl raised in the clergyman's house', a poor second.

Phillip also commented that Barangaroo 'thought herself drest when her nose was occasionally ornamented with a small bone or a bit of stick'. The stick or bone in the nose was a male adornment, highly unusual for a woman. Phillip had seen only one other woman with her septum perforated. Yet Barangaroo wore the adornment as she chose.

Consider now Barangaroo's determined nakedness. Despite direct exhortation—despite the accommodations made by other Australian women to the British preference for clothing inside the settlement—Barangaroo went naked. I suspect that was an early decision. Tench paints a pretty picture of her dewy confusion on her first meeting with British men on that day of reconciliation in mid-September 1790, a week after the spearing. He reports that Barangaroo, hovering at a shy distance, resisted Baneelon's urgings to come nearer to the male group, so Boorong was sent to coax her into approaching. Finally she did—but only after Boorong had put a petticoat on her. That did not suit the watching men at all: as Tench expansively puts it, 'This was the prudery of the wilderness, which her husband joined us to ridicule, and we soon laughed her out of it. The petticoat was dropped, and Barangaroo stood armed cap-a-pee [head to toe] in nakedness.'

Tench then ruminates on 'the feminine innocence, softness and modesty' to be found 'amidst a hoarde of roaming savages in the desert wastes of New South Wales'. At this initial meeting Tench, who would later decide she was a vixen deserving whatever she got, was charmed by Barangaroo's bashfulness as she stood naked before an audience of grinning, yelling white men, and her grinning, yelling husband.

If we extricate ourselves from the syrup of Tench's sentimentality and look again at the sequence of events he describes, we see something other than bashful modesty. Boorong goes to Barangaroo, and somehow persuades her to put on the weird garment we call a 'petticoat'. She is then led over to the strangers—who laugh, shout and gesticulate at her. Barangaroo, recognising, resenting the men's mood, strips off the alien garment which has brought her into public ridicule, and stands...blushing? or glowering? before them.

Barangaroo had taken the petticoat off for good. She would not endure that humiliation again; and she would make no more concessions to the strangers. Collins might comment on Australian women's tactful pretence of modesty when they were in the settlement; Baneelon and Colbee might politely don genteel British clothing when dining at the governor's table; Barangaroo went superbly naked, wearing at most that slim bone in her septum. On the one occasion she 'dressed' she did so Australian-style, when she came to the governor's table direct from a major ceremony in full ceremonial fig, with the upper half of her face painted with red ochre highlighted with white pipeclay spots, and more red ochre rubbed at the small of her back.

Barangaroo had made one concession. On that long-ago September day on the beach she submitted to having her hair cut, at Baneelon's request. That seems to have been the end of her acquiescence. On that day the girl Boorong, sent after Barangaroo to persuade her to come to the settlement, had instead been so effectively coaxed to abandon the strangers and rejoin her own people that she returned to the boat very reluctantly, and only after 'often repeated injunctions'. And on the memorable 8 October when Baneelon prepared for his first visit to Sydney Cove, Barangaroo angrily refused to go with him, and staged a furious protest against his going.

We have seen how Baneelon's plottings to have her bear their child in the governor's house or, failing that, in the hospital, foundered on the rock of her stubbornness. (Could that have been the reason for her ferocious beating on the morning of the birth?) While she cheerfully exchanged her net for Phillip's convict crochet, she did so only after taking out of it a paperbark 'blanket', 'nicely folded up', as Phillip remembered it. This was, presumably, the blanket on which the new baby was lying when Collins came upon the birth scene. If Baneelon wanted a British blanket, that was not her affair.

Not long after the birth, with her baby girl Dilboong still at the breast, Barangaroo died. Her funeral, which took place close to the end of 1791, presents its own anomalies. When the accidental outlaw Boladeree died from the illness which brought him back into the governor's care and affection, he was buried in the governor's garden, and coffined, poignantly enough, in one of his beloved canoes. His interment came only after elaborate ceremonial mourning which went on for the best part of a night and a day and involved ritual combats and much wailing from the women and children, and Boorong, who must have been a close kinswoman, having her head deeply gashed by Boladeree's mother. When the corpse was at last carried to rest it was accompanied by a large escort, and shrubs were carefully cleared from the burial site 'so that the sun might look at it as he passed'. The British made their own contribution to the obsequies: while the grave was being prepared Phillip's drummers, at Baneelon's request, beat out 'several marches'.

The funeral of Colbee's secondary wife who died in childbirth at about the same time was treated with much the same formality, with the corpse paraded through the town before it was laid in its grave with the living baby beside it. The mourning was less prolonged and less intense than the outpourings for Boladeree, but Boladeree was a well-loved young warrior dead in his prime, as well as a local hero. Women wailed for the young mother, and her death rites concluded with a shower of spears, presumably signifying her friends' determination to seek vengeance.

Barangaroo's funeral was an altogether more hushed affair. The governor, White and Collins attended at Baneelon's request, along with seven Australians: Baneelon, three of his men friends, and three women, one of them his sister—and none of them, we note, Daringa. The warriors threw their spears, but there seems to have been no wailing, no flurries of mock combat, no body-painting, no self-wounding. Barangaroo's body, wrapped in an old British blanket, was simply laid on a pyre with her basket of fishing gear beside her, and burnt. Phillip, White and Collins were present at the gathering of her ashes the next day, again at Baneelon's invitation, with no other Australian attending. The three Englishmen watched as Baneelon scraped the ashes into a little pile, placed a log on each side of the mound, and crowned it with bark. Collins was moved to sentiment by the solemn tenderness Baneelon brought to the task; a tenderness which 'did honour to his feelings as a man, as it seemed the result of a heartfelt affection for the object of it, of whose person nothing now remained but a piece or two of calcined bone'. Collins later reports a large formal combat (he calls them 'funeral games') where 'many' were wounded. Baneelon himself had 'a severe contest' with Willemerin, the Botany Bay curer who had speared Phillip, and who had failed to attend Barangaroo when Baneelon had summoned him, but this performance seems to have had as much to do with formal protocols and placating the formidable Cameragal as with personal grief.

There is another possibility in this hall-of-mirrors world: that Barangaroo's funeral rites were muted not because of Barangaroo's social isolation, but because of Baneelon's ongoing ambition to impress the British, in this case with the reverent sedateness of his mourning. After all, he had watched enough British burials.

Then Baneelon took another unorthodox step. Immediately after Barangaroo's death he solicited Phillip's help in finding a convict woman to wet-nurse the baby: a remarkably emancipated request given that Australians did not practise wet-nursing. When Colbee's wife died in childbirth, Colbee followed tradition by laying her living suckling child in the mother's grave, and crushing its head with a stone. What else could he do, with no one to feed it? Yet Baneelon took the radical step of asking Phillip to find a British wet-nurse. Was this another example of his adventurous thinking as he sought to strengthen the political bond?

Long after the events I am describing here, the assiduous Collins shed oblique light on what Baneelon might have had in mind in all his approaches to the governor. Even in their stormiest moments Baneelon persisted in calling the governor Be-anna, 'Father'. Buried in one of his long appendices Collins tells us that while Be-anna was a courtesy title bestowed on the oldest man in any group, it also had another usage:

We observed it to be frequently applied by children to men who we knew had not any children of their own. On inquiry we were informed, that in the case a father should die, the nearest kin, or some deputed friend, would take care of his children; and for this reason those children styled them, Be-anna, though in the lifetime of their natural parent. This Bennillong [sic] (the native who was some time in England) confirmed to us at the death of his first wife, by consigning the care of his infant daughter Dil-boong (who at the time of her mother's decease was at the breast) to his friend Governor Phillip, telling him he was to become the Be-anna or Father to his little girl.

Baneelon knew Phillip had no children. So—a formal claim to adoption and its rights? Possibly; to my mind even probably. But it is possible to overemphasise the political. Little Dilboong—named, Collins tells us, for 'a small bird which we often heard in low wet ground and in copses'—was Baneelon's only issue. She was also his well-loved Barangaroo's daughter. Was he desperate to save her? When Dilboong died he asked that she be buried in Phillip's garden, where he and a couple of Australian friends sat vigil for her through the night. Because these actions might strengthen his dwindling claim to intimate connection with the British, the land they occupied, the goods they possessed? Or to comfort her baby spirit?

I am left wondering at the absence of personal mourners from both parts of Barangaroo's funeral ceremony. In life we commonly encounter her either alone or with Baneelon, sometimes in the company of children, but not of other women. Aloof in life, she remained so in death. As an outsider and a Cameragal she may have been feared as a witch. (The Cameragal had some reputation for witchcraft.) My own suspicion is that we have simply run into historians' good or bad luck, however you choose to look at it, in that the woman who emerges most vividly from the documentation we happen to have is, simply, atypical—a natural-born loner, a natural-born rebel. That exaggeratedly erect carriage, together with the masculine nose ornament and the extreme touchiness, look like direct appropriations from the male repertoire of symbols of social domination. Even when she undertook what might be in another woman the conventional role of protecting the weapons and the honour of her man, she did so flamboyantly, as in the ferocious scene she made at the governor's house when Baneelon yielded up his spears. Making her assault on the crumpled girl at the surgeon's house, she was inhibited neither by the alien location nor by her scandalised British audience: she simply attacked. She quietened only when Baneelon slapped her, presumably acknowledging in this situation his authority to do so.

Phillip, deeply shocked by the violence Baneelon habitually used against her, was equally shocked by Barangaroo's violence in the canoe-wrecking scene, and was bewildered to know 'what inducement this woman could have had to do an act she must have known would be followed by a severe beating?' Time and again we watch her behaving as provocatively as she was able, staging scenes and engaging in direct aggression not only against women, but against men, including British men: think of the flogger flogged, and the guard, the surgeons, the governor himself, defied on their home ground.

Presumably Baneelon liked a fierce woman: one who could challenge and match his own volatile temper. He must also have valued her beauty, as did other men. He was ready to make concessions to her: it is likely that she was ailing when he withdrew from a planned sortie to Norfolk Island in the company of its new lieutenant-governor Philip King in mid-October 1791 (we do not know the date of her death). What I admire is her intransigence. Despite the massive pressures brought to bear upon her by her warrior society, Barangaroo always remained her own woman.

NOVEMBER–DECEMBER 1791
TENCH GOES HOME

On 18 December 1791 Watkin Tench finished his tour of duty and embarked with most of his fellow marines on the *Gorgon*, bound for England. Great things were happening in the world. The French were still up to mischief but wreaking most of it at home, with their king losing his liberty and soon to lose his head. Tench himself would lose his liberty to them three years hence, taken captive after a battle at sea, but in those final months of 1791 his concerns remained strenuously local. He made two more expeditions with his friend Dawes, commenting time and again on the remarkable kindness of the Australians met along the way, and we wonder how much that kindness had to do with the sense and sensibility of the two young explorers. He is brief and regretful on the trouble with Boladeree, and careful to record other gratuitous acts of kindness by Australians close around Sydney. But with the arrival of the *Gorgon* on 21 September, he knew his departure was imminent. His last gift to us is his survey of the colony which had consumed four years of his young manhood.

He had come to view the settlement with a disillusioned eye. Sydney Town's urban pretensions were dead: now it was no more than a depot for stores. He was not much more sanguine about Parramatta, or 'Rose Hill', as he still preferred to call it. Some 'petty erections' might masquerade as public buildings, but the so-called 'town' was no more than a few hundred hovels built of twigs and mud. Despite the pathetic actuality, dreams remained huge: 'We feel consequential enough already to talk of a treasury, an admiralty, a public library, and many other edifices, which are to form part of a magnificent square.' And the settlement was expanding physically: with the promise of free land and the financial cushion of accumulated back pay to sustain them, sixty or so marines had elected to stay on in the colony as settlers, most of them, Tench thought, because of 'infatuated affection' for female convicts. He hoped they wouldn't regret their decision, and was sure that they would.

He also thought local estimations of agricultural yields to be inflated. Both soil and climate remained unfriendly, with even the hardy Indian maize not cropping reliably. Too many settlers lacked both the skills and the steady work habits to make farmers, and even experienced men were finding the soils and the seasons baffling. And the most promising and ambitious cultivator, with four convicts in his service, had decided to specialise in wine and tobacco, which Tench thought were not the most desirable products for a struggling colony.

Tench summed up the harshness of the new land in a near-biblical flourish: 'He who looks forward to eat grapes of his own vine; and to sit under the shade of his own fig-tree, must labour in every country: here he must exert more than ordinary activity.'

The human scene was no more encouraging. In church on the eve of his departure, Tench carefully scanned the 'several hundred convicts…present, the majority of whom I thought looked the most miserable beings in the shape of humanity, I ever beheld...they appeared to be worn down by fatigue'. He lamented the lack of a sense of community: from the first days of settlement convicts and soldiers had stolen from one another, and from the government stores as well, and they continued to steal. No community, and no compassion either: when the Second Fleet was arriving from mid-1790 and discharging its dreadful cargo of sick and decrepit convicts, dying men had their bread and their share in a blanket snatched from them by their stronger fellows. Even at Rose Hill, where long cohabitation and communal work should have generated solidarity, theft was chronic. Men returning to their miserable huts after a long day's work might find their rations pillaged, so hunger was added to exhaustion. The spread of settlement had decreased physical security: now the more intrepid settlers were living in solitary huts or scattered hamlets, vulnerable to attack from both unreconciled Australians and the dangerous new tribe of convicts-turned-bushrangers. Sickness continued rife. A couple of weeks before he embarked Tench took a medical inventory, and found 382 people listed as sick and twenty-five men and two children dead the previous month from a 'putrid fever'.

Perhaps Tench was looking too hard. In such circumstances improvement has to be measured in small things. Collins had been delighted to record that a few days before Christmas in 1789 Mr Dodd, the highly efficient superintendent at Rose Hill, sent a cabbage down to Sydney which weighed not much under fifteen kilos, with celebrations and congratulations all round. Tench was leaving a place where a simplified caricature of British civilisation had been set down on the edge of a wilderness: a caste system of officers and gentlemen, soldiers, free settlers, convict men and convict women. It would take time for that skeleton structure to develop a natural vital substance. Collins farewelled the marine contingent thus: 'On board the *Gorgon* were embarked the marines who came from England on the first ships, as valuable a corps as any in His Majesty's service...They were quitting a country in which they had opened and smoothed the way for their successors and from which, whatever benefit might hereafter be derived, must be derived by those who had the easy task of treading in paths previously and painfully formed by them.' His statement stands as a fair epitaph for Tench and his fellows.

It is easy to be so seduced by Tench's generosity of spirit as to think it was universal in application. It was not. For example, he seems to have talked little with subordinates. When Marine Private Jonathan Easty referred to 'Captain Tench', as he occasionally did, he did so with antiseptic impersonality. From Easty's text we would think there were no interactions between ranks beyond orders crisply delivered and swiftly obeyed. Could such social distance really have been sustained in the messiness of camp life, or the necessary intimacies of military and exploratory expeditions? On the evidence we have, it seems it was—except when the subordinates were drunk, which they quite often were. Then hard words might be spoken, and paid for in lashes. Keeping the skeleton of hierarchy bone-hard was a political necessity if the colony were to survive, but it was also a habit of mind.

Nor did Tench speak with convicts, unless they happened to provide diverting anecdotal material. He took convict executions easily, noting the death by hanging within a month of landfall of 'Thomas Barrett, an old and desperate offender who died with that hardy spirit which too often is found in the worst and most abandoned class of men' only in passing. The next convict execution, in May, also failed to move him, because the sufferer, 'a very young man', 'met his fate with a hardiness and insensibility which the grossest ignorance and the most deplorable want of feeling alone could supply'. It was salutary remorse Tench wanted, and in June he got it. Two more men were hanged; they acknowledged 'the justice of their fates'; and Tench's pen took tender fire. He cited in full the text of the letter twenty-year-old Samuel Peyton had a friend write to Samuel's mother. It was signed 'from your unhappy dying son', and oozes with elevated sentiment, and we wonder, cynically, whether young Peyton had his letter concocted in a last-ditch hope of a reprieve, which could sometimes happen after a dramatic display of remorse. We also have to suspect that Tench might be moved by an individual tragedy, but not by the general convict condition.

A final example of his perspective on hierarchy in this convict society is drawn from his last month in the colony, November 1791, when he was making his final rounds before taking ship to England. It was that frightening month of November at Rose Hill, with 382 sick and the 'hospital', two long thatched sheds, holding only two hundred people. Half of the invalids must have lain alone in their huts, but four hospital mattresses had been allotted to 'a few of the Chinese travellers', as Tench gaily dubbed them, now under arrest. Twenty Irish convicts and a pregnant woman had fled the colony early in the month in a dash for 'China', which they had been persuaded lay only a hundred miles away to the north. They thought they could walk there, sustaining themselves with shellfish gathered along the way. The old fantasy was still compelling: there would be a river, and on the other side a copper-coloured people who would receive them kindly and treat them well. (In this racial fantasy it is the white men, not the coloured, who are cruel.) They had suffered the slave-trade horrors of passage in the Second Fleet, and now there was only labour, starvation and death to look forward to. Who would not fear dying in that desolate place? Why not try for 'China'?

They found only the grey, death-haunted bush. One man died

of exhaustion on the third day out. Then natives attacked, killing another man and wounding others. There was no food: only hunger, terror, death. Over the next days some came tottering back, found by people from the camp or stumbling in alone, and the bones of others would be discovered from time to time. Tench's response reveals how different his sensibility is from ours. He talks with four of these desolate creatures, lying on their hospital mattresses, waiting for their floggings, and makes them the butt of an Irish joke.

When he visited the 'Chinese travellers' Tench knew he would be leaving for home in a matter of days, but he drew no comparisons between his situation and theirs. Always tender to abstract notions of 'liberty', his intuitive sympathy failed when he considered the convict condition, foundering on the rocks of convention and caste.

As we would expect, Tench saved his most important subject for the last: his attempt at a scientific description of the Australians. Baneelon had obligingly allowed himself to be measured; now we know the girth of his thigh, his leg at the small, his belly. Tench describes the precise texture of Australian hair, approves the typical Australian profile, deplores the typical Australian smell. It is a dutiful account, but it lacks his usual flair—until he begins to celebrate those 'large black eyes' with their 'long sweepy lashes', and suddenly a girl looks shyly from the page. It is here, on the verge of leaving forever, that he at last tells us about the girl Gooreedeeana and her gentle beauty.

He briskly reverts to duty by raising the key British question to determine the Australians' level of civility: do these people believe in a superior invisible power? He concludes (strenuously massaging the evidence) that they do. He acknowledges that as a race they stand low on the scale of savagery: although 'they may perhaps dispute the right of precedency with the Hottentots or the shivering tribes who inhabit the shores of Magellan', they are deficient in those twin signs of civility, the wearing of clothes and the cultivation of the earth. He sums up, with the awkwardness pomposity always imposes on him: 'A less enlightened state we shall exclaim can hardly exist.'

Then he abandons puffy generalisation for accounts of individuals, and the text takes fire. He memorialises the kindness of Arabanoo, the wit of Baneelon, the steady affability of Colbee. He celebrates the ingenuity of Australian tools and Australian skill in using them. He is baffled as to why their curiosity is so uneven—why they care nothing for the tools and techniques of farming and building—but he acknowledges their expertise in everything to do with the hunt or with battle, and he notes that while they lack surgeons their wounds heal clean and fast. As to character: while he cannot defend 'their levity, their fickleness, their passionate extravagance of character', he insists on their loyalty, especially to those British they have cause to love, and we think that Tench was among them.

He admits finding their songs tedious and their dances alarming, but vehemently defends Australians on another key issue for the British, their honourable conduct in war: 'Unlike all other Indians, they never carry out operations at night, or seek to destroy by ambush and surprise.' Pursuing the comparison with American Indians, viewed by the British as singularly treacherous, Tench lauds the Australians' 'ardent fearless character [which] seeks fair and open combat only', so conveniently forgetting those stealthy midnight assassinations.

There were some things about Australian society he did not see. Australian structures of thought, of religion, of deference and hierarchy, quite escaped him. He never grasped the respect owed to age or accumulated ritual experience. And he could not see British society at all. He did not think to contrast the freedom and the material equality achieved by Australians living around Sydney Cove against the oppression, inequality and unrelenting toil he had just been describing in his own society, where order was sustained by the whip, and the sanctity of property required that some of his country-men should die by the noose to preserve it.

The lack of fit between these visions is beautifully if inadvertently dramatised in the sketch *Mr White, Harris and Laing with a party of soldiers*, probably by the hand of the prolific 'Port Jackson Painter' (reproduced in the plate section). To the left, three tall, behatted Britishers, every bit of their bodies covered except their hands and faces, muskets in hand, stand around naked Australians, some of them connubially entwined, lounging on the grass around a fire. To the right an Australian warrior, identified in a pencilled note as 'Colebee' (not 'our' Colbee but a Botany Bay warrior of the same name) is sitting peaceably on a log, spear propped beside him, gazing off slightly to the right. Meanwhile a dozen red-coated marines are sweating their way in their hot, tight uniforms through close-order drill behind the strict example of their sergeant. They are so tight packed, so rigid, that they look like a line of cardboard cut-outs, ready to topple at a breath.

Thanks to Tench's eager eye and honest pen, I think we can sometimes glimpse the view from the log.

PHILLIP GOES HOME

Unlike the Australians they saw moving freely among them, convicts had to endure a strict regime of physical labour, and suffer the 'cruel discipline' of the 'merciless wretches' who were their supervisors. There could be no personal dignity, no blow-for-blow retaliation for them. Now more were choosing the hardship and the freedom of the bush, fleeing the settlement not in search of a phantom 'China', but to join the bushrangers; the runaways who occasionally co-operated with the 'wild' Australians and participated in their depredations.

Hunger was securely alleviated only in July 1792, six months before Phillip's departure, first with the arrival of the *Atlantic* from Calcutta, and then the *Britannia* from London, with two more store ships in her wake. By the end of August rations had been restored to a bare adequacy, and Richard Atkins, newly arrived and deeply shocked by the miserable condition of the people ('the convicts dying very fast, merely through want of nourishment…O shame, shame') soon noticed a major drop in the crime rate. By October the maize crop was beginning to yield, and the ships continued to arrive. Their arrival brought not only supplies but opportunity for a new crime: men plundered each others' hidden stores of money to buy their passage back to England.

Through all Phillip's time in office the colony's suffering was largely due to the neglect of the colonial authorities. As David Collins had observed, recording yet another downward adjustment of the rations:

> It was impossible to make the deduction without reflecting that the established ration would have been adequate to every want; the pleas of hunger could not have been advanced as the motive and excuse for thefts; and disease would not have met so powerful an ally in its ravages among the debilitated and emaciated objects which the gaols had crowded into transports, and the transports had landed in these settlements.

The case of the *Pitt*, arriving in February 1792, three months after the departure of Tench and his marines, is exemplary of the mix of neglect, cheese-paring and stupidity inflicted on the colony. Assuming the colony to be adequately supplied with flour, she had brought only salt provisions for her cargo of more than 350 convicts, many of them ill. To find the space to install the fully constructed frame of a forty-ton vessel (at last their masters had heard the colonists' call for another workhorse ship) she had simply left behind 'all the Clothing, Stores and some Provisions, which were intended to be sent in her, except for a few Shoes, and some Leather'. David Collins' fury was only lightly disguised as sarcasm as he recounted the series of accidents which had provided the colony with a single ship's carpenter capable of masquerading as a qualified shipwright long enough to turn the frame into a useable ship:

> A person who came out to this country in the capacity of a carpenter's mate on board the *Sirius*, having been left behind when

that vessel sailed for England, offered his services to put together the vessel that arrived in frame on the *Pitt*; and being deemed sufficiently qualified as a shipwright, he was engaged at two shillings per diem and his provisions to set her up. Her keel was accordingly laid down on blocks placed for the purpose near the landing-place on the east side.

Then—this equable man is beginning to snarl—'as this person was the only shipwright in the colony, the vessel would have much sooner rendered the services which were required of her' (replacing the indispensable *Supply*) 'had she been put together, coppered, and sent out manned and officered from England; by these means too the colony would have received many articles which were of necessity shut out of the *Pitt* to make room for her stowage'.

This was mismanagement to the point of malice. Even Phillip's self-command must have faltered. But he refused to despair, continuing to write optimistic letters to Sir Joseph Banks and Lord Sydney advising them to ignore ill reports of the colony, and enclosing an independent report 'made by a man who was bred a Gardener' on the great potential of the soil of the colony. He also included elegantly selective images which evoked a little paradise of kine and vine: 'The few cattle we have grow exceedingly fat…all our fruit trees thrive well, and I have this year gathered about three hundred pounds of very fine grapes.' Nor was the vision wholly illusory: Major Grose, arriving in March 1792 and the man who would succeed Phillip, could enthuse that instead of the rock he had been told to expect he found himself in an Eden, 'surrounded by gardens that flourish and produce fruit of every description', where all that could be desired was 'one ship freighted with corn and black cattle'. By September 1795, Elizabeth Macarthur was confiding to her friend Bridget Kingdon that, when the capture of a ship off the coast of Brazil had left them with no news from Europe for twelve months, many colonists 'firmly believed that a revolution or some national calamity had befallen Great Britain & believed that we should be left together to ourselves until things at home had resumed some degree of order'. Elizabeth then proceeded to so radiant an account of the productivity of the soil that we have to assume that the prospect of having to survive independent of the mother country's support did not much alarm her. A change indeed, over a mere seven years. Two months after that, in November 1795, the two bulls and four cows lost from the infant settlement in July 1788 were found again, multiplied to 'a fine herd upwards of forty in number'. Major Grose would have his black cattle after all.

By the last months of 1792, with his health failing fast, Phillip knew he must take ship for England. The colony he handed over to Grose would survive, even thrive, materially. But it would not be the society he had dreamed of. Along with the influx of newcomers and the amelioration of supply came the opportunity to subvert Phillip's conscientious democratisation of rations: Grose sought Phillip's official approval for a plan by which the *Britannia* would bring cattle and comforts for the men he commanded, the New South Wales Corps, beyond the 'reduced and unwholesome' rations available from the public store. True to his principles, Phillip refused his approval, but he could not prevent what became the first private enterprise in the colony. Grose also demanded that his officers be granted land, together with the convicts to work it. Again Phillip refused; there were already too few convicts to serve the public interest. But his vision would not prevail. The spirit of free enterprise and of faction had been imported into the colony along with the New South Wales Corps.

Grose initiated his revolution almost before Phillip's ship had cleared the heads. The military hierarchy took over the civil administration first at Parramatta, then at Sydney; on the second issue of rations after the governor's departure the convict ration was reduced vis-à-vis that issued to free men. Settlers began selling the breeding stock Phillip had freely given them to officers eager to establish their own herds. And Lieutenant-Governor Grose joyfully purchased 'seven thousand five hundred and ninety-seven gallons of (new American) spirits at four shillings and sixpence per gallon', as David Collins icily records, from an American ship which had put in to Sydney Harbour, as its master declared, merely for wood and water. The spirits were to be traded at the commissary. Soon spirits would become the new currency, and intoxication, even among convicts, rampant. Sydney also fought its first serious bushfire.

By the time of his leaving Phillip must also have known that his grand enterprise of civilising the Australians and integrating them into British economy and society would not succeed, not least because of the locals' stubborn refusal to see their condition as impoverished. But affection and hope prevailed over experience. When Phillip left for England he took with him his durable friend Baneelon and the 'good-tempered lively lad' Imeerawanyee, who had been living for much of the time in the governor's house: 'Two men,' Collins tells us, 'very much attached to his person; and who withstood at the moment of departure the united distress of their wives, and the dismal lamentations of their friends.' Imeerawanyee would die in that strange cold country. After three years there, Baneelon would return, to find his own country transformed.

DECEMBER 1793 AND AFTER
COLLINS GOES HOME

As early as the end of 1791 David Collins was being pressed by his family to come home on the *Gorgon* with Tench and his friends. Both family affection and family finances urgently required his presence. Collins had to explain to his father that he could not. Much as they longed to embrace him—much as he longed to embrace them—there were insurmountable objections. The first was formal: he had not been officially relieved of his post, which could only be done from England. The next two were personal. If he were to leave on the *Gorgon* he would have to take ship with Major Ross, and this he absolutely refused to do. 'I would not sail were wealth and honours to attend me when I landed,' he writes, and we are reminded how vast animosity can grow within the narrow confines of a colony. But love could grow there, too. The man who earlier had viewed Phillip with scepticism, especially for what he saw as his impetuous romanticism regarding the Australians, wrote to his father in October 1791: 'I could not reconcile it in my mind to leave Governor Phillip, with whom I have now lived so long that I am blended in every concern of his.'

Now Phillip was gone, along with the rest of his old comrades, and Collins was left to deal with new men and different ways. The officers of the New South Wales Corps were seizing every chance to enrich themselves collectively, individually, and often enough fraudulently. Collins had little to say in his journal about their doings, beyond noting their endless squabbles. Along with Phillip had gone some of his old compulsion to record. Now he was ready to accept some things as constant. He thought the convicts, apart from the few who had become effective farmers, remained hopelessly depraved, with no possibility of moral reform. If the more ignorant persisted in their fantasies of China-over-the-river despite the scarecrows that came tottering back with tales of companions starved or speared in the bush, the realists knew that escape by land was impossible and that the sea was the road to liberty. They were always stowing away on ships, to be discovered, or not discovered. Others, especially after William Bryant's brilliant getaway in 1791, made off in small boats. So many boats were being hijacked by late 1797, the year after Collins went home, that Governor Hunter had to order any boat left unguarded at night, or with oars, rudders, masts or sails on board, be burnt.

And now harder men were being dumped in Sydney, among them Irishmen shipped straight from rebellious Ireland to Botany Bay; men who thought of themselves as political prisoners, and who arrived and remained intractable. Collins had always despised the Irish. Back on 13 July 1791, he had taken pleasure reporting that 'Patrick Burn, a person employed to shoot for the commanding officer of the marine detachment, died…and the hut what he had lived in was burnt down in the night a few hours after his decease by the carelessness of the people, who were Irish and were sitting up with the corpse, which was with much difficulty saved from the flames, and not until it was much scorched'. Unstated: the mourners were not only Irish, but drunk. The tone is more condescending than outraged. Compare it with his reporting, admittedly at second hand, of a later incident in a maize field at a government farm in April 1798. Exciting rumours had been circulating among the convicts of French warships about to descend on the settlements, to destroy them, liberate the convicts and repatriate them to Europe and to freedom (so much for British patriotism). Collins reports:

> One refractory fellow, while working with a numerous gang in Toongabbie, threw down his hoe, advanced before the rest, and gave three cheers for liberty. This for a while seemed well-received; but a magistrate fortunately being at hand, the business was put an end to, by securing the advocate for liberty, tying him up in the field, and giving him a severe flogging.

A very physical response to a metaphysical cry made in a paddock at the edge of the world. (Note too Collins' confidence of the docility of the local representative of the law.) Later again, after an account of a bungled escape attempt in January 1798 which collapsed into desperate betrayals and abandonments as it unravelled:

> Here we find extreme ignorance, accompanied by great cunning, producing cruelty…Could it be imagined that at this day there was existing in a civilised, polished kingdom a race of beings (for they do not deserve the appellation of men) so extremely ignorant, and so little humanised as these were, compared with whom the naked savages of the mountains were an enlightened people?

We might think he was talking about the Australians. He was talking about the Irish.

These later sentiments are different in texture from those expressed in his first volume, which he had carried with him to

England in manuscript form at the end of 1796. That volume, along with its twelve bulky appendices, was published in 1798, but Collins was so dedicated to his annalist's task that he compiled a second volume from reports from the colony throughout the five-year governorship of his friend John Hunter, ending in 1800.

Collins' second volume appeared in 1802. It makes dreary reading. Even before he left the colony Collins thought disorder was increasing, with convicts once kept under proper control enjoying disgraceful liberties, and those who had served out their terms adding dangerously to the social turmoil. Some of the freed convicts had joined the soldiery, but, not having 'changed their principles with their condition', they continued to embroil themselves in shameful plots and assaults. Sexual offences were becoming frequent and increasingly brutal, with gang rape now so common despite savage punishments (one man was sentenced to one thousand lashes), that a cant term, which the discreet Collins does not disclose, had been coined to further humiliate the victims. And the colony was drenched in drink: even the Sabbath, when the licensed public houses were kept closed during the hours of worship, was commonly spent 'in every abominable act of dissipation', and illicit stills were sprouting everywhere. When found they were immediately destroyed, 'to the great regret of the owners, who from a bushel of wheat worth at the public store ten shillings distilled a gallon of new and poisonous spirit, which they retailed directly from the still at five shillings per quart bottle'. With a chronically thirsty public and that profit margin, we can assume the stills would keep sprouting. And already the New South Wales government was finding itself implicated in less-than-desirable activities. Black Caesar, a famous convict, repeat escapee and local legend, was loose in the bush again, with armed men about him. (The government had lost its monopoly over the possession of guns.) Black Caesar had sent a formal defiance to the custodians of law and order, saying 'that he would neither come in, nor suffer himself to be taken alive'. It had become essential to put an end to his dangerously glamorous career. Accordingly, 'notice was…given, that whoever should secure and bring him in with his arms should receive a reward'. The reward nominated was five gallons of spirits.

Civilisation itself seemed to be dropping away. The terror of irreversible disorder which had haunted Phillip haunted later governors, too. They responded, as he had, by elaborating punishments. In November 1796 five men, some of them convicts, some soldiers, were hanged, four for theft from the public stores, and one, Francis Morgan, for wilful murder. The court, now under the direction of Richard Atkins, the new judge-advocate, distinguished between the capital offences by embellishing the murderer's penalty. His corpse was hung in chains on the tiny island the British called Pinchgut because they used it as a place of exile on minimal rations.

The whites took the gruesome tableau lightly, with 'many', Collins says regretfully, 'inclined to make a jest of it'. The Australians were appalled: by the corpse, 'his clothes shaking in the wind, the creaking of his irons'; by their fear that this ghost-creature 'might have the power of taking hold of them by the throat'—and also, I think, by horror of a people who could devise and inflict so barbarous a punishment, and so casually desecrate a whole location. Thereafter they shunned the island where the blackening corpse hung, 'which, until this time, had ever been a favourite place of resort'.

Governor Hunter's court would mete out more obscene posthumous punishments. In 1799 a missionary gentleman, fled for his life from the ungrateful savages of Tahiti, was murdered by British savages in Australia when his skull was split by a settler, in collusion with a soldier and his wife, to extinguish a ten-pound debt.

All three were hanged at the site of the crime, the house of iniquity pulled down and burnt, and the corpses of the men hung in chains before the ruins. The woman's body was awarded a worse fate. It was handed over to the surgeons for dissection. We are left to wonder how John White, returned to England five years before, would have responded to that.

Although the time of imposed scarcity was over, convicts still in servitude were approaching an Australian insouciance regarding clothing: Collins was told that during the harvest of 1798 'several gangs were seen labouring in the fields, as free of clothing of any kind as the savages of the country'. Reading, we wonder whether 'the civilising process' was not beginning to reverse itself, with Australian example silently subverting British complacencies regarding the moral virtues of submission, modesty, property, decent housing and unremitting toil. The Australians' sociability and their obvious preference for exciting pursuits like fishing or hunting or fighting must have been a siren song for Europeans whose lives had been spent not tilling fields, labouring for the morrow and internalising the work ethic but hunting and gathering in the London jungle. Taking to the bush might not have seemed so great a step for them. The convict taste for binge drinking, along with their improvident consumption of rations, with seven days' rations gobbled in two and then living by scavenging, begging or borrowing until the next issue, suggests that many of these British men had never learnt the practised frugalities of the working poor, but had lived by their wits, consuming resources as they found them. Could they have been coming to share Botany Bay Colbee's 'demoralised' view from the log?

This is as good a time as any to discuss the elusive issue of 'racism'. The force and incidence of racism imported by the First Fleeters is impossible to measure with any confidence. Consider the range of attitudes even within the few members of the officer caste we have investigated. Consider also the thinness of what we can discover of convict attitudes to Australians. To some convicts, possibly to many, they were animals, to be pillaged and punished at will. Australian men responded with violence, and the dread of native attack circumscribed convict freedom more effectively than any musket-bearing guard, with a pleasurable task beyond the confines of the settlement turning in an instant into fatal terror. Later, convicts would see Australian hostages treated like pampered gentlefolk; after the official reconciliation of the last months of 1790 they had to watch as passing savages were welcomed into the governor's house and fed in the governor's yard, while the British-born went hungry, and worked under the threat of the lash.

The gentleman convict Thomas Watling gives literate expression to what must have been common grievances. Watling was a forger who, after taking an unauthorised vacation in Capetown on the voyage out, was recaptured and taken on to Sydney in October 1792. He remained in the colony until Governor Hunter pardoned him in 1797, when he had served eight years of his fourteen-year sentence. During his convict years he served as draughtsman and illustrator to several amateur natural scientists, among them Surgeon John White, David Collins and Hunter himself. He wrote dutifully to his loyal aunt back in Dumfries, describing the landscape, the weather, and the local animal life: the dearth of quadrupeds, the abundance of highly coloured birds and fish.

Then he moved on to the local humans. He disliked them heartily. He thought them 'in general very straight and slim, but extremely ill-featured; and in my opinion the women more so than the men'. (Women's appearance and conduct were commonly taken to be an index of civility.) As for their natures: 'Irascibility, ferocity, cunning, treachery, revenge, filth and immodesty are strikingly their dark characteristics,' while their virtues, if any, 'are so far from conspicuous, that I have not, as yet, been able to discern them'— although he does allow they were not cannibals, and were good mimics. He also grants they are attracted to the visual arts: 'The natives are extremely fond of painting, and often sit hours by me when at work.' Clearly, a few of the things these peculiar pale people did were worth studying.

Then we come to the root of his anger. Watling was writing in mid-1793. The Australians had been living in and around the settlements for months, and the one-time gentleman Watling had to watch while his betters pampered these sorry creatures:

> Our governors, for they all are such, have carried philosophy, I do not say religion, to such a pitch of refinement as is surprising. Any of these savages are allowed…a freeman's ration of provision for their idleness. They are bedecked at times, with dress which they make away with at the first opportunity, preferring the originality of nature; and they are treated with the most singular tenderness.

Meanwhile Watling and his fellow-convicts were left ill-clad, half-starved, and held to endless labour.

So says Watling, and he must have spoken for many others. Yet we know, almost by accident, that some convicts always responded differently. It is difficult to imagine the narrowness of convict life in those early years, with boredom a more savage enemy than want. With near-starvation chronic, I think it was the hopelessness embedded in the boredom which made the physical deprivation intolerable; that the wild schemes of 'walking to China' were concocted in response to the social and psychological anomie of convict life. Other episodes speak to the same motivation, like the Great Goldmine Scam Collins outlines: a beguiling way of beguiling the time by the exercise of old tricks, even with exposure and punishment inevitable. I also suspect the tireless internecine thieving was as much sport as necessity. But others sought escape, psychological or physical, by seeking the company of Australians. We remember those 'large parties of convicts of both sexes' Collins mentions regularly visiting their Australian friends as early as July of 1788. This suggests both that convict life was rather less constricted than the formal regulations implied, and that, as a category, convicts did not bear animus towards the locals. Given the swift and early spread of venereal disease among the native population we have to assume sex was one of the attractions of the social exchanges, but so, presumably, were the singing and dancing and the general conviviality of the Australian camp. Expressive good humour was a rare commodity in early convict Australia.

Later, after the 'coming in', the officers' narratives naturally focused on their own interactions with the natives, but they still offer the occasional snapshot of convivial social relationships, even friendships, between particular convicts and particular Australians, like the mysterious convict woman in men's dress taking refuge with Baneelon's people out at the point, or the Australians who regularly caroused in the military barracks of an evening.

Collins had made his sour remark about wasting time and energy on 'amusing ourselves with those children of ignorance' immediately after the governor's spearing, when Phillip's conciliatory policy seemed to lie in tatters. When the local Australians decided to 'come in' to Sydney Town, Phillip's persistence seemed vindicated, but the suddenness of their change of heart had not impressed Collins, and their exuberant behaviour once in the town only added to his dismay.

Surely the convicts posed enough threats to order, without importing more trouble?

Over the years, however, we watch a moving transformation as Collins, watching, and reflecting on what he was watching, becomes our best and most sensitive informant on Australian ways of life and thought, especially in matters of justice and rights. Over those years (and it did take years) Collins became increasingly sensitive to indicators of cultural habits of mind, in time surpassing, for example, Tench, whose swift sympathy for individuals could sometimes blind him to systematic cultural differences.

unbreached, especially on conceptual matters. Remember, too, the difficulty of translating layered cultural meanings and emotions into words even for the native speaker. Nonetheless, Collins doggedly recorded the details of his watching, attaching his devoted observations of Australian conduct as those twelve appendices to his already weighty narrative of events in the British colony. And once again we are made aware of the vulnerability of what have become for us indispensable historical materials. His publisher, faced with that huge work, and with the first spate of curiosity regarding Australia already waning, decided nonetheless to include the appendices.

One example of both the riches and the limitations: Collins provided a detailed account of a great male puberty ceremony, along with an elaborate sequence of drawings. He tells us that the ceremony was performed in late summer every four years: in February 1791, and again in February 1795, when he had watched it. His account is as detailed as a film's shooting-script. He hazards guesses as to possible representations ('now they are dingoes, now kangaroos'); he recognises enactments of the capture, terrorising and then comforting of the juvenile stars; he shows us the boys after their teeth have been knocked out, blood drying on their breasts and magically transformed into men, tearing back into the town driving gleefully screaming men, women and children before them. But what we are most aware of as we read is that we, like Collins, are blind and must be blind to much of what is going on before our eyes. The deeper symbolism of movement, gesture, sequence and regalia remained obscure to him, as it does to us. Here is Collins' conclusion regarding this particular ceremony, which holds for the whole of his tenacious investigations into the Australian world of the sacred: 'For its import I could discover very little. I made much inquiry; but could never obtain any other answer, than that it was very good; that the boys would now become brave men; that they would see well, and fight well.' And that was all.

Where Judge-Advocate Collins excelled was in his recording and analysis of the working of tribal law. At first he had thought the Australians savages, the playthings of passion whose only law was violence. Then, as he watched graduated degrees of violence being visited on different offenders, he realised that 'law'—a system of ranked punishment for ranked social transgressions—was indeed controlling the action. He still suspected the action was essentially expressive and arbitrary: a collective venting of emotion. And then, with more watching and longer reflection, he began to see the principles ordering the violence.

His enlightenment came through watching warriors facing the clubs and spears of tribal justice. As he watched—as he marvelled at their courage—he came to realise that these men lived under a code of honour as rigorous as any he knew: a code informed by what must have seemed to him as an educated English gentleman a classic stoicism. Towards the end of December in 1793 Collins described the execution of a punishment for murder in terms so admiring it deserves quoting in full:

> The natives who lived around Sydney appeared to place the greatest confidence in us, choosing a clear spot between the town and the brickfield for the performance of any of their rites and ceremonies; and for three evenings the town had been amused with one of their spectacles, which might have been properly denominated a tragedy, for it was attended by a great effusion of blood. It appeared from the best account we could procure, that one or more murders having been committed in the night, the assassins, who were immediately known, were compelled, according to the custom of the country, to meet the relations of the

deceased, who were to avenge their deaths by throwing spears, and drawing blood for blood. One native of the tribe of Cammeray [Cameragal], a very fine fellow named Carradah, who stabbed another in the night, but not mortally, was obliged to stand for two evenings exposed to the spears not only of the man whom he had wounded, but of several other natives. He was suffered indeed to cover himself with a bark shield, and behaved with the greatest courage and resolution. Whether his principal adversary (the wounded man) found that he possessed too much defensive skill to admit of his wounding him, or whether it was a necessary part of his punishment, was not known with any certainty; but on the second day that Carradah had been opposed to him and his party, after having received several of their spears on his shield, without sustaining any injury, he suffered the other to pin his left arm (below the elbow) to his side, without making any resistance; prevented, perhaps, by the uplifted spears of the other natives, who could have easily destroyed him, by throwing at him from different directions, Carradah stood, for some time after this, defending himself, although wounded in the arm which held the shield, until his adversaries had not a whole spear left, and had retired to collect the fragments and piece them together. On his sitting down his left hand appeared to be very much convulsed, and Mr. White was of the opinion that the spear had pierced one of the nerves. The business was renewed when they had repaired their weapons, and the fray appeared to be general, men, women, and children mingling in it, giving and receiving many severe wounds, until night put an end to their warfare.

Collins also notes that Carradah 'had not entirely expiated his offence, having yet another trial to undergo from some natives who had been prevented by absence from joining in the ceremonies of that evening'.

Collins was profoundly impressed, as anyone would be. But he was bewildered by the attitude of all combatants during and after these ritualised combats:

> What rendered this sort of contest as unaccountable as it was extraordinary was, that friendship and alliance were known to subsist between several that were opposed to each other, who fought with all the ardour of bitterest enemies, and who, though wounded, pronounced the party by whom they had been hurt to be good, and brave, and their friends.

The words we need here are not only 'good' and 'brave' and 'friend', but 'trial', and 'expiation', and 'offence'. It is clear that male courage and skill were being tested; that expiation would not be achieved until all those wronged had engaged with the offender; that while the offence was individual, retaliation was tribal. It is also clear that the combat was unequal, and was meant to be—several against one. Blood was necessary, but not death. How much blood? A single wound, even a crippled hand, was not sufficient to purge Carradah's offence. It seems there was no fixed penalty beyond that which was marked by the bystanders' collective decision to join the combat…and then, when all involved considered honour and justice to be satisfied, to desist. The degree of injury—above all, whether it would include death—would be decided in the course of the combat.

What Collins is showing us is a contest which echoes medieval European trials by ordeal, with the amount of retributive justice decided not by the offended parties, although they are its instrument, but by some higher source, whose judgment is revealed by the course of the action, which also signals that the offence is fully purged. Despite the yells, the blood, the violence, we are watching law at work.

Paradoxically, it was Collins' developing sensitivity to the web of invisible rules within which Australians lived which would lead him to repudiate his one-time friend Baneelon, who, forced to inhabit the void between two worlds, fetched up rejecting the laws of both. Collins would finally dismiss him simply, decisively, as a 'savage'.

Increased understanding does not necessarily entail tolerant acceptance. Within three years of his departure Phillip's dream of a unitary commonwealth of whites and blacks living peaceably under British law was dead, as 'wild' Australians plundered the new settlers along the Hawkesbury and around Parramatta, and settlers and soldiers took horrible revenge. Now, with settlers and freed convicts encroaching into new areas, and with some recovery among local populations after the smallpox deaths, the contest for the land was becoming explicit. In August 1794 there were seventy settlers on the Hawkesbury flood plains. Ten months later there were close to five hundred. The spring of that year saw the first murderous 'dispersals' of the original inhabitants which were to scar our shared history.

Collins sketched an early episode which prefigured many others. A settler and his servant had been 'nearly murdered in their hut' in a surprise attack. A few days later there was another raid, the raiders this time carrying off their victims' 'clothes, provisions and whatever else they could lay their hands on'. Then 'the sufferers collected what arms they could, and following them, seven or eight of the plunderers were killed on the spot'.

Collins knew the injustice of this vigilante 'justice'. He knew where the blame lay:

> Whatever the settlers had suffered was entirely brought on them by their own misconduct: there was not a doubt but many natives had been wantonly fired upon; and their children, after the flight of the parents, have fallen into the settlers' hands, they have been detained at their huts, notwithstanding the earnest entreaties of the parents for their return.

He would put it more economically and depressively a year later in a letter to a friend recently returned to England: 'We have little or no news. The natives at the Hawkesbury are murdering the settlers. Abbot and MacKellar with Co. soldiers are in turn murdering the natives (but it cannot be avoided...)' As early as the autumn of 1795 Collins was ready to talk of 'an open war' along the Hawkesbury between Australians and settlers. Australian families were carrying out what look very like organised raids on the ripening maize. When word was received that a settler and a free labourer had been killed, troops were sent from Parramatta 'with instructions to destroy as many as they could meet with of the wood tribe (Be-dia-gal); and, in the hope of striking terror, to erect gibbets in different places, whereupon the bodies of all they might kill were to be hung'. Black bodies hanging in the trees would mark the whites' territory. We have come a long way from Phillip's theatrical headhunt.

In the event the soldiers found no bodies, which had probably been carried away by comrades. They captured only one man—a 'cripple', they said—five women and some children. The man managed to escape, but one of the women had a child at the breast, and the baby, wounded when the mother took a musket ball through the shoulder, died. Another of the captured women went into labour and was delivered of a boy-child, who also died.

So the sinister dance began. When the soldiers withdrew a group of Australians attacked an isolated farm, and in accordance with their take-no-prisoners practice on revenge-raids, slaughtered the settler along with 'a very fine child', and severely wounded the wife before she managed to hide. From that time on soldiers were permanently stationed among the settlers. With December came a freak ice-storm—Collins reports that a day after the storm unmelted fragments were up to twenty centimetres long, and at least two fingers thick—and obliterated the disputed crops anyway.

By early 1796, Collins' last year in the colony, firearms had been issued to remote settlers. While it remained forbidden to fire at Australians 'wantonly', Hunter ruled that the settlers must come to each others' aid when there was risk of an attack. By that act vigilantism was licensed.

Collins' attitudes were also hardening. He had believed that selected Australians could be tolerated inside the settlements and even make themselves useful in small ways, because inside the settlements the violence was typically between whites, or—if between blacks—battles between rival clans which the colonists treated much as we do football matches, if with less understanding of the rules. Once back in England, with the whites reporting to him ignorant of the political and social rivalries animating these clashes and therefore treating them as anarchic outbursts of violence, Collins' views darkened, especially as he heard evil news of the doings of one-time Australian friends.

In May 1797 a young Australian woman raised in the colony was first shockingly beaten by her husband, a man well known to Collins and also raised in the colony, and then speared to death by Colbee, who had participated in the beating. In August 1798 Baneelon's sister Warreweer, wife to his own namesake 'Collins', was found murdered in what was probably a payback killing. Colbee's kinsman Nanbaree had also been badly speared, and in the flurry of retaliatory violence which followed Colbee and Baneelon were in the forefront of the avengers. Baneelon had been seriously wounded—by treachery, Collins insisted—only to be wounded again in a mass battle.

The killing venom of these battles persuaded Collins, or perhaps only his informants, whose views he presumably felt bound to reproduce, that the whole land was thinly populated because of the

Australian taste for this kind of violence, reinforced by casual resort to abortion and infanticide: that is, that these people's defects were chronic, innate, and cultural. Knowing, as Collins could not, how comprehensively destabilising the British presence was of the Australian social order, we wonder whether the radical reduction in resources and the imbalances of tribal power effected by that presence had exacerbated normally tempered conflict to fatality.

In the course of his second volume Collins set down his final judgment. He knew how possessive Baneelon's people were of their access to the settlement and their special relations with the whites; how determined they were to repel other tribes' efforts to establish an equivalent intimacy. They knew the value of what they enjoyed. Nonetheless, he lamented that they displayed not the least gratitude to their benefactors, nor did their jealous grip on privileges bind them to white ways. At last he was to ready to declare them incorrigible by nature, quite lacking the sense of reciprocity essential in a civil society. He writes:

> although they lived among the inhabitants of the different settle-
> ments, were kindly treated, fed and often clothed, yet they were
> never found to possess the smallest degree of gratitude for such
> favours. It is an extraordinary fact that even their children, who
> had been bred up among the white people, and who, from being
> accustomed to follow their manner of living, might be supposed to
> ill relish the lives of their parents, when grown up, have quitted
> their comfortable abodes, females as well as males, and taken to
> the same mode of savage living, where the supply of food was
> often precarious, their comforts not to be called such, and their
> lives perpetually in danger.

We see a naked Boorong paddling away in her canoe, and a lad named Nanbaree running through the scrub to warn his friend Boladeree that the soldiers were after him.

With increasingly bloody clashes over land, and with no end to the conflict in sight, Collins came to think that Phillip's whole experiment in tolerance, continued in wizened form by Hunter and later by King, was mistaken, being derived from a wrong reading of the Australian character. His conclusion: 'Could it have been foreseen that this was their natural temper, it would have been wiser to have kept them at a distance, and in fear, which might have been effected without so much of the severity which their conduct has sometimes compelled him to exercise towards them.'

In retrospect we can see as Collins could not that different understandings of law placed a giant, invisible stumbling block in the way of peace between the two peoples. Three months after Collins left the colony, in December 1796, there was an event which distilled his disillusionment with 'the savage inhabitants of the country, [who] instead of losing any part of their native ferocity of manners by an intercourse with the Europeans among whom they dwelt, seem rather to delight in exhibiting themselves as monsters of the greatest cruelty, devoid of reason, and guided solely by the impulse of the worst passions'. A little girl estimated to be six or seven years old had been 'rescued' from the running battles along the Hawkesbury River. The British had shot both her parents and most of her kin in a reprisal raid, but someone scooped up the child and took her back to Sydney to be cared for, where she, as Collins recorded with no trace of irony, 'being a well-disposed child, soon became a great favourite with her protectors'. Some time later her body was found 'in the woods near the governor's house...speared in several places, and with both the arms cut off'. Her British protectors gathered the poor remains, gave them a Christian burial, and lamented the savagery of her compatriots.

Collins thought the motive was jealousy: 'As she belonged to a tribe of natives that was hostile to the Sydney people, they could not admit of her partaking in those pleasures and comforts which they derived from their residency among the colonists, and therefore inhumanly put her out of the way.' It may have been a payback killing for some earlier offence. Her sex and her years would not exempt her from that. Orphaned by the whites, murdered by tribal enemies, she was a victim of the gulf between two unlike systems of law. Each had grievously wronged her. Neither could protect her.

When Baneelon sailed for England with Phillip in December 1792, his star stood high with the governor, although we notice that Phillip also took with him Imeerawanyee. (He had planned to take Boladeree, only recently dead.) Imeerawanyee's company mitigated Baneelon's loneliness, but it also signalled the end of his unique status. What he hoped to achieve by that journey is obscure, but it is likely he sought to strengthen his alliance with Phillip and the British through the ordinary courtesy of visiting his friend's home country. He had proudly shown David Collins his own 'country', inherited from his father: the little island he called Me-mel, named by the British Goat Island. He also told him he would in time pass it on to his friend (Baneelon had no issue). He could have had not the least notion of how far it was to the land of Phillip's father.

Despite some kindnesses—he was taken to London to see the King, which I think he would have enjoyed—Baneelon had a cold and lonely time of it, with that cool snuff-taking gentleman earlier mentioned providing one of his warmest memories. Both men suffered badly from homesickness, and both were often ill.

Imeerawanyee died in England from a chest infection 'when he was supposed to be about 19 years of age', and was buried in a Kent churchyard. Baneelon finally got his longed-for passage home only in 1795, travelling back to Sydney on the *Reliance* with his old acquaintance John Hunter, appointed governor to replace Grose. Phillip had hoped that one or both Australians would become fluent in English during their stay, but Hunter records that despite his long exile Baneelon's English was little improved.

Over the seven months of the voyage Baneelon probably hoped to forge a special relationship with the incoming governor. Certainly his behaviour once home was confident to the point of arrogance, and determinedly in the British style: he appeared on the shore most elegantly clad, and publicly rebuked his sister for coming to greet him (she had run all the way from Botany Bay) without taking the time to dress. 'He declared,' Collins reports, 'in a tone and with an air that seemed to expect compliance, that he would no longer suffer them to fight and cut each other's throats, as they had done; that he should introduce peace among them, and make them love one another.' He also required them to be 'somewhat more cleanly in their persons, and less coarse in their manners'. So, at least, says Collins, and we might wonder how Collins understood so much of what was said. But it seems clear that Baneelon had decided to commit himself to the British account of things.

As other expatriates have learnt since, absence does not make the Australian heart grow fonder. The first sign that he had lost prestige within his own group was that, despite his gift of a rose-coloured petticoat, jacket and gypsy bonnet, his reclaimed wife refused to stay with him. Baneelon beat her new lover with his fists in the proper British way, but he could not get her back. Another girl he grabbed took her first opportunity to escape back to her mother's country.

Thereafter Baneelon had no luck with women, being reduced to random sexual attacks which were usually foiled by their guardian menfolk, as when Colbee split his lip for molesting Colbee's wife. His humiliation was necessarily public, and grievous. The incapacity of a mature man to keep even one woman was a painful indication of lost prestige.

Baneelon also found that his old privileged role among the British was being usurped by younger, less ambitious men, ready to live alongside the white men, ready to take material benefit from them, but with no discernible political aspirations. Some of the new favourites were not of his kin or his territory. He must have known that his power in both camps was slipping away.

At first he clung to his privileges, spending most of his time within the settlement, but Phillip was gone, and loneliness and celibacy must have been hard to bear. Collins tells us that after a few months he was regularly escaping the settlement for days at a time: doffing his clothes, stowing them at his house, and vanishing 'into the woods with his sisters and other friends'.

An episode from late 1797, two years after his return, marks the swiftness of Baneelon's political and social decline. Collins records it almost by accident, after he has given his admiring account of a young man who (like the formidable Carradah) had faced the required ordeal for killing a man in a quarrel, and 'stood manfully up against all their spears, and defended himself with great skill and address. Having two shields split in his hand, by the two spears passing quite through them, his friends, who were numerous, attacked his opponents, whom they disarmed, and broke their shields with many of their spears'. Thus courage was displayed, grievance satisfied, anger purged, and key loyalties displayed and strengthened—as was proper.

Baneelon should have faced the spears that day. A dying woman had dreamed that Baneelon had killed her, and after her death her kin accused him of achieving her death by sorcery. Some claimed he had wounded her physically before her death. Baneelon denied involvement, insisted that he didn't even know the woman and refused to submit to the prescribed trial, either because his courage failed or (more sadly) because his confidence in both traditional laws and traditional explanations had gone.

The interest lies in why the woman, whom Baneelon insisted he didn't know, should have dreamt that he had injured her. Collins supplies a plausible explanation. He tells us when Baneelon was drunk in the town, as he often was, he 'amused himself with annoying the women and insulting the men, who, from fear of offending his white friends, spared those notices of his conduct which he so often merited, and which sooner or later he would certainly meet with'. (This aggressive, disoriented behaviour is painfully familiar, in Australia and elsewhere, following on dispossession and systematic humiliation.)

We can guess at a deeper cultural division. While his friend Hunter might be prevailed on to extricate Baneelon from a personal difficulty by having soldiers protect him from retaliation, the motive for any such intervention was purely personal and individual. It could not be parlayed into enduring political capital. Tragically, the distinction between the personal and the political so effortlessly drawn by the British was one which Baneelon, for all his swift wit, would never grasp.

As Baneelon's star declined, Colbee's was steadily rising. Colbee is an interesting figure. He had been a prisoner of the British for only a week, but from the moment of renewed contact he had moved smoothly in Baneelon's wake. Within days of Baneelon being given his hatchets and received into Sydney and the governor's house, Colbee and his immediate kin made their approach, and were accepted in too; while Baneelon failed to coerce Barangaroo into bearing her child inside the British hospital, Colbee brought his wife and a baby only two or three days old all the way from Botany Bay to present his child to the governor, and Daringa and her baby quickly became the darlings of Elizabeth Macarthur, who fed them regularly and spoke of them tenderly. Colbee kept a sure footing in both camps, perhaps because he was never tempted to make any accommodation to British values, but remained always a tribal man. He was able to pull off at least two night assassinations of men who had offended him, winning applause from his fellows, and without losing credit among the British. Collins admiringly noted that in one such exploit Colbee had gently lifted aside a child asleep on the intended victim's chest, speared the man, and then, with the killing accomplished, carried the child back to Sydney to be cared for. He beat women at least as often as Baneelon, and with less provocation, beating Boorong ferociously and, as we have seen, spearing a girl at the request of her angry husband. As a warrior and a kinsman, Colbee could be relied upon—while somehow he retained his reputation among the British for being a steady, good-tempered fellow. For me he has come to be an Australian Collins, ready for genial coexistence, but with no desire for conversion in either direction.

Collins himself reports another tangled episode in December 1797, three months after Baneelon had refused to face tribal justice. Colbee had put himself outside Australian law by a major breach of warrior etiquette. In the thick of a desperate one-to-one combat his opponent's shield had come away from its handle, and as he bent to pick it up Colbee had clubbed him once, and then again. This was in the warrior code a reprehensible action, and Colbee fled. But he could not run far enough: even while the man still lingered, Colbee and a kinsman were severely beaten by the victim's people; when he died the kin sought formal revenge. The body had been buried 'by the side of the public road, below the military barracks' (note the confident use of what we would think of as core British territory) and a large body of Australians gathered at the grave 'breathing revenge'. Privileged status among the whites might lend brief protection, but it could not cancel tribal obligations and affiliations: Colbee's kinsman Nanbaree (the lad raised in Surgeon White's household), who had unwisely approached the scene, was grabbed and beaten, and rescued only 'by the appearance of a soldier who had been sent to the place with him'.

It was clear the vendetta would not stop until Colbee yielded himself up to justice. So he did. Meeting with the offended kin and their friends near the barracks, presumably close by the grave site, Colbee put up a sturdy fight, but he could not prevail against such numbers and, we might want to add, such anger at so rank an offence. Soon he was on the ground, with death a club's length away. And then 'several soldiers rushed in, and prevented them putting him to death where he lay'; they 'lifted him from the ground, and between them bore him into the barracks'.

Did the soldiers intervene through personal friendship, or were they simply offended by a murderous brawl being staged on their doorstep? What happened next was even more mysterious. Baneelon had played a major role in the young man's burial, which suggests at least a courtesy kin relationship, but he had taken no part in the attack on Colbee. Armed, 'unencumbered by clothing of any kind', he had been 'a silent spectator of the tumultuous scene'—until the soldiers rushed in to extricate the fallen Colbee. And suddenly Baneelon was enraged. He hurled his spear at a soldier, wounding him horribly. The soldiers would have killed him on the spot but for a British official who 'interfered and brought him away, boiling with the most savage rage; for he had received a blow on the head with the butt-end of a musket'. Baneelon was held overnight, as much 'to prevent the mischief with which he threatened the white people, as to save him from the anger of the military, and on the following morning he quitted town'. Collins implies that from this point on Baneelon became a pariah among his own people: 'The natives who had so constantly resided and received so many comforts in the settlement were now afraid to appear in the town, believing that, like themselves, we would punish all for the misconduct of one.'

Why had Baneelon hurled that fatal spear, and at a soldier, too? Because of the intolerable intrusion into properly conducted tribal justice? If so, there is an irony here. He had himself actively begged protection from Hunter only a year before, when he claimed a great body of Australians was assembled near the brickfields on the edge of the settlement swearing to kill him in retaliation for the death of a man near Botany Bay; a killing Baneelon insisted he had not done. The governor had yielded to his pleas: he sent him back with some of the military to inform the assembled Australians that he was innocent of the killing, that the governor would not allow him to be ill-treated, and that he would drive them away from Sydney if they should attempt any violence against him. Collins recalled that 'many of them were much alarmed when they saw in what manner and by whom he was attended; and to be driven from a place whence they derived so many comforts, and so much shelter in bad weather, would have been severely felt by most of them'. By invoking British protection to avoid the consequences of his actions, Baneelon had placed himself beyond the reach of tribal law, and forfeited the respect of his own people.

We might have expected that the recollection of his own dependence on British power would mitigate Baneelon's fury at the soldiers' intervention, but clearly it did not. Perhaps our own circumstances always look special. And why should he have been so enraged by the musket-butt blow on the head? Because it was an illegal intervention by an outsider? Because it was a foul blow delivered from behind, with an inappropriate weapon? Because it was the kind of blow only women should suffer? We cannot know. We only know that 'this most insolent and troublesome savage', as Collins was now ready to call him, had fallen into a blind rage and speared a soldier, in British eyes a cardinal sin, and that this time there would be no reconciliation. This time, he would remain disaffected. When finally readmitted to the town, he drank more, stalking the Sydney streets defiantly naked, carrying his spear and threatening violence against the governor. Who simply closed his doors to him.

It was at about this time that the last of the great initiation ceremonies was held at the traditional meeting place at Middle Harbour. Presumably the complex reciprocities needed to sustain such supra-group ceremonies were finally fracturing under the strains of the British presence.

Thereafter Baneelon, with his anger and his anguish, simply drops from British notice. He did not die until 1813. On 3 January of that year an obituary appeared in the *Sydney Gazette*, and we hear the official British summary of the meaning of his life:

> The principal officers of the government had for many years endeavoured, by the kindest of usage, to wean him from his original habits and draw him into a relish for civilised life; but every effort was in vain exerted and for the last few years he has been but little noticed. His propensity to drunkenness was inordinate; and when in that state he was insolent, menacing and overbearing. In fact, he was a thorough savage, not to be warped from the form and character that nature gave him by all the efforts that mankind could use.

Baneelon, that fluent, perceptive man, memorialised in death as an unchanged, unchanging icon of 'the savage'. At our greater distance he is a both a more dynamic and more tragic figure. His constant endeavour was to establish his clan, as embodied in his person, in an enduring reciprocal relationship with the British—the relationship of profitable intimacy and mutual forbearance Phillip, for a time, seemed to offer. Early in his captivity he gave Phillip the name Be-anna; Phillip had responded by calling him Dooroow, son. Thereafter Baneelon consistently read what were to Phillip mildly sentimental professions of regard as the recognition of coercive kinship obligations; and time and again he was brutally disappointed. The early history of their relationship was studded with frustrations and disappointments as Phillip refused his clear duty to support Baneelon, and Baneelon's people, against their enemies.

During Baneelon's English sojourn the claim of his clan to special privileges was submerged into the socially depressed category of 'native'. Only a few individuals continued to be privileged, and they were privileged as individuals, regardless of tribe. For Baneelon this was betrayal. I suspect that the soldiers' intervention to save Colbee affronted him on both the political and the individual level: for its arrogant disruption of the proper execution of tribal law, but also its reminder that Colbee, once his friend, always his rival, could count on personal protection from the whites, too.

Over the last years of his life Baneelon abandoned the British in his heart, as they had long abandoned him in the world. At fifty he fumed his way to an outcast's grave. He should have died earlier, in the days of hope.

A man from the Broken Bay tribe the whites called Bungaree was to prove more successful than Baneelon in managing the quicksilver experience of being a colonised black male. He was early known as an excellent man with boats. Matthew Flinders chose him to be part of his northern explorations in mid-1799, and again in 1802 when the *Investigator* set out to circumnavigate the continent. On that second voyage Bungaree had Nanbaree, now a young man, as companion. Flinders found himself relying on Bungaree for his skills as a seafarer and fish-taker, his tact in negotiating with newly met Australians, and for his steady good humour. A year later and back on land it was Bungaree's warrior skills which were being celebrated, the *Sydney Gazette* commending him for the killing force of his boomerang during a fight at Farm Cove, and also for his 'courtesy', surely an odd quality to remark in a battle. Presumably they meant his scrupulous observance of the warrior combat code. Later again he was one of the men selected for Governor Macquarie's doomed experiment of turning nomads into farmers, with specially selected Australians having huts built for them on little slices of land and being provided with tools, seeds and animals. Two years after the unlamented death of the irremediably 'savage' Baneelon, the Governor's Lady herself presented Bungaree, in his new role as Chief of the Farmers, with 'a Breeding Sow and 7 pigs—and also a pair of Muscovy Ducks—together with Suits of Clothes for his Wife and Daughter': a poignant echo of Phillip's dream of seeing the Australians settled, clothed and self-supporting.

The dream was again disappointed. Bungaree and his people abandoned the nascent farms, ate, sold or lost the animals, and stripped the huts of saleable items. The one gift they prized was a boat. They used it to catch fish to peddle in Sydney Town.

In the same year the governor recognised the vitality of Bungaree's authority by investing him with a metal chest ornament proclaiming him to be 'BOONGAREE—Chief of the Broken Bay Tribe—1815'.

Macquarie continued to distinguish his self-created 'chief'. In February 1822, on the day before he was to leave for England, the governor went to visit Bungaree at Pittwater, taking the incoming governor Thomas Brisbane with him. Macquarie feasted Bungaree and his people, and then presented him with 'an old Suit of General's uniforms to dress him out as Chief', perhaps in genial mockery, perhaps in recognition of his role as mediator between the races. There was some reality in the title: in 1824, when the Frenchman d'Urville was recording his impressions of Sydney, he watched Bungaree lead his people into battle against another tribe, and was impressed by Australians' skill with the boomerang.

A remarkably flexible career, to be put together by a man who had lived through 'interesting times', as the old Chinese curse has it. But Bungaree was ageing and his alcohol addiction worsening. The protean man was transforming again, this time into chronically drunken 'King Bungaree', a figure of fun in a plumed hat and a British jacket, with a brass plate around his neck which now proclaimed him 'Bungaree, King of Sydney Cove'. He would have himself rowed out in a decrepit whaleboat to welcome newcomers to Sydney, collect his kingly 'tax', and then divide the spoils in the form of drink among his disreputable followers. It seems that Bungaree, 'whose good disposition, and open and manly conduct' had won him Flinders' enduring regard, had been extinguished by the alcoholic clown. He fell seriously ill in 1830, was restored to fragile health in the Sydney General Hospital, and thereafter received a full ration from the government. For a time he was cared for in the house of a Catholic priest, but he died among his own people at Garden Island in November 1830.

What had happened to this man, who had accommodated so flexibly to the colonial regime, expanding the narrow role allocated to Australians within it to something like autonomy? Why did the disciplined seafarer fall victim to alcohol and indulgent contempt? Why was alcohol so lethal a solvent of Australian social bonds and individual dignity, which had seemed the central passions of their lives? In those first encounters on the beach most Australians had shunned the wine or rum pressed on them—except for Baneelon. Restless for glory in this as in so much else, he was soon quaffing wine with all the flourishes with which white gentlemen surrounded it. The general refusal did not last. The Europeans discovered the only lures which could coax services from the Australians were flour, sugar, tea—and alcohol and tobacco. The Russian navigator Bellingshausen, who met Bungaree and his rowdy entourage in 1820, noted that 'the magic charms of drink and tobacco' had attracted swarms of Australians to Sydney Town, and had become indispensable to them, so they 'willingly become hewers of wood and drawers of water for the sake of tobacco and spirits,' and we remember Dampier's frustration with his intransigent 'savages'. Yet Bungaree, and others—too many others—seemed to tumble suddenly into a condition of obsessive addiction: an addiction remarked on and jeered at even in that society of obsessive European drinkers.

The drinking may have been a symptom of the multiple losses incurred under the new imposed system. Perhaps, after the eruption of smallpox and of venereal diseases and the malignant erosion of other imported diseases; after the cognitive shocks of trying to fathom the true nature and intentions of these powerful, chronically unreliable intruders, alcohol provided a fast passport to the familiar and well-loved place they had once achieved through the slow preparation and joyful performance of ceremony: a broad avenue to the sacred. In other better documented countries (I am thinking of my own territory of sixteenth-century Mexico under the blows of Spanish colonisation) we watch the decay of formal traditional ceremonial life as the conditions necessary to sustain it disintegrated, then the inflow of alcohol to fill the void—and then the quick slide into the abyss. We also see that the 'hopelessness, powerlessness, poverty and…confusion' diagnosed by Stanner two centuries after contact were already evident by the second decade after European intrusion.

Captain Bellingshausen was puzzled by the tension between Bungaree's earlier reputation as a multi-skilled seafarer, and the broken-down figure he saw before him. He was sufficiently moved by the puzzle to describe the shape of the life the older Bungaree had created for himself, in which we discern a patchwork of fragments drawn from the old and from the new. With the clowning and begging done, Bungaree and his makeshift clan would go out fishing, exchange their catch for rum and tobacco, and row back to their camps on the north shore. The Russian remembered that 'they had to pass near our ships, and every evening they came back drunk, shouting savagely and uttering threats: and often their quarrels with each other ended in a fight...' (I am writing these words just before Christmas. Other people's parties often sound very like brawls.)

The Russian's observations raise another teasing possibility. We notice that Bungaree managed to keep his people together, and free from white supervision, in desperately oppressive circumstances. Not long after the 'coming in' and the Australians' adoption of what the British called begging as a technique of survival, they began preening in bits of European gear. They were also often drunk. To British observers they were pathetic inebriates, miming a glory forever beyond them. But given their passion for mimicry and their rapturous imitations of European absurdities, might not the strutting and preening have functioned as an impromptu secular corroboree, a running Australian joke on the British, invisible to its victims, radiantly clear to its perpetrators? There were few roles open to warriors under British rule. Baneelon found himself thrust into a suicidal performance of 'irreconcilable savage'. Did Bungaree choose 'tolerated clown'? Look again at the poise and the ironic flourish of Augustus Earle's representation of Bungaree which closes the plate section. Bungaree's beautifully florid performances won some goods, money and a modicum of freedom from the whites, while it parodied European pretensions before an appreciative Australian audience.

However complex the Australians' accommodations, and despite moments of affection and good will, the die was now cast. The years of negotiation and hopeful experiment were gone, along with most of the people, black and white, who had lived through them. As all young colonies do, Sydney regularly lost its memory with the old hands going home, and newcomers entering what they took to be an unchanging colonial reality. As drunken Australians fought, danced and shouted in the streets of the town, most Britishers came to think they had always been like that, and Augustus Earle could reliably supplement his income by representing the Australians as clownish caricatures.

Bungaree died in 1830. A year before, on 7 July 1829, which is a wintry month in Sydney, the *Sydney Gazette* reported an apparition. Citizens walking through the Government Domain had been startled to see an Australian man 'in a state of perfect nudity, with the exception of his old cocked hat, graced with a red feather'. The spectre of Baneelon, returned in a comic hat. He was identified as 'the veteran native Chief, Bungaree'.

After the hectic engagements of Phillip's time, the social gulf between the races had been fixed. But multiple interactions and influences continued. We remember that even in the first days, when we were firmly told of convicts' fear and loathing for Australians, we would also see that some sought each other's company, like that family in the bay adjacent to Sydney where convicts and Australians made merry together, and a scatter of other glimpses of trans-racial trust and affection. Pleasure was taken in each other's company. A series of foreign travellers would comment on the relaxed style of black–white relations in and around Sydney, as they would on the curious persistence, beyond the towns, of the Australians' independent way of life.

To end, as we began, with Charles Darwin, this time in 1836, in New South Wales, somewhere between Sydney and Bathurst. This is what he saw late one afternoon:

At sunset, a party of a score or more of the black aborigines passed by, each carrying, in their accustomed manner, a bundle of spears and other weapons...They were all partly clothed, and several could speak a little English: their countenances were good-humoured and pleasant, and they appeared far from being such utterly degraded beings as they have usually been represented. In their own arts they are admirable...In tracking animals or men they show the most marvellous sagacity; and I heard of several of their remarks which manifested considerable acuteness, they will not, however, cultivate the ground, or build houses and remain stationary, or even take the trouble of tending a flock of sheep when given them...It is very curious thus to see in the midst of a civilised people, a set of harmless savages wandering about without knowing where they shall sleep at night, and gaining their livelihood by hunting in the woods.

He also notes, regretfully, the unequal contest over the land, and points to a consequence: the Australians' infants are dying because of the difficulty, in these changed times, of procuring sufficient food, 'so their wandering habits increase...and the population, without any apparent death from famine, is repressed in a manner extremely sudden'.

So the Australians walk on to their unknown camp, and their uncertain future. For a while longer they would dance their dances, but now they would dance alone.

ENTER MRS CHARLES MEREDITH

Nearly forty years after Watkin Tench had quit the colony an Englishwoman, upper class, cool, and free from the least desire to flatter the colonials, came to Sydney with her husband. Already recognised as a poet of some note, she wrote elegant literary letters to beguile the time and her friends at home, mainly by astonishing them with the crudity of life in Australia.

The main tale she has to tell is of colonists' drunkenness. Men, women and near-children all drank with ferocious determination. She was especially impressed by the inebriation, regardless of age, sex or time of day, among all those 'keeping a public'. Her explanation points to the colonists' natural indolence: 'Idleness and drinking are such besetting sins, and money to provide them both so easily earned by "keeping a public" in this Colony, that nothing demanding bodily exertion is attempted.' She tells eye-stretching stories about some of the inns she encountered along her way between Sydney and Bathurst just three years after Darwin, and we think how differently individuals travel (Darwin ate, slept, and tranquilly moved on). Mrs

Meredith also intersperses her horror stories with heartfelt abuse for the trailblazing explorer Major Mitchell and his taste for the picturesque as his road clambered painfully up and over the very 'summits of hills, while level valleys lay within a few hundred feet'. 'Prospects' can come at a high price in time and comfort.

But it is 'the demoralising passion for rum' which most offended her: 'No threats, no bribe, no punishments avail to keep the besotted creatures from the dram bottle.' Even young chambermaids would snatch a swig of eau de cologne or lavender-water or anything else they thought might contain spirits if it were left within their reach. After a squalid breakfast in a squalid public house—'nice sweet milk poured into a dirty glass' by a 'stupid, dirty, half-dressed, slipshod woman' in a house still full of unmade beds and clothes lying about at ten o'clock in the morning!—she commented: 'This universal addiction to drink, and the consequent neglect of all industry and decency, are truly shocking.' The only exceptions to the general rule, she thought, were the families of poor English emigrants, who clung to the frugalities, industry and virtues of home. Mrs Meredith accordingly shunned local whites as servants, choosing to employ only sober, respectable, respectful persons from England, not yet corrupted by the colonials.

She had little sustained contact with Aboriginal Australians, whom she called 'Aborigines' or 'natives' (she reserves the word 'Australian' for locally-bred whites), but she was, like Tench, curious about them and like him, although quite lacking his imaginative sympathy, she had a good eye. Her general summation dents the stereotype. She saw them as a cheerful bunch, stubbornly refusing the white man's gifts of garments, steady labour, and a sensible frugality; and demonstrating instead an irresponsible preference for their own feckless ways. Nonetheless, she regarded them more highly than she did most of the local whites. The native taste for strong drink was eclipsed by white excesses, and they usually drank to rowdy cheerfulness, not sodden inebriation. She heard them singing, and found their songs to have more melody and variety than those of the Maori, 'which surprised me, as the latter people are so immeasurably superior to the natives of New South Wales in everything else'. (She had seen quite a few Maoris in Sydney; by the 1820s a useful trade in flax and timber had been established with New Zealand, so despite their penchant for eating people Maoris were judged to be fine, sensible folk.) She acknowledged that the civilising process among the Australian natives was moving slowly, if it moved at all, especially in the matter of housing. While they took grateful shelter in weather-proof European houses during downpours, they flatly refused to build any dwellings for themselves, being content to risk the weather and 'raise a few strips of bark slantingly against a tree', with the result looking, to Mrs Meredith's untutored eye, no more than 'accidental heaps of bark'.

As for clothing: she noticed how well native men looked in coachmen's livery, which she thought showed off their splendidly erect postures to advantage, and we remember William Bradley's comment made during the first month after his landing: 'They walk very upright, and very much with their hands behind them', a stance designed to display the masculine chest to advantage. Mrs Meredith also noted the men's particular talent for managing horses, which made them stylish and efficient coachmen even over long tough journeys like that between Sydney and Adelaide. Then follows a now-familiar lament: once they got home even the most stylish and efficient refused to stay in service, and neither example nor exhortation nor vanity nor shame could keep them in their clothes: 'Even after a sojourn of many months with Europeans, and in a comparatively civilised state, they invariably return to their old habits, and relinquish their smart and comfortable clothes for the corrobbory [sic] costume of nudity and pipe-clay.'

She also noticed something else: male pride in physical prowess. Aborigines shinning up trees after possums seemed to leap upwards: they would make tiny notches in the bark 'just large enough to rest the end of the big toe', and up they would go—and we flash back to Phillip and his intrepid bushwalkers marvelling at the agile old man leaping up the tree on the Hawkesbury. On horseback, a European skill 'which many of them do, well and fearlessly', 'they never put the flat foot in the stirrup, but only lay hold of it with the great toe', so dramatising natural balance. These men clearly exulted in displays of prowess and courage.

Mrs Meredith was also astonished by their talent for mimicry, 'one learn[ing] to waltz very correctly in a few minutes' (shades of Darwin) while:

> the slightest peculiarity of face or figure never escapes their observation, so that in speaking of any person you know, though his name be not mentioned, their accurate impersonation of his gait, expressions of countenance, or any oddity of manner, is so complete as to leave no doubt of the identity.

Fifty years of white presence had only sharpened that passionate, gleeful talent for re-presentation.

A less attractive quality also remained noticeable. The men's mistreatment of their women drove her to a fury of underlinings:

> Female children are sometimes 'promised' in infancy to their future husbands (frequently decrepit old men), and others appear to be taken by means of force and ill-usage, as is the case among many savage nations, The men are always tyrannical, and often brutally cruel to their unfortunate wives, who really do seem to

occupy as miserable and debased a position, in <u>every</u> respect, as it is possible for human beings to do…<u>Severe</u> personal chastisement is among the lesser grievances of the poor Gins.

She goes on to tell a horrible story of a man's pipe having been broken, by accident, by his wife—and the breaking of the culprit's arm as punishment. She concludes: 'These poor unhappy wretches are <u>slaves</u>, in every social sense.'

Mrs Meredith also unwittingly gives us news of an enduring legacy. I am a part-time North Queenslander these days, and proud of it. But I still can't master the local lingo, especially the way locals of all colours use the sound 'Ay'. They can just about make a conversation out of it.

Listen to Mrs Meredith a hundred and fifty years ago:

> The various expressions conveyed by the peculiar 'Ay, Ay', so constantly used by the natives in speaking, is perfectly indescribable. It is used doubtfully, interrogatively, or responsively, as the case may be, and contains in itself a whole vocabulary of meanings, which a hundred times the number of words could not convey in writing. Suppose you inquire of a native if he has seen such and such a person pass, as he had gone that way:—'Ay, ay?' (interrogatively.) 'Yes, a tall man.'—'Ay, ay' (thoughtfully). 'A tall man, with great whiskers.' 'Ay, ay (positively). Good way up cobbra, cabou grasse; ay, ay (corroboratively).'—'Good way up cobbra' meaning 'head high up', 'grasse' meaning hair or beard, and 'cabou' meaning a great deal, or very much.

Identification achieved. This small act of reverse colonisation pleases me very much.

During an early and relatively benign phase of their imperial adventure the British—or rather the selection of them we have just met—chanced to encounter in Australia one of the few hunter-gatherer societies left on the earth. (Today, to my knowledge, there are none.) Despite or perhaps because of the width of the cultural chasm between the two peoples, each initially viewed the other as objects not of threat, but of curiosity and amusement; through those early encounters each came to recognise the other as fellow-humans, fully participant in a shared humanity.

Unseen conflict lay in the path. If less peripatetic than their inland brothers, the people around Sydney Cove were nonetheless compelled to exploit the seasonal resources of all of their territories if they were to survive. During those first years, both the complexity and the fragility of the nomad economy were masked from the newcomers by local population losses and the fortuitous provision of British rations to supplement the diet of those Australians most directly affected by the British presence. Only a handful of First

Fleet observers began to grasp the great fact of the Australians' intimate dependence on what the British continued to think of as 'wild', indeed empty, land. And then it was too late. The British, with labour enough from convicts, would find no place for Australians in their colony-building enterprise. What they wanted was land, and they took it. Once that conflict became explicit, racial frontiers, pushing irresistibly outwards, would be marked in blood, and many Australians would die; some from British bullets, more from disease and starvation.

Milan Kundera reminds us that we humans proceed in a fog. By coming to see the fogs through which people in other times battled in the direction they hoped was forward, we may be better able to recognise and penetrate our own. Fast-evolving colonial situations demand swift responses. Our two main protagonists, Phillip and Baneelon, were given no space for reflection, revision or even explanation of their positions. Each failed, to their own and their people's injury, and to ours. They cannot be blamed for that failure.

We have a duty to the people of the past: to rescue them from the falsifying simplifications we impose if we refuse to see the fog through which they were trying to make their way. W. E. H. Stanner has called the Australians 'a high-spirited and militant people', and it is as a high-spirited, militant people they leap from the eighteenth-century page. They should be honoured not only for their ingenious adaptation to life on this, the least manipulable continent on earth, but also for their inventive resourcefulness in dealing with the strangers. The men of the First Fleet deserve honour too, for their openness, their courage, and their stubborn curiosity. In the end, it was the depth of cultural division which defeated them, not any lack of energy, intelligence or good will.

Every indigenous people has walked their trail of tears, but few others enjoyed that springtime of trust. Our first shared Australian story is a tragedy of animated imagination, determined friendship and painfully dying hopes. Through time and accumulated disillusionments each group, despite their domestic proximity, lost both curiosity and concern for the other, and imagination atrophied into settled mistrust. Now, with hope for reconciliation renewed over this past decade, it is time to think again about that atrophy: how it came about, and how we might climb out of it.

Accordingly I have introduced a rather more expansive concept of culture into the discussion of race relations in this country than is currrently in use. I hope I have persuaded the reader that 'culture' is more than a bundle of legal prinicples, a matter of going clothed or naked, of cherishing privacy or ignoring it, of sharing or not sharing. It is best understood as the context of our existential being: a dynamic system of shared meanings through which we communicate with our own. Because those meanings are rarely made explicit, understanding another culture's meanings is and will always be a hazardous enterprise.

History is not about the imposition of belated moral judgments. It is not a balm for hurt minds, either. It is a secular discipline, and in its idiosyncratic way a scientific one, based on the honest analysis of the vast, uneven, consultable record of human experience. To understand history we have to get inside episodes, which means setting ourselves to understand our subjects' changing motivations and moods in their changing contexts, and to tracing the devious routes by which knowledge was acquired, understood, and acted upon. Only then can we hope to understand ourselves and our species better, and so manage our affairs more intelligently. If we are to arrive at a durable tolerance (and it is urgent that we should), we have only history to guide us.

Inquiry into our confused beginnings suggests that the possibility of a decent co-existence between unlike groups must begin from the critical scrutiny of our own assumptions and values as they come under challenge. We might then be able to make informed decisions as to which uncomfortable differences we are prepared to tolerate and which we are not, rather than to attempt the wholesale reformation of what we identify as the defects of the other. A lasting tolerance builds slowly out of accretions of delicate accommodations made through time; and it comes, if it comes at all, as slow as honey.

There remains a final mystery. Despite our long alienation, despite our merely adjacent histories, and through processes I do not yet understand, we are now more like each other than we are like any other people. We even share something of the same style of humour, which is a subtle but far-reaching affinity. Here, in this place, I think we are all Australians now.

These [two black swans] had with very
great care been brought alive to England;
but unfortunately one of them soon died in
moulting; and the other having, after that
operation, with his health also recovered the
perfect use of his wings, availed himself of
the liberty they gave him… and was shot by
a nobleman's gamekeeper as it was flying
across the Thames.

David Collins, An Account of the English
Colony in New South Wales*, 1802*

NOTES ON SOURCES

INTRODUCTION

There were significant territorial divisions among the Australians, with the boundaries marked by fighting, mutual feasting and ritual obligations, and the exchange of women on the established anthropological principle, 'they are our enemies; we marry them'. The primary division was between what David Collins called 'families' and we might call clans, each family being named for its territory: 'Thus the southern shore of Botany bay is called Gwea, and the people who inhabit it style themselves Gweagal [while] those who live in the north shore of Port Jackson are called Cam-mer-ray-gal.' (I will refer to them throughout as 'Cameragal'.) The Cameragal was the dominant tribe, the most numerous, 'robust and muscular', and controlled the most important male initiation rite which centred on the knocking-out of the right upper incisor. (British observers were to notice that the inland people retained their teeth, so were presumably beyond the Cameragal zone of influence.) John Hunter confirms and expands Collins' information, and contributes his own intrepid spelling:

The tribe of Cammera inhabit the north side of Port Jackson. The tribe of Cadi inhabits the south side, extending from the south head to Long-Cove, at which place the district of Wanne, and the tribe of Wangal, commences, expanding as far as Par-ra-mata, or Rose-Hill. The tribe of Wallumede inhabit the north shore opposite Warrane, or Sydney-Cove, and are called *Walumeta*. I have already observed that the space between Rose-Hill and Prospect-Hill is distinguished by four different names, although the distance is only four miles.

Time and time again during those first years we are shown that tribal divisions could cut deeper than race. Nonetheless I have made only the best-attested clan identifications, because too often the evidence we have is unclear. For example: because I remain in doubt as to the precise referent of 'Eora', the most popular collective term, which seems to have meant 'we people here', with the referent depending on context, I have avoided using it.

For the 'tribes' David Collins, *An Account of the English Colony in New South Wales,* vol. 1, London, 1798, A. H. and A. W. Reed, Sydney 1975, Appendix I, esp. p. 453, and John Hunter, *An Historical Journal of Events at Sydney and at Sea 1787–1792*, [1793], edited John Bach, Angus and Robertson, Sydney, 1968, pp. 274–5.

For a persistent inquiry into these obscure matters, see Keith Vincent Smith, *Bennelong: The Coming In of the Eora, Sydney Cove, 1788–1792*, Kangaroo Press, Sydney, 2001.

DANCING WITH STRANGERS

Friendly encounters were not restricted to the British. French explorers in Australia, transient visitors and some with Rousseau's writings tucked into their kits, were typically even readier to project active good will than were the British. When some officers and men from de Freycinet's voyage landed at Shark Bay in Western Australia and suspected they might be under threat of attack, one of the officers had his men begin to dance in a circle, an old Australian man joined them—and laughter expunged aggression. Jacques Arago tells us that the French navigator Bruny d'Entrecasteaux's sailors were so moved by their enthusiastic welcome in Van Diemen's Land in February 1793 that they stripped off their clothing to present to their new friends. A naturalist graciously helped a young girl into his pantaloons while the expedition's botanical artist submitted to having the visible parts of his person blackened with charcoal, so being made a more agreeable colour. We also know that Baudin's expeditioners, either in a burst of patriotic fervour, covert imperialism or sheer mischief, taught 'La Marseillaise' to Western Australian people in 1802, so preparing a fine surprise for later visitors.

Paul Carter makes much—perhaps rather too much—of such moments of mimicry in his *Living in a New Country: History, Travelling and Language.* See especially chapter 8 for his account of what happened in 1801 when Matthew Flinders' *Investigator* visited 'St. George's Sound'.

For Tierra del Fuego, Charles Darwin, *A Naturalist's Diary,* chapter X.

For dancing, see page 3 of the plate section, William Bradley, *A Voyage to New South Wales: The Journal of Lieutenant William Bradley R. N. of HMS* Sirius, *1786–1792.* Facsimile reproduction, Trustees of the Public Library of New South Wales, Sydney 1969. Original manuscript held in Mitchell Library, Sydney.

For 'Marlbrooke' and singing, Watkin Tench, *Watkin Tench: 1788*, edited and introduced by Tim Flannery, The Text Publishing Company, Melbourne, 1996, pp. 42–3; John White, *Journal of a*

Voyage to New South Wales by John White Esq., edited A. R. Chisholm, The Royal Australian Historical Society, Angus and Robertson, 1962, pp. 110–11, 152–4.

For solving the sexual puzzle, Philip Gidley King, *The Journal of Philip Gidley King: Lieutenant, R. N. 1787–1790*, edited by Paul Fidlon and R. J. Ryan, Australian Documents Library, Sydney, 1980, pp. 32–5.

For clowning pantomimes, John Bayley, *Iris: A Memoir of Iris Murdoch*, Duckworth, London, 1998, p. 43.

For 'La Marseillaise', J. Arago, *Narrative of a Voyage Around the World*, London, 1823, p. 172.

MEETING THE INFORMANTS
For full references see bibliography, and for the mutual borrowings the 'Note on Sources' which precedes it.

For David Collins' letters to his father dated 23 March 1791 and 17 October 1791, see John Currey, *David Collins: A Colonial Life*, Melbourne University Press, Melbourne, 2000, p. 71, p. 76.

GOVERNOR ARTHUR PHILLIP
Arthur Phillip, *The Voyage of Governor Phillip to Botany Bay,* [1789], edited and annotated by James J. Auchmuty, Angus and Robertson, Sydney, 1970, *passim*. This is a composite work, incorporating 'Contributions from Other Officers of the First Fleet', maps and natural history illustrations. The volume was pulled together for publication in 1789 to catch the market with the first news from the new colony. It incorporates reports from Phillip to various recipients up to November 1788. While it cannot be relied on for exact wordings, it is reasonable to assume the tenor and emphases are his.

See also Phillip in John Hunter, *An Historical Journal of Events at*

Sydney and at Sea 1787–1792, [1793], edited John Bach, Angus and Robertson, Sydney, 1968, pp. 299–375. Another selective account drawn from Phillip's official reports for the period from July 1790 to the departure of the *Gorgon* in December 1791. Hereafter 'Phillip in Hunter'.

For accounts of his first meetings with the Australians see Phillip to Lord Sydney, 15 May 1788, *Historical Records of New South Wales,* vol. 1, part 2, p. 129, and Phillip, *Voyage,* chapter 6, esp. pp. 48–9.

For the material benefits he intended to bring, e.g. Phillip, *Voyage,* pp. 76–9.

For Phillip's letter of July (?) 1788, see Mitchell ms C 213, transcribed in Alan Frost's unpublished, unpaginated notes. (I thank Professor Frost for his generosity here, and throughout this enterprise.)

For Phillip the hasty sailor, Bowes Smyth, *Journal,* pp. 47, 62–4. For Phillip on land e.g. *Journal,* pp. 67–9, 74–6. For Bowes Smyth's radiant account of another Tahitian idyll, the month he spent in the islands on his voyage home, again on the *Lady Penrhyn,* in July 1788, see pp. 99–110. A sample of his euphoria:

> There cannot be a more affectionate people than the Oteheiteans nor is any country more capable of affording refreshments of various kinds both animal and vegetable, to Ships long at Sea, or any people more ready to part wt. them & all for the trifling barter before mention't vizt. Hatchetts, Knives, old Hoop, Lookg. glasses, red feathers &ca. &ca.

(*Ibid.* p. 106.) On p. 105: 'These Girls are total strangers to every idea of Shame in their Amours…This day I was tattowed on both arms…'

For Worgan's opinions, George B. Worgan, *Journal of a First Fleet Surgeon*, The Library Council of New South Wales, Sydney, 1978, esp. p. 3.

For the Morton discussion, see Anne Salmond's absorbing study, *Between Worlds: Early Exchanges between Maori and Europeans, 1773–1815*, University of Hawaii Press, Honolulu, 1997.

On the later trade with Tahiti, see Collins, *Account,* 2, p. 238.

For a lesson not learnt, William Dampier, *A New Voyage Around the World: The Journal of an English Buccaneer*, [1697], Hummingbird Press, London, 1998, p. 221.

For the English intellectual world most elegantly analysed see Alan Atkinson's *The Europeans in Australia: A History. Vol.1; The Beginning*, Oxford University Press, Melbourne, 1997, and for 'a panorama of his [Phillip's] life and times', and the literary dimensions of that world, Alan Frost, *Arthur Phillip 1738–1814: His Voyaging*, Oxford University Press, Melbourne, 1987. For the dynamic controversies centring on the transportation of convicts, John Hirst, *Convict Society and its Enemies: A History of Early New South Wales*, Allen and Unwin, Sydney, 1983.

CAPTAIN JOHN HUNTER

Jane Austen, quoted Gillian Dooley, *Australian Book Review*, March 2002, p. 47. Dooley draws attention to Noel Purdon's pursuit of the nautical connection in Austen in 'a splendid brace of articles written for the *Adelaide Review* in 1987'. *Ibid.* p. 45.

For a magnificent brief essay on the great Stubbs, Robert Hughes, *Nothing If Not Critical*, The Harvill Press, London, 1999, pp. 43–6.

For Hunter, *An Historical Journal, passim;* for the shooting scene, Hunter, *Journal,* pp. 56–7, and chapter 3 *passim*; for the Australian woman and the baby, pp. 96–100; for the quoted comment on savages, pp. 41–3.

Granted, the rescue of the woman and baby was a single case. E. P. Thompson has taught us how little chivalry or compassion tempered 'Old Corruption' at home. There is an occasional whiff of that pervasive corruption in the colony, too, but I think there it was challenged by an emerging culture of professionalism, especially in its naval manifestation. However—for a necessary corrective to Jane Austen, see any of the works of E. P. Thompson, but most conveniently 'The Peculiarities of the English', in his *The Poverty of Theory,* Merlin Press, London, 1978, pp. 35–91, esp. p. 49, and 'The Patricians and the Plebs', in his *Customs in Common*, Merlin Press, London, 1991, pp. 16–96.

Surgeon-General John White

For White's establishing of the health regimen on board ship, White, *Journal*, pp. 48–50; for the amputation, pp. 85–6; for his amorous adventures in port, pp. 83, 97–9.

For the airy grating between the sexes, p. 63; for the girl and the buttons, p. 160.

Arthur Bowes Smyth reports a fine compliment paid to Phillip in Rio. 'At night the town was most beautifully illuminated & the Tops of the Churches & several Monasteries also, in honour of the Commodore who had some years ago been employ'd with much credit in the Portuguese Service...' See Bowes Smyth, *Journal*, esp. pp. 28–30.

For the officer's comment on the slave trade, Rienits, Biographical Introduction, White, *Journal*, p. 21; for White's figures on the numbers lost on the voyage over, *ibid.* p. 231 n. 11; Phillip to Sydney, 12 February 1790, *Historical Records of Australia*, ser. 1, vol. 1, p. 144; Rienits p. 20. For discrepancies see Collins, *Account*, 1, p. 534.

On birds' songs, or noises. Tench, *1788*, pp. 73–4; Collins, *Account*, 2, p. 66. Jacob Nagle noticed when he was charting around Botany Bay that when they landed on a 'small island with lofty trees and no under wood, but like a grass plat', it was 'so numerous with smal birds call'd parrekeets that we could scarcely hear when we spoke to each other'. Jacob Nagle, *The Nagle Journal: A Diary of the Life of Jacob Nagle, Sailor, from the year 1775–1841*, edited John C. Dann, Weidenfeld & Nicolson, New York, 1988, p. 100. Nagle's life as represented in his journal is so picturesque as to raise doubts regarding its authenticity, but his distinguished editor is persuaded that Nagle really was at all the places he claimed he was, and his account of how he handled the surf at Norfolk Island after the *Sirius* was wrecked persuaded me he was there. See esp. *Nagle Journal*, pp. 121–2. See also the shipwright Daniel Paine: 'Of Birds there are great numbers of all Sorts excepting singing birds of which none have as yet been found'—and Paine was writing in 1796. His assessment of the Australians is even bleaker than those of the most dismissive First Fleeters. *The Journal of Daniel Paine 1794–1797*, edited R. J. B. Knight and Alan Frost, Library of Australian History, Sydney, 1983, p. 37, p. 39.

For White's biographical details, Rex Reinits' fine 'Biographical Introduction' to White's *Journal, passim*.

JUDGE-ADVOCATE DAVID COLLINS

For Collins' motives in keeping his *Account*, see Fletcher, Introduction, Collins, *Account*, 1, App. XV; for George Worgan's comments to Dick Worgan, 2 July 1788, quoted in John Cobley, *Sydney Cove, 1788*, Hodder and Stoughton, Sydney, 1962, p. 173, pp. 180–90.

For an agricultural metaphor painfully elongated see Collins' 'Advertisement' for his second volume, *Account*, 2, xiii; for convict solidarity, Collins, *Account*, 1, p. 28; for the raid on the British fishing party, Collins, *Account*, 1, p. 29.

For Collins' life, Fletcher in Collins, *Account*, 1, p. 519, n. 33, and especially Currey, *David Collins: A Colonial Life*.

WATKIN TENCH, CAPTAIN-LIEUTENANT OF MARINES

Tench, *1788*. See also L. F. Fitzhardinge's superb backnotes to his edition of Tench's narratives: *Sydney's First Four Years, being a reprint of A Narrative of the Expedition to Botany Bay and A Complete Account of the Settlement at Port Jackson by Captain Watkin Tench of the Marines, with an introduction and annotations by L. F. Fitzhardinge*, Library of Australian History, Sydney, 1979.

On language, Tench, *1788*, fn. p. 195; Tench on sharks, p. 76.

For W. E. H. Stanner see *After the Dreaming: The Boyer Lectures 1968*, ABC, Sydney, 2001, pp. 44–5. For Stanner's terse history of Aboriginal–European interactions over that early period, see his 'The History of Indifference Thus Begins' (1963) in *White Man Got No Dreaming*, pp. 165–97. As will become clear, I think more can be done to retrieve Australian intentions than Stanner allows.

For the probable identity of the little boy on the beach, see Fitzhardinge, *Sydney's First Four Years*, pp. 82–3, n. 6.

On canoes, James Cook, *The Journals of Captain James Cook on his Voyage of Discovery* edited by J. C. Beaglehole, 4 vols., Hakluyt Society Extra Series xxxiv, Cambridge, 1955, vol. 1., p. 283, p. 301; Bradley, quoted in Tim Flannery, *The Birth of Sydney*, Text Publishing, Melbourne, 1999, p. 55; Hunter in Hunter, p. 44.

SETTLING IN

For La Pérouse and for the islanders' attack on his men, and the order to settle Norfolk Island, Philip Gidley King, *The Journal of*

Philip Gidley King: Lieutenant, R. N. 1787–1790, edited by Paul Fidlon and R. J. Ryan, Australian Documents Library, Sydney, 1980, pp. 36–40. King gives an envious description of the 'Philosophic instruments' on the French ships which were 'fitted out with the greatest liberality'.

For the attack see also Phillip, *Voyage*, chapter 7, for a typical disclaimer: 'This fatal result from too implicit a confidence may, perhaps very properly, increase the caution of Europeans in their commerce with savages, but ought not to excite suspicion. The resentments of such people are sudden and sanguinary, and, where the intercourse of language is wanting, may easily be awakened by misapprehension.' For the (utopian) instructions to King regarding Norfolk Island, pp. 71–4.

For the wild night of the landing of the convict women see, e.g., Bowes Smyth, *Journal*, p. 67, and Flannery, *The Birth of Sydney*, pp. 60–1. Bowes Smyth, luckily for his peace of mind, slept on board ship that night.

For the King's Birthday festivities, Worgan, *Journal*, p. 28, p. 40; White, *Journal*, pp. 140–4. Phillip's account corrects the women convicts' issue to a quarter pint. See also Cobley, *1788*, p. 158, and for the White/Balmain quarrel, Cobley, *1788*, p. 220. For Tench on the play, Tench, *1788*, p. 109. Note: *pace* Thomas Keneally's *The Playmaker*, there is no evidence that Ralph Clark had anything to do with the play's production.

On dogs and dingos: Ralph Clark, *Journal and Letters 1787–1792*, Sydney, 1981, p. 32, p. 50; Hunter, *Journal*, pp. 46–7; Collins, *Account*, 1, App. VI, p. 469; Phillip, *Voyage*, chapter 22, p. 275.

For Major Ross's letter to Nepean, Flannery, *The Birth of Sydney*, pp. 81–2.

For Collins' existential swoon in the harbour inlet, Collins,

Account, 1, p. 57, note.

For the body on the path to Botany Bay, Collins, *Account*, 1, p. 34. See also Tench, *1788*, pp. 55–6; for the durability of the 'China' story, Tench, *1788*, pp. 211–12.

On the deteriorating conditions in the colony see e.g. Collins, *Account*, 1, p. 81, pp. 96–7; for Maxwell, see Nagle, *The Nagle Journal*, pp. 85, 105–6, 109, 111, 131; Collins, *Account*, 1, pp. 80, 83, and also p. 551, n. 8.

For Collins on the condition of the convicts, Collins, *Account*, 1, pp. 99–100.

WHAT THE AUSTRALIANS SAW

For White on the fishing incident, *Journal*, pp. 153–4.

For Furneaux in Van Diemen's Land, 'The History of New Holland' in Phillip, *Voyage*, p. 305.

For the old man and the spade, Tench, *1788*, p. 146; Phillip, *Voyage*, p. 45.

For Australians' hunger and the consequences of the British presence, Phillip to Sydney, 2 July 1788, in Alan Frost's transcription in his 'The Papers of Arthur Phillip (1738–1814)', unpublished ms.

For Tench's reflections on the landing, Tench, *1788*, pp. 43–5.

For the how-will-we-cross-the-water story see Hunter, *Journal*, p. 107.

For W. E. H. Stanner's reflections, *White Man Got No Dreaming*, p. 218, p. 162.

For an unforgettable account of the physical toughness of Arnhem Land hunters seventy years ago, see Nicolas Petersen's compilation from Donald Thomson's papers, *Donald Thomson in Arnhem Land*, Currey O'Neil Ross, South Yarra, 1983. Note especially the rigours of the goose hunt.

For an elaboration on the austere ecological hand dealt the Australians, and a penetrating analysis into the consequences, see Jared Diamond, *Guns, Germs and Steel: A Short History of Everybody for the Last 13,000 Years*, Chatto and Windus, London, 1997, especially chapter 15. This volume deserves to be read end to end, with its steady exposition of facts too large for us to notice. It contains the most comprehensive and systematic arguments against cultural arrogance, or even cultural complacency, I know.

ARABANOO

For the friendly incidents of July 1788, Collins, *Account*, 1, p. 29.

For Arabanoo's anguish, Collins, *Account*, 1, p. 496.

For Tench on Arabanoo, Tench, *1788*, pp. 95–108.

For the smallpox hypothesis, Judy Campbell, *Invisible Invaders: Smallpox and Other Diseases in Aboriginal Australia 1780–1880*, Melbourne University Press, Melbourne, 2002.

ENTER BANEELON

For the seizing of Baneelon and Colbee and its aftermath, Hunter, *Historical Journal*, pp. 114–16; Tench, *1788*, pp. 117 *et seq.* For Bradley's participant account, *A Voyage to New South Wales*, pp. 181–3. I urge readers to seek out a copy of Bradley, which is reproduced in facsimile, to enjoy both the smooth elegance of his handwriting and his skill as a watercolourist.

For Australian naming practices, Collins, *Account*, 1, App. XI, p. 504. For Tench on Baneelon's prowess as a fisherman, Tench, *1788*, p. 260. For Baneelon's many names see Keith Smith's list in his *Bennelong*, Appendix, pp. 159–6.

For Plains Indians, see e.g. Karl N. Llewellyn and E. Adamson Hoebel, *The Cheyenne Way: Conflict and Case Law in Primitive*

Jurisprudence, University of Oklahoma Press, Norman, 1941.

On Phillip and his clothing strategy, and a description of Baneelon, Phillip in Hunter, *Historical Journal*, pp. 269–70; on Colbee and Baneelon's comparative rank, p. 116.

On Baneelon's flight, Phillip to Banks, July 1790, Frost, 'The Papers of Arthur Phillip (1738–1814)'.

SPEARING THE GOVERNOR

For Collins' account of the spearing, Collins, *Account*, 1, p. 111.

For the *non-sequitur*, Collins, *Account*, 1, pp. 111–12.

Elizabeth Macarthur, *The Journals and Letters of Elizabeth Macarthur*, introduced and transcribed by Joy N. Hughes, Historic Houses Trust of New South Wales, 1984: Elizabeth Macarthur to Bridget Kingdon, 7 March 1791, pp. 28–30.

On language, Collins *Account*, 1, Appendix: General Remarks, p. 451.

For Phillip's account of the spearing and its aftermath, 'Narratives from the Official Despatches of Governor Phillip', Phillip in Hunter, chaps. 17–23, pp. 305–14.

For the Bradley kidnap, Bradley, *A Voyage*, p. 183.

For the Waterhouse account, Bradley, *The Journal*, Sydney, 1969, pp. 225–30.

For Tench, *1788*, pp. 134–40.

For Collins' account, Collins, *Account*, 1.

For the spear-deflecting techniques, Hunter, *An Historical Journal*, p. 39. For Collins' awed description of the ritual spearing of the warrior Carradah, where everyone knew their parts and played them superbly, see Collins, *Account*, 1, pp. 275–6.

For Stanner's comment, *White Man Got No Dreaming*, p. 174; for Phillip's final analysis, Phillip in Hunter, *Historical Journal*, p. 308.

Consider also Keith Vincent Smith's interesting hypothesis in his *Bennelong: The Coming In of the Eora, Sydney Cove, 1788–1792*, Kangaroo Press (Simon and Schuster), East Roseville, 2001. While Smith constructs his narrative of the spearing from discordant sources, he recognises that the spearing was masterminded by Baneelon, arguing that the motive was a personal payback. I think my argument clings more closely to the complicated contours of events. See also Keith Willey's elegant retrieval of events in his *When the Sky Fell Down: The Destruction of the Tribes of the Sydney Region 1788–1850s*, Collins, Sydney and London, 1979. While Willey is sensitive to the opacities blurring our understanding of Australian action, and while he acknowledges that the parleys between the British and Baneelon and his party would have looked very like a progressive peace conference from an Australian point of view, he describes the 'coming-in' after the spearing as a 'surrender' (p. 116).

For the reactions of the Australians from around Rose Hill, Tench, *1778*, p. 140; Collins, *Account*, 1, p. 112, and Phillip in Hunter, p. 312.

For the Port Jackson Painter: Bernard Smith has emphasised that the 'Port Jackson Painter' is more properly identified as a cluster of stylistic traits rather than an individual, but allows Henry Brewer, an accomplished draughtsman and 'an old friend of Governor Phillip [who had] acted as a clerk for him on several of his ships', to be a major contributor to the collective. Bernard Smith, *European Vision and the South Pacific*, 2nd ed., Oxford University Press, Melbourne, 1989, p. 347, n. 6. As well as a painter Brewer was a director of the Night Watch, Provost-Marshal of the courts and a devoted drinker.

'COMING IN'
For the hair-clipping and the romping, Collins, *Account*, 1, p. 452; for

the reconciliation in general, Tench, *1778*, pp. 141–50. Tench, who was present at the second meeting if not at the first, habitually uses the collective 'we', whether present or not.

For the hints of the survival of the traditional Australian hierarchy, Thomas Watling, *Letters from an Exile at Botany Bay, to his Aunt in Dumfries, 1794*, quoted in Bernard Smith (ed.), *Documents on Art and Taste in Australia*, p. 13, and Collins, *Account*, 1, p. 452.

On Baneelon's 'hut', Tench, *1778*, p. 160, Collins, *Account*, 1, p. 71, p. 117, and Phillip in Hunter, p. 316 and *passim*. For the formal reconciliation with Colbee, Phillip in Hunter, p. 314.

HOUSE GUESTS

For the population figures, Collins, *Account*, 1, p. 120; for John Harris, quoted Alan Frost, *Arthur Phillip: His Voyaging*, p. 195.

For the troubles with Baneelon, Phillip in Hunter, pp. 316–34. See p. 344 for the comment about the woman 'granting favours' to convicts. This is the first explicit mention of convict–Australian sexual relations of which I am aware.

For Tench's dramatised version of the episode, Tench, *1788*, pp. 160–4.

BRITISH SEXUAL POLITICS

For the Australian girls going on board ship, Collins, *Account*, 1, Appendix V; for the woman convict discovered in men's clothing, Collins, *Account*, 1 p. 159.

For Gooreedeeana, Tench, *1788*, p. 244, p. 246–7.

On Dawes: to follow the life of this reluctant imperialist in an imperialist age a little further; L. F. Fitzhardinge tells us that Dawes had intended to return to New South Wales 'either with an official appointment or as a settler', but that he was persuaded to go instead as first governor to Sierra Leone, the colony for liberated slaves established by an abolitionist company in the aftermath of the American War of Independence. There he remained until 1796, a lion on behalf of his adopted people. Then after a breakdown in health he removed to the West Indies in 1823. By 1827 he was living in Antigua, and his old friend Watkin Tench, now lieutenant-general in the Army and colonel of the Royal Marines, was warmly supporting his application for compensation for his service as Officer of Engineers and Artillery back in Port Jackson, when they had been young together. Dawes died in Antigua in 1837. He was a man most at home on the fringes of empire—and looking outwards. Fitzhardinge, Tench, *Sydney's First Four Years*, xix-xx, pp. 82–3, n. 1; p. 331, n. 51. See also *Australian Dictionary of Biography* entry for William Dawes.

For William Dawes and Patyegarang, Daniel Southwell, quoted Fitzhardinge p. 118, n. 7; Dawes, quoted Flannery, *The Birth of Sydney*, pp. 112–15. Copies of the Dawes notebooks are held in the Mitchell Library. For more on Dawes and Patyegarang see Keith Vincent Smith, *Bennelong*, pp. 108–9.

For wistful Elizabeth Macarthur, *The Journals and Letters*, letter to Bridget Kingdon, 7 March 1791.

AUSTRALIAN SEXUAL POLITICS

I do not suggest this is a universal law—what is, among humans? For a different ordering in a warrior society of habituated impulses and political relations between the sexes, see my *Aztecs: An Interpretation*, Cambridge University Press, London and New York, 1991.

For Baneelon's boasting, Tench, *1788*, p. 118; for other styles of assault, 261–4; for Baneelon's attack on Colbee's woman, and his punishment, Collins, *Account*, 1, p. 390, and his Appendix V

('Courtship and marriage') *passim*; for Barangaroo's pre-parturition beating, Collins, *Account*, 1, footnote p. 465; and for the pitiable condition of women in general, Collins, *Account*, 1, pp. 485–6; for damage to skulls, male and female, p. 497; for the two Australian women who chose to go to Norfolk Island, p. 327.

For British offences against women see, e.g., Collins, *Account*, 2, p. 3.

For Boorong and the witches, Collins, *Account*, 1, App. VII, p. 494.

For the picnic, Collins, *Account*, 1, App. VI, p. 493; for Warreweer's murder, 2, p. 89; for Me-mel, 1, p. 497; for the teeth, 1, p. 483.

For warrior protocols, Collins, *Account*, 1, App. VI, *passim*. See also his moving homage to the Cameragal 'Carradah' enduring a ritual spearing, December 1793, 1, pp. 275–6.

BOAT TRIP TO ROSE HILL

For Phillip's boats, see Nagle, *The Nagle Journal*; for the events, Phillip in Hunter, pp. 325–6.

HEADHUNT

For Phillip's account of the McEntire spearing and its consequences, see Phillip in Hunter, *Journal*, pp. 326 *et seq*.

For Tench's account of his expeditions and Colbee's ruse, see Tench, *1788*, pp. 168–76.

For engrossing investigations into the rhetorical dimensions of late eighteenth-century British law see Douglas Hay *et al.*, *Albion's Fatal Tree*, Allen Lane, London, 1975.

For Collins' opinion of the affair, Collins, *Account*, 1, p. 119.

On Discipline

For Phillip's thoughts regarding the uses of Polynesians for punishment and reward, Phillip, quoted Willey, *When the Sky Fell Down*, p. 41.

For Nagle's report of Phillip's shipboard speech, Nagle, *Journal* pp. 85–6.

For the hanging of the six marines, Tench, *1788*, p. 102; Collins, *Account*, 1, pp. 48–51, 72; on the trial and its aftermath, Jonathan Easty, *Memorandum of the Transactions of a Voyage from England to Botany Bay, 1787–1793: A First Fleet Journal by John Easty, Private Marine*, Trustees of the Public Library of New South Wales, Sydney, 1965, p. 111.

For Joseph Hunt's floggings, Collins, *Account*, 1, p. 46; for the Botany Bay convicts, Collins, *Account*, 1, pp. 47–8. For a detailed, vivid and very horrible eye-witness account by an ex-Irish rebel, Joseph Holt, of the flogging of four 'rebel' convicts, two receiving one hundred lashes apiece, and two three hundred lashes, see Flannery, *The Birth of Sydney*, pp. 171–3.

For Tench's involvement in the stealing-through-hunger case, and his eye-witness account of a death by starvation, Tench, *1778*, p. 125.

On British law, Douglas Hay *et al.*, *Albion's Fatal Tree*, esp. chapters 1 and 2.

On shipboard punishments Marcus Rediker, *Between the Devil and the Deep Blue Sea*, Cambridge University Press, Cambridge, 1987, e.g. p. 226, and N. A. M. Rodgers, *The Wooden World: An Anatomy of the Georgian Navy*, Collins, London, 1986. The most penetrating discussion of flogging and all forms of discipline at sea remains Greg Dening, *Mr Bligh's Bad Language*, Cambridge University Press, Melbourne, 1992. See esp. pp. 113–56, and for the German armourer, p. 114.

For Phillip to Dundas 2 October 1792 see Egan, *Buried Alive*, p. 296.

For a rich account of what happened later to convicts in Australia, see Robert Hughes, *The Fatal Shore: A History of the Transportation of Convicts to Australia 1787–1868*, The Harvill Press, London, 1986, *passim*.

POTATO THIEVES

For the barefoot guards, Flannery, *The Birth of Sydney*, p. 99.

For the potato thieves, Phillip in Hunter, pp. 331–2.

For the confrontation over the fish, Phillip in Hunter, pp. 333–4.

For John White and his Australian friends finding the corpse, and its condition, Tench, *1788*, p. 177; for the mishap with the fishing boat, Phillip in Hunter, p. 338.

For the flying fox, Phillip in Hunter, p. 337; for the emu chicks, p. 361. Tench remembered the emu chicks, or 'cassowaries' as he called them, as living for only a few days. Tench, *1788*, p. 240.

EXPEDITION

For Bowes Smyth, *Journal*, pp. 76–8.

'I enjoy these little rambles, and I think you would. However, I think it is hardly worth your while to come and try them.' George Worgan to his brother, quoted Egan, *Buried Alive*, p. 59.

For the governor's illness on the early expedition, White, *Journal*, p. 127.

My reconstruction of the expedition rests on Tench and Phillip. For Phillip's account, see Phillip in Hunter, pp. 340–8; for Tench's, *1788*, pp. 185–99. Tench is clear that 'our two natives carried each his pack, but its weight was inconsiderable, most of their provisions being in the knapsacks of the soldiers and gamekeepers'. By contrast

Phillip claims that the Australians 'carried their own provisions'. Why insist on so small a matter? Because Phillip feared critical comment? Having white men carry provisions for black men would scandalise readers back in Britain. Is this another of Phillip's politic rearrangements of the truth?

CRIME & PUNISHMENT: BOLADEREE

For the attempted kidnap-rape, see Phillip in Hunter, pp. 314, 316, 350.

For the flagpole colours, Collins, *Account*, 1, p. 122.

For Boladeree, Phillip in Hunter, pp. 353–9, p. 374; Collins, *Account*, 1, pp. 137–9, 146, 499–502 (Collins calls him 'Balloodery').

On the suit of clothes in payment for the canoe, Collins, *Account*, 1, p. 148.

BARANGAROO

On reductions in the rations, Phillip in Hunter, pp. 348–9.

For Collins on Barangaroo, Warreweer and birthing practices, Collins, *Account*, 1, Appendix VI, pp. 464–5. For a different reading of the British women's intervention with Warreweer, and the claim that Barangaroo shared Baneelon's political interest in bearing her child at Government House, see Patricia Grimshaw *et al.*, *Creating a Nation*, chapter 1, McPhee Gribble, Ringwood, 1994, and Ann McGrath, 'Birthplaces Revisited' in Ross Gibson, ed., *Exchanges: Cross-cultural Encounters in Australia and the Pacific*, Historic Houses Trust of New South Wales, Sydney, 1996, pp. 219–42.

On Barangaroo's nakedness, Tench, *1788*, pp. 142–3; Phillip in Hunter, p. 332.

On noses and bones, Phillip in Hunter, p. 317 *et seq*. Collins claims that some girls had their septums bored, Collins, *Account*, 1, p. 458.

For the funerals, Collins, *Account*, 1, pp. 500–4.

For the bestowal of names and their implications, Collins, *Account*, 1, p. 452.

For a possible confusion: Colbee's wife Daringa, who had exchanged names with Barangaroo, and whom Collins seems to confuse with the girl dead in childbirth, lived at least to 1792, when the convict artist Thomas Watling sketched her.

TENCH GOES HOME
For Tench's farewell survey, Tench, *1788*, pp. 212–26.

For the monster cabbage, Collins, *Account*, 1, p. 74.

For Tench's spell as a prisoner-of-war of the French 'between the month of November 1794, and the month of May 1795', see his *Letters from Revolutionary France*, edited by Gavin Edwards, University of Wales Press, Cardiff, 2001. Piquantly, Tench's Australian 'Narrative', which had appeared in England in 1789, appeared in Paris in a French edition (*Relation de une expédition a la Bay Botanique*) in that same year. Edwards generously provides us with the French editor's introduction in which he praises the experiment of the English ('these people, who we would do better to copy in their political conduct than their fashions') in reforming their criminals, and in putting them to use.

For convicts and repentance, Tench, *1788*, p. 66, pp. 68–9; for the Chinese Travellers, pp. 211–12.

For his considered reflections on the convict condition, pp. 268–71.

PHILLIP GOES HOME
On rations, e.g., Collins, *Account*, 1, p. 188, pp. 202–3. For Atkins' comments see Egan, *Buried Alive*, pp. 285, 295.

On the *Pitt*, John Palmer, purser to the *Sirius*, quoted Cobley,

Sydney Cove, 1792, p. 219; Collins, *Account,* 1, pp. 168–72.

On the changing state of the colony, Phillip quoted Cobley, *Sydney Cove, 1792,* pp. 241–3; Grose to Nepean, H. R. N. S. W., vol. 1, part 2, p. 613; Elizabeth Macarthur, *Journals and Letters,* p. 40; Collins, *Account,* 1, pp. 211–19, p. 365.

For Baneelon and Imeerawanyee, Collins, *Account,* 1, p. 211.

COLLINS GOES HOME

For convicts and boats, Collins, *Account,* 2, p. 39.

On Irish convicts, Collins, *Account,* 2, p. 77, p. 56.

For alcohol and for Black Caesar, Collins, *Account,* 1, pp. 363, 375–7, 380; for Caesar's ambush killing by bounty hunters, p. 381.

For Pinchgut and the corpse, Collins, *Account,* 2, p. 7.

For the killing of the missionary and the posthumous dissection, Collins, *Account,* 2, p. 156.

For convict 'aboriginalisation', see e.g. Collins, *Account,* 2, pp. 88, 102–3.

For early conviviality between Australians and some convicts, Collins, *Account,* 1, p. 29.

For Watling, 'Letters from at Exile at Botany Bay', pp. 10–15.

COLLINS RECONSIDERS

For the initiation ceremony, Collins, *Account,* 1, App. VI, esp. p. 446. Despite his respect for the Australians, Collins makes a strangely myopic remark regarding the ceremony's timing: 'As they have no idea of numbers beyond three, and of course have no regular computation of time, this [coincidence in time of the ceremonies] can only be ascribed to chance, particularly as the season could not much share in their choice, February being one of the hot months.' A 'coincidence' indeed.

For Carradah's magnificent defence, Collins, *Account*, 1, pp. 275–6. See also his account of another trial-by-spear reported to him after he had left the colony in Collins, *Account*, 2, p. 34.

For attacks on the settlers, their retaliation and Collins' response, Collins, *Account*, 1, pp. 348–9; 2, p. 9. Alan Frost, 'The growth of settlement', *Art of Australia*, p. 129; Collins, *Account*, 1, pp. 326–7, and for a horrible episode of torture and murder then denied, 1, pp. 329–30. For the tit-for-tat killings, *Account*, 2, pp. 348–9; for Hunter's ruling, Collins, *Account*, 1, pp. 382–3. For the Australian fights and British theories about the thinness of the Australian population, Collins, *Account*, 2, pp. 89–90; for his repudiation of Phillip's policy of conciliation, Collins, *Account*, 2, pp. 256.

For the little girl murdered, Collins, *Account*, 2, p. 9.

For a fine discussion of law as a cultural system, see Clifford Geertz's analysis of three distinctive forms of jurisprudence, Arabic *haqq*, Malaysian–Indonesian *adat* and Indian *dharma*, each one with its own way of deciding what constitutes relevant evidence; of defining and determining guilt and innocence; of applying appropriate punishments or penance—and each resting on and reinforcing its own system of social distinctions. Clifford Geertz, 'Local Knowledge: Fact and Law in Comparative Perspective', chapter 8 in *Local Knowledge*, Basic Books, New York, 1983, pp. 167–234.

BANEELON RETURNED

For Me-mel: en route to Rose Hill three weeks after the spearing, Phillip was told by a local that Baneelon was at 'Me-mel', diverted there, and found Baneelon and Barangaroo enjoying themselves there. Phillip in Hunter, p. 313.

For Collins' report on Baneelon's conduct, Collins, *Account*, 2, p. 5, p. 34; for the Colbee affair, *Account*, 2, pp. 47–9.

Collins, *Account*, 2, p. 5.

For a touching letter from Baneelon written from Sydney and dated 29 August 1796 to an English patron whose wife had nursed Baneelon through illness, asking for shoes and stockings, see Flannery, *The Birth of Sydney*, pp. 146–7.

For Baneelon's obituary, *Sydney Gazette*, quoted Flannery, *The Birth of Sydney*, p. 217.

For Imeerawanyee's death, Smith, *Bennelong*, p. 98.

Bungaree

For the psychological tensions imposed on the presentation of the masculine self in colonial situations, see Ashis Nandy, *The Intimate Enemy: Loss and Recovery of Self under Colonialism*, Oxford University Press, Delhi, 1983.

For Bungaree and Flinders, and a charming account of Bungaree's special friendship with Flinders' remarkable seafaring cat Trim, see Keith Vincent Smith, *King Bungaree: A Sydney Aborigine Meets the Great South Pacific Explorers, 1799–1830*, Kangaroo Press, Kenthurst, 1992. Smith tells us that Bungaree was also one of the party which went out from Sydney in 1801 to examine the entrance to Hunter's River.

For more about the Lane Cove fight and a fine discussion of the treatment and condition of Australians around Sydney through the first half of the nineteenth century, see Keith Willey, *When the Sky Fell Down*, p. 201 and *passim*.

For the view of one foreign visitor to Sydney the year after Phillip's departure, see Alexandro Malaspina, *The Secret History of the Convict Colony: Alexandro Malaspina's Report on the British Settlement of New South Wales*, trans. Robert King, Allen and Unwin, Sydney, 1990. This makes fascinating reading throughout. A sample:

Both Boys and Girls [were] received and cared for with great attention in the houses of the principal persons of the colony. Both men and women…have been admitted to the dining room in our presence, and have enjoyed delicacies from the same table. At times we heard whole families salute us in English. Sometimes we saw Aborigines dancing and singing in the principal streets about a fire the whole night, without anyone disturbing them.

The Spaniard did not approve.

For the Russian, Bellingshausen, Frank Debenham (ed.), *The Voyage of Captain Bellingshausen to the Antarctic Sea 1819–1821*, 2 vols, Hakluyt Society, Cambridge, 1945, p. 189, p. 335.

For Stanner's comment, 'After the Dreaming: 1968', in *White Man Got No Dreaming*, p. 230.

For the *Sydney Gazette* report of Bungaree in the Domain in the year before his death, Smith, *King Bungaree*, p. 143. For Bungaree's death, Flannery, *The Birth of Sydney*, pp. 230–1.

For Darwin's sunset meeting, *A Naturalist's Voyage*, chapter 19, pp. 443–4.

ENTER MRS CHARLES MEREDITH

Mrs Charles Meredith, *Notes and Sketches of New South Wales (1839–1844)*, Ure Smith for the National Trust, Sydney, 1973, *passim* (see chapter headings). For her use of the word 'Australians' p. 38, p. 90.

For William Bradley on the Australian male posture, quoted Flannery, *The Birth of Sydney*, p. 58.

For the surprising informalities, Malaspina, *The Secret History of the Convict Colony*, *passim*.

Bradley, William *A Voyage to New South Wales: The Journal of Lieutenant William Bradley R.N. of HMS* Sirius, *1786–1792*. Facsimile reproduction, Trustees of the Public Library of New South Wales, Sydney, 1969.

Clark, Ralph *Journals and Letters, 1787–1792*, Sydney, 1981.

Collins, David *An Account of the English Colony in New South Wales,* vol. 1. London, 1798. A. H. and A. W. Reed, Sydney, 1975; vol. 2, London, 1802. A. H. and A. W. Reed, Sydney, 1975.

Cook, James *The Journals of Captain James Cook on his Voyage of Discovery* edited by J. C. Beaglehole, 4 vols, Hakluyt Society Extra Series xxxiv, Cambridge, 1955, vol. 1.

Dampier, William *A New Voyage Around the World: The Journal of an English Buccaneer,* [1697], Hummingbird Press, London, 1998.

Darwin, Charles *A Naturalist's Voyage around the World (...the Voyage of H.M.S. 'Beagle', 1839)*, Oxford World Classics, Oxford University Press, Oxford, 1930.

Easty, John (Jonathan) *Memorandum of the Transactions of a Voyage from England to Botany Bay, 1787–1793: A First Fleet Journal by John Easty, Private Marine*, Trustees of the Public Library of New South Wales, Sydney, 1965. See also 'Marines' Petition', 1793, published in *Historical Records of New South Wales*, 2, pp. 44–5.

Fowell, Newton *The Sirius Letters: The Complete Letters of Newton Fowell, 1786–1790, Midshipman and Lieutenant aboard the Sirius Flagship of the First*

Fleet on its Voyage to New South Wales, the Fairfax Library, Sydney, 1988.

Historical Records of New South Wales, vol. 1, part 2; vol. 2.

Hunter, John *An Historical Journal of Events at Sydney and at Sea 1787–1792,* [1793], edited John Bach, Angus and Robertson, Sydney, 1968. Note: while the collection of writings which appeared under John Hunter's name in 1793 contained ten chapters from a journal of Hunter's, beginning in 1786 and ending 1792, six chapters were from the journal Philip Gidley King kept during his first stint on Norfolk Island, seven were based on Arthur Phillip's dispatches for 1790–1, and a final chapter presented Lieutenant Ball's account of his voyage back to England in the *Supply.* Hunter also aimed at coverage: for example, because he had been at Norfolk Island when Governor Phillip was speared at Manly Cove, he carefully incorporated Lieutenant Waterhouse's participant account of what happened that day, identifying Waterhouse only as 'someone who was there'. Given its contents, Hunter's *Historical Journal* could more properly be called *A Collective Report from the Antipodes.*

Hunter, John *The Hunter Sketchbook,* National Library of Australia, Canberra, 1989.

King, Philip Gidley *The Journal of Philip Gidley King, Lieutenant, R. N., 1787–1790,* edited P. G. Fidlon and R. J. Ryan, Australian Documents Library, Sydney, 1980. See also *Journal, Norfolk Island (1791–94)* unpublished mss. A1687m M.l. Sydney.

Macarthur, Elizabeth *The Journals and Letters of Elizabeth Macarthur,* introduced and transcribed by Joy N. Hughes, Historic Houses Trust of New South Wales, Sydney, 1984.

Malaspina, Alexandro *The Secret History of the Convict Colony: Report on the British Settlement of New South Wales,* trans. Robert King, Allen and Unwin, Sydney, 1990.

Meredith, Mrs Charles *Notes and Sketches of New South Wales (1839–1844),* Ure Smith for the National Trust, Sydney, 1973.

Nagle, Jacob *The Nagle Journal: A Diary of the Life of Jacob Nagle, Sailor, from the Year 1775–1841,* edited John C. Dann, Weidenfeld & Nicolson, New York, 1988.

Paine, Daniel *The Journal of Daniel Paine 1794–1797,* edited R. J. B. Knight and Alan Frost, Library of Australian History, Sydney, 1983.

Phillip, Arthur *The Voyage of Governor Phillip to Botany Bay, [1789],* edited and annotated by James J. Auchmuty, Angus and Robertson, Sydney, 1970. See also Hunter, *Journal*.

Smyth, Arthur Bowes *The Journal of Arthur Bowes Smyth: Surgeon,* Lady Penrhyn, *1787–1789,* edited Paul Fidlon and R. J. Ryan, Australian Documents Library, Sydney, 1979.

Southwell, Daniel 'Journal and Letters of Daniel Southwell', *Historical Records of New South Wales,* vol. 2, ed. F. M. Bladen, Sydney, 1893, pp. 668 *et seq.*

Tench, Watkin *Letters from Revolutionary France,* edited by Gavin Edwards, University of Wales Press, Cardiff, 2001.

Tench, Watkin *Sydney's First Four Years, being a reprint of A Narrative of the Expedition to Botany Bay and A Complete Account of the Settlement at Port Jackson by Captain Watkin Tench of the Marines*, with an introduction and annotations by L. F. Fitzhardinge, Library of Australian History, Sydney, 1979.

Tench, Watkin *Watkin Tench: 1788*, edited and introduced by Tim Flannery, The Text Publishing Company, Melbourne, 1996.

Watling, Thomas *Letters from an Exile at Botany Bay to his Aunt in Dumfries*, Penrith, 1794, edited George Makanass, Australian Historical Monographs, no. 12, Sydney, 1945.

White, John *Journal of a Voyage to New South Wales by John White Esq.*, edited A. R. Chisholm, Royal Australian Historical Society, Angus and Robertson, Sydney, 1962.

Worgan, George B. *Journal of a First Fleet Surgeon*, Library Council of New South Wales, Sydney, 1978.

Compilations

Cobley, John *Sydney Cove, 1788*, Hodder and Stoughton, Sydney, 1962.

Cobley, John *Sydney Cove, 1789–1790*, Angus and Robertson, Sydney, 1963.

Cobley, John *Sydney Cove, 1790–1792*, Angus and Robertson, Sydney, 1965. These are curious compilations, because while they consist of a chronology of dated entries from contemporary sources, I can identify no consistent principle of selection. For Cobley's own statement of his intention to provide a daily record of events until the *Sydney Gazette* began publication in March 1803, while avoiding 'the intrusion of [his] own opinion', see his *Prefaces* to vol. 1, *Sydney Cove, 1788,* and vol. 2, *Sydney Cove, 1789–1790.*

Egan, Jack *Buried Alive: Sydney 1788–92, Eyewitness Accounts of the Making of a*

Nation, Allen and Unwin, St Leonards, 1999. Note Egan's helpful bibliography of First Fleet writings.

Flannery, Tim *The Birth of Sydney*, The Text Publishing Company, Melbourne, 1999.

Other books referred to

Atkinson, Alan *The Europeans in Australia: A History. The Beginning*, Oxford University Press, Melbourne, 1997.

Bayley, John *Iris: A Memoir of Iris Murdoch*, Duckworth, London, 1998.

Campbell, Judy *Invisible Invaders: Smallpox and Other Diseases in Aboriginal Australia 1780–1880*, Melbourne University Press, Melbourne, 2002.

Carter, Paul *Living in a New Country: History, Travelling and Language*, Faber, London, 1992.

Clendinnen, Inga *Ambivalent Conquests: Maya and Spaniard in Yucatan 1517–1570*, Cambridge University Press, Cambridge, Melbourne and New York, 1987, 2002.

Clendinnen, Inga *Aztecs: An Interpretation*, Cambridge University Press, Cambridge, Melbourne and New York, 1991.

Currey, John *David Collins: A Colonial Life*, Melbourne University Press, Carlton, 2000.

Dening, Greg *Mr Bligh's Bad Language*, Cambridge University Press, Cambridge, Melbourne and New York, 1992.

Diamond, Jared *Guns, Germs and Steel: A Short History of Everybody for the Last 13,000 Years*, Chatto and Windus, London, 1997, especially chapter 15.

Frost, Alan *Arthur Phillip 1738–1814: His Voyaging*, Oxford University Press, Melbourne, 1987.

Geertz, Clifford 'Local Knowledge: Fact and Law in Comparative Perspective', chapter 8 in *Local Knowledge*, Basic Books, New York, 1983, pp. 167–234.

Grimshaw, Patricia *et al. Creating a Nation*, McPhee Gribble, Ringwood, 1994, chapter 1.

Hay, Douglas *et al.* (eds) *Albion's Fatal Tree*, Allen Lane, London, 1975.

Hirst, John *Convict Society and its Enemies: A History of Early New South Wales*, Allen and Unwin, Sydney, 1983.

Hughes, Robert *Nothing If Not Critical*, The Harvill Press, London 1999.

Hughes, Robert *The Fatal Shore: A History of the Transportation of Convicts to Australia, 1787–1868*, The Harvill Press, London, 1986.

Llewellyn, Karl N. and E. Adamson Hoebel *The Cheyenne Way: Conflict and Case Law in Primitive Jurisprudence*, University of Oklahoma Press, Norman, 1941.

McGrath, Ann 'Birthplaces Revisited' in Ross Gibson, ed., *Exchanges: Cross-cultural Encounters in Australia and the Pacific*, Historic Houses Trust of New South Wales, Sydney 1996, pp. 219–42.

Nandy, Ashis *The Intimate Enemy: Loss and Recovery of Self under Colonialism*, Oxford University Press, Delhi, 1983.

Petersen, Nicolas *Donald Thompson in Arnhemland*, Currey O'Neil Ross, South Yarra, 1983.

Read, Peter *Belonging*, Cambridge University Press, New York, Cambridge and Melbourne, 2000.

Rediker, Marcus *Between the Devil and the Deep Blue Sea*, Cambridge University Press, New York and Cambridge, 1987.

Rienits, Rex and Thea *Early Artists of Australia*, Angus and Robertson, Sydney, 1963.

Rodger, N. A. M. *The Wooden World: An Anatomy of the Georgian Navy*, Collins, London, 1986.

Rose, Deborah Bird 'Hard Times: An Australian Study,' in *Quicksands: Foundational histories in Australia and Aotearoa New Zealand* ed. Klaus Neumann, Nicholas Thomas and Hilary Ericksen, UNSW Press, Sydney, 1999, pp. 2–19.

Salmond, Anne *Between Worlds: Early Exchanges between Maori and Europeans, 1773–1815*, University of Hawaii Press, Honolulu, 1997.

Smith, Bernard (ed.) *Documents on Art and Taste in Australia: The Colonial Period 1770–1914*, Oxford University Press, Melbourne, 1975.

Smith, Bernard *European Vision and the South Pacific,* 2nd ed., Oxford University Press, Melbourne, 1989.

Smith, Bernard and Wheeler, Alwynne (eds) *The Art of the First Fleet*, Oxford University Press, Oxford, 1988.

Smith, Keith Vincent *Bennelong: The Coming In of the Eora, Sydney Cove 1788–1792*, Kangaroo Press, Kenthurst, 2001.

Smith, Keith Vincent *King Bungaree: A Sydney Aborigine Meets the Great South Pacific Explorers, 1799–1830,* Kangaroo Press, Kenthurst, 1992.

Stanner, W. E. H. *After the Dreaming*, the 1968 Boyer Lectures, ABC, Sydney, 2001.

Stanner, W. E. H. *White Man Got No Dreaming*, Australian National University Press, Canberra, 1979.

Thompson, E. P. *Customs in Common*, Merlin Press, London, 1991, esp. pp. 16–96.

Thompson, E. P. *The Poverty of Theory,* Merlin Press, London, 1978, esp. pp. 35–91.

Willey, Keith *When the Sky Fell Down*: *The Destruction of the Tribes of the Sydney Region 1788–1850s*, Collins, Sydney and London, 1979. Willey has constructed a near-continuous narrative from the major sources to provide the most coherent account we have of Aboriginal–European interactions through the early decades of settlement.